PRAISE FOR *THE POWER MANUAL*

This book provides not only an outline for the basis of positive psychology, it also applies to the reality of police work. . . . I would strongly encourage police officers, psychologists, and counselors to read this book.

—**JOHN M. VIOLANTI, PHD,** RESEARCH PROFESSOR, DEPARTMENT OF EPIDEMIOLOGY & ENVIRONMENTAL HEALTH, SCHOOL OF PUBLIC HEALTH & HEALTH PROFESSIONS, UNIVERSITY AT BUFFALO STATE UNIVERSITY OF NEW YORK, BUFFALO, NY; NEW YORK STATE POLICE, RETIRED

Will be a "go-to" resource for me, and something I intend on sharing with as many law enforcement and mental health professionals possible.

—**DR. MICHAEL T. WILTSEY,** LAW ENFORCEMENT OFFICER & NJ LICENSED PSYCHOLOGIST; ASSOCIATE PROFESSOR, PROFESSIONAL SECURITY STUDIES, NEW JERSEY CITY UNIVERSITY (NJCU)

The most realistic training book for police officers that is currently available. . . . I have never seen a manual that combines an understanding of the relationship between stress, wellness, and ethics.

—**PATROL SERGEANT BETH MILLIARD, PHD,** YORK REGIONAL POLICE, AURORA, ONTARIO, CANADA

The police culture is unique, and a manual written by professionals with an intimate understanding of this culture is of vital importance. . . . This manual successfully fills the void.

—**BRIAN A. CHOPKO, PHD, PC,** PROFESSOR, CRIMINOLOGY & JUSTICE STUDIES/DEPARTMENT OF SOCIOLOGY, KENT STATE UNIVERSITY AT STARK

It's not just another academic process, but a practical manual containing actionable, implementable material to help police navigate the excesses of stress and trauma they face each day.

—**GRANT EDWARDS, APM,** RETIRED POLICE COMMANDER, AUSTRALIAN FEDERAL POLICE SURVIVOR, POLICE MENTAL HEALTH ADVOCATE AND AMBASSADOR

This book works to remove the stigma associated with these topics and increase the dialogue among our law enforcement professionals so to improve the overall health and wellness of our brothers and sisters in blue.

—**DR. CHUCK RUSSO,** PROGRAM DIRECTOR, PROFESSOR, EDUCATION & BUSINESS CONSULTANT, RETIRED LAW ENFORCEMENT OFFICER

A real game-changer. . . . A must for anyone with an interest in this most rewarding and fascinating of occupations.

Blue Line magazine would like to make it known it fully endorses *The POWER Manual* . . . an absolutely crucial read to continue the work of building modern-day wellness in law enforcement and beyond.

As a police psychologist with over 20 years of experience, I highly recommend *The POWER Manual* and will be using it in my practice. Very readable and practical, I think the book will be widely accessed and valued by clinicians and cops for years to come.

THE
P·O·W·E·R
MANUAL

THE
P·O·W·E·R
MANUAL

A STEP-BY-STEP GUIDE TO IMPROVING

POLICE OFFICER WELLNESS,

ETHICS, AND **RESILIENCE**

DANIEL M. BLUMBERG

KONSTANTINOS PAPAZOGLOU

AND MICHAEL D. SCHLOSSER

 AMERICAN PSYCHOLOGICAL ASSOCIATION

Published by
American Psychological Association
750 First Street, NE
Washington, DC 20002
https://www.apa.org

Order Department
https://www.apa.org/pubs/books
order@apa.org

In the U.K., Europe, Africa, and the Middle East, copies may be ordered from Eurospan
https://www.eurospanbookstore.com/apa
info@eurospangroup.com

Typeset in Sabon by Circle Graphics, Inc., Reisterstown, MD

Printer: Gasch Printing, Odenton, MD
Cover Designer: Mark Karis, Frederick, MD

Library of Congress Cataloging-in-Publication Data

Names: Blumberg, Daniel M., author. | Papazoglou, Konstantinos, author. |
   Schlosser, Michael D., author.
Title: The POWER manual : a step-by-step guide to improving police officer
   wellness, ethics, and resilience / by Daniel M. Blumberg, Konstantinos
   Papazoglou, and Michael D. Schlosser.
Other titles: Police officer wellness, ethics, and resilience
Description: Washington, DC : American Psychological Association, [2022] |
   Includes bibliographical references and index.
Identifiers: LCCN 2021019005 (print) | LCCN 2021019006 (ebook) |
   ISBN 9781433836305 (paperback) | ISBN 9781433838347 (ebook)
Subjects: LCSH: Police—Health and hygiene. | Police ethics. | BISAC:
   SELF-HELP / Personal Growth / General | PSYCHOLOGY / Forensic Psychology
Classification: LCC HV7936.H4 B58 2022 (print) | LCC HV7936.H4 (ebook) |
   DDC 613.6/20243632—dc23
LC record available at https://lccn.loc.gov/2021019005
LC ebook record available at https://lccn.loc.gov/2021019006

https://doi.org/10.1037/0000272-000

Printed in the United States of America

10 9 8 7 6 5 4 3 2 1

We would like to dedicate this book to all members of law enforcement who put their lives on the line every day to help keep us safe.

—Drs. Blumberg, Papazoglou, and Schlosser

And I would like to dedicate the book to my beautiful daughters, Dominiki and Maria, who bring sunshine into my life every day.

—Dr. Konstantinos Papazoglou

CONTENTS

Contents

FOREWORD

When I was asked by Dan, Konstantinos, and Mike to share my thoughts on the topic of their new book, *The POWER Manual: A Step-by-Step Guide to Improving Police Officer Wellness, Ethics, and Resilience*, I was honored. They had, however, a rather unusual request. Instead of writing a recommendation or testimonial for their book, which is typically the case in writing forewords, they requested instead my perspective on the importance for law enforcement professionals of developing and using a comprehensive wellness program.

Having worked in law enforcement and particularly in the behavioral sciences area since the early 1970s, when the area first began receiving attention, I appreciated this opportunity to share my perspective. Watching the field of law enforcement mental health services emerge and evolve over the past decades and seeing law enforcement mental health grow into a unique specialty field has been rewarding personally, while also raising concerns for the focus of the field. For the past several decades, the concept of psychological well-being for law enforcement officers has been considered almost synonymous with providing competent and confidential counseling services. If a departmental counselor or employee assistance program were available, it was believed all bases were covered. The infusion of traditional clinical mental health services into the law enforcement culture has been highly helpful but too narrow in scope, in my opinion. In recent years, this clinical approach has increased its focus and attention on the specific area of dealing with the psychological aftermath of trauma exposure for the prevention of posttraumatic stress disorder. Effective and available posttraumatic response teams have proliferated in agencies across the United States, Canada, and Australia. These necessary intervention services have assisted many law enforcement professionals in moving forward in their lives after trauma exposure, yet missed the overall target of comprehensive officer wellness and resiliency. I believe this is because, over the past decades, psychological services to law enforcement appear to fall into a compartmentalized silo-like effect with several areas of potential services operating in their specific independent spheres. Each sphere is making contributions but missing the overall comprehensive goal of officer wellness by lack of coordination or interactive focus.

The first encounter law enforcement personnel experience with psychological professionals is the gatekeeper functioning silo marked "preemployment evaluations." Here it is determined whether the candidate for a law enforcement career has the psychological suitability to move forward and actually enter the profession. Successful candidates might then experience the second psychological silo of academy stress training. This training is valuable for the entry-level recruit to raise awareness of the stresses inherent in the profession. Many times, this training is presented competently by the specific agency clinician. Often, this clinician or instructor is the same mental health professional available to a given agency's personnel for confidential counseling services if the officer seeks assistance. These confidential counseling services constitute the third silo. After traumatic events, officers might volunteer or be mandated to attend a critical incident stress debriefing, often coordinated by a peer support officer in coordination with a mental health professional. Again, this intervention service would be a beneficial experience for the officer and yet again constitutes an additional silo of independent assistance, silo number four.

If an officer along the journey across a law enforcement career begins engaging in behavior deemed problematic to management, or engages in a behavior that raises the question of agency liability, such as being involved in the use of lethal force, this officer might experience a fifth independent silo, the fitness for duty evaluation. This clinical assessment determines whether psychological impairment existed and whether it was of a magnitude precluding the officer from performing their professional duties. Each of these silos of service is essential for effective law enforcement but not sufficient for comprehensive wellness. Each silo has a mental health professional practicing competently but not comprehensively. An overall perspective to maintain and coordinate long-term mental and physical wellness is long overdue in law enforcement.

Assuming, in a best-case scenario, that each of these silos of independent psychological services is performed competently and effectively, the goal of a comprehensive approach to officer wellness and psychological resiliency is still not achieved. Officers enter the field of law enforcement idealistic, committed, and physically fit. Even casual observation at any law enforcement agency yields the obvious casualties of the profession. Idealistic recruits can transition into angry, cynical veteran officers. The transition to a cynical worldview might not meet a threshold of clinical concern in traditional mental health diagnostic circles but, certainly, if unaddressed, reduces the overall quality and wellness of the law enforcement professional's life. Physically fit recruits can transition within a few years to clinically obese officers. One researcher puts the level of obesity at 40% of the officer ranks. The link between physical exercise and psychological resiliency is not drawn for officers in a silo-like mental health services delivery system.

For example, as ever-increasing amounts of expense and resources are placed into each of these independent silos of psychological services, such as expanding preemployment evaluations or more readily available counseling services, a reasonable prediction would be a significant reduction in the tragedy of law enforcement suicides. Yet, the opposite appears to be the case. When a discussion about the tragedy of law enforcement suicide does take place, the blame is often immediately placed on the concept of stigma. The tragedy of suicide happened because the officer could not overcome the "stigma" of seeking help. Yet, in reality, many police suicides occur among officers who have, in fact, sought help. So perhaps the concept of stigma as an explanation only projects the responsibility onto the deceased officer: "If only they could have overcome the stigma of seeking help, this could have been avoided." Perhaps the tragedy occurs because, as a profession, law enforcement too often pays only lip service to comprehensive officer wellness and psychological resiliency. Each silo of service is competently provided, but each acts alone in only time-limited and situation-specific circumstances. The key concept that is lacking is the term *comprehensive*. A medical analogy is a patient who has excellent specialists available but lacks a primary care physician who can coordinate comprehensive overall health care for the patient, taking the input from each silo.

Comprehensive wellness and psychological resiliency of law enforcement professionals need to be woven into the basic fabric of the law enforcement culture at all agencies and not seen merely as a "program" that is available if the officer chooses to use it. The law enforcement profession might do well to look at a parallel concept that has come and gone and then come back again in law enforcement, community policing. I often hold in my mind's eye a direct parallel between psychological services and the old term *community policing*. I have lost count of how many times community policing as the "new" cutting edge concept of law enforcement services has come and gone in the profession. The parallel exists in how problems are conceptualized and solutions generated. Do we define problem-solving strategies as knee-jerk reactions or use well-thought-through proactive approaches? When done correctly, community policing defines what is taking place in a given zone and then generates a solution proactively to address the problem: Identify the offenders, identify the potential victims, identify the potential locations where they might intersect, and generate a solution to prevent the next call for services from ever even needing to take place. Without a proactive problem-solving approach, law enforcement services are provided reactively: a rapid response to a call for service, retrospectively investigate what just happened, and hopefully generate closure and resolution in the form of an arrest if it is a criminal matter, then just wait for the next call for services and reactively perform the entire process all over again and again and again . . . ad infinitum. Comprehensive community policing addresses the precursor issues and breaks the repetitive cycle.

Similarly, in mental health services without a comprehensive wellness approach to psychological services in law enforcement, the same Groundhog Day reactive-only experience is replicated: You can see the counselor if you would like to; you've been in a shooting, so you have to see the psychologist; the event was traumatic so you must attend the critical incident debriefing. These are all good beneficial services, just like rapid response to a 911 call, but alone they will just feed into a never-ending cycle.

Psychological services to law enforcement will not provide the correct answers for officers until it begins asking the right questions. Why do over 80% of law enforcement officers report inadequate sleep, yet most agencies provide no ongoing training to officers and their significant others in sleep hygiene? Reaction time and judgment studies clearly demonstrate the significant impairment to law enforcement officers due only to chronic sleep impairment, yet it goes unaddressed. As mentioned earlier, obesity is significant in the ranks of law enforcement, yet virtually no training is given to raise the awareness of the role the chronic adrenal–cortical stress response plays in incremental weight gain. Obesity is clearly a precursor to heart disease and stroke, which in a number of states are considered compensated presumptive injuries for police, yet no resources are invested in prevention. Research has demonstrated that as little as 22 minutes per day of moderate exercise yields the same effect on depression as antidepressant medication and also reduces the risk of Type 2 diabetes between 60% and 70%, yet almost no law enforcement agencies mandate daily physical fitness. As long as an overall comprehensive approach to officer wellness is ignored in favor of the clinical silo type services, the extreme physical and psychological costs of policing will continue.

I am going to violate one of the requests of the authors of the book you are about to read and give a testimonial. This book outlines a comprehensive road map for officers. The continuingly interacting parts of the puzzle of law enforcement wellness are presented. It addresses the issues of exercise, sleep, trauma, nutrition, and emotional balance. Law enforcement would not send you to the range at the academy and assume your firearm skills are sufficient to last a career. You go back to the range regularly. Officer wellness requires the same approach. Wellness needs to move from the external clinical realm where you go to "see the doctor" to an internal coaching and maintenance realm. Officers would need to routinely have profession-specific wellness appointments and be coached in specific areas such as those outlined in this book. Physical fitness must be mandated as one tool to address the issues physically and depression psychologically.

Looking forward into the future, I hope the conceptual subject areas contained in this book are comprehensively utilized by our behavior science and management professionals to create an ongoing proactive approach to overall wellness for our law enforcement professionals, and I hope that the silo model is abandoned. I hope the time is not far off when routinely scheduled wellness appointments for law enforcement professionals with their wellness coordinator are as routine as going to the range. Also, every law enforcement professional will finish every shift with a mandated 30-minute exercise session. This book provides the information to facilitate that change to a comprehensive wellness model. It will yield dividends to officers as individuals across their life span, as well as to the communities they service.

Kevin M. Gilmartin, PhD

THE
P·O·W·E·R
MANUAL

ACHIEVING BALANCE

This book is about staying healthy during and after your career in law enforcement. It is written by folks who have spent decades working with and as police officers. We have seen lots of officers who have struggled, but we've also seen many officers thrive, despite all the crap they face on the job every day. We use the term *police* as a kind of shorthand throughout the book; however, we wrote the book for everyone in law enforcement, including deputies, agents, correctional officers, parole and probation officers, investigators, and those who work in civilian positions, such as dispatchers and crime lab techs.

This is not your typical police wellness book. We will discuss, but not dwell on, the stressors of policing. We won't rehash every threat to officers' wellness. We don't need another account of how tough the job is. This book does not only focus on trauma or troubles. Rather, it is intended as a straightforward guide to wellness in all its forms. We've compiled a wide range of specific strategies that you can use on duty and off duty to help you thrive in both your professional and personal life. The book includes practical suggestions, examples, and scenarios of the strategies in action and lots of encouragement. But let's be clear: We won't give you random ideas to try; the book provides you with strategies backed by research and practice-based evidence.

The information, advice, skill-building exercises, and resources that we provide are meant to help you create and maintain a healthy lifestyle. We know that some of our tips will be difficult to do on duty, given that you may have little downtime while at work. You can adapt these as you are able and focus your attention on the off-duty exercises. However, the exercises are not meant to feel like homework; they are suggestions for you to jump-start a commitment to your health and wellness. We'll leave it to you to make the time to incorporate these activities into what we know is an already busy schedule. Also, we have provided some references to key research literature on these topics for those who want to dig deeper.

Throughout the book, you'll hear from Officer Mike. He is not a fictional character we created to help us convey the material. Officer Mike is one of the authors of this book who will tell you directly what has worked for him and other officers he has known over his 30-year law enforcement career.[1] Officer Mike, as you'll see, is not a perfect person; none of us is. However, he is an excellent role model and someone whose experience is well worth sharing.

Some police officers may not need any convincing to start using new wellness skills. And some are content with the steps they currently take to stay healthy. However, we bet you know plenty of cops who still think that this psychological stuff is for the birds. Although those may be the folks who need this book the most, we think everyone in law enforcement can benefit from reassessing their wellness program. When you examine your health, you may see that some bad habits have gradually crept in, which seem to have come out of nowhere. The book provides alternatives that you can use to start building some better habits. Maybe your current approach to your health has become somewhat lopsided or incomplete. Our approach to health involves a lot more than just fitness and nutrition. We want to show you a different view of wellness, which focuses on achieving and maintaining balance in many areas of your life.

WHAT IS POWER?

Let's take a moment to tell you about our philosophy on police officers' health and well-being. The power of a police officer does not come just from your badge, your gear, or your tactical skills. The power of a police officer comes from your POWER: police officer wellness, ethics, and resilience. The literature is pretty clear. Optimal health involves preserving wellness in many domains of your life: physical, cognitive, emotional, social, and spiritual. The skills described in this book will improve your wellness in these areas, regardless of how healthy you currently are. Beyond these topics, though, optimal health requires you to maintain your personal integrity. Well-being includes taking steps to ensure that your moral compass does not get compromised. There are many moral risks in policing, so this book offers strategies to strengthen your ethical commitments. Finally, no matter how much time and energy you spend staying healthy, sometimes, as the saying goes, shit happens. That is why your POWER requires you to learn and actively use techniques to boost your resilience. Police work changes those who serve. It's up to you to make sure that those changes are for the positive; this happens only when you are willing to improve your ability to grow through the adversities.

Although many things in the world of policing have changed since we began writing this book, our intent is not to address policy or organizational issues. Our focus is not on issues such as civil unrest or what law enforcement agencies should or should not be doing. Our intent is for you to focus on yourself so that you can do your job effectively and grow personally and professionally. And after all, if we can't individually stay grounded in the basics of wellness, how can we hope to have any meaningful impact on larger social problems? When people are divided and the social media–fueled blowups show no sign of abating, it's more important than ever to tend to our relationships, health, and POWER.

WHAT'S IN THE BOOK

This book is organized into three parts. Part I is about your health and wellness. Although you may have heard some of this content before, we emphasize how these techniques can be used on duty and off duty, given the demands of shift work and the other responsibilities in your life. Beyond the specific recommendations, this section provides tips to achieve more balance and inoculate yourself against many of the common job stressors. And you may find that you haven't considered some of these areas (e.g., cognitive, social, spiritual) to be so important to your health and wellness. We hope that we can convince you that your overall wellness needs you to be functioning optimally in all of these areas. Enhancing your health and wellness is not always a solitary endeavor, so we include plenty of ideas for you to enlist family and friends in some of these activities.

The chapters in the wellness section focus on strategies for you to maintain your health and fitness. You've heard it before: Wellness involves body, mind, and spirit. This section addresses all of these dimensions. The job makes it difficult to always eat well, find time to exercise, get enough sleep, and avoid too much caffeine and alcohol. But Chapter 1 provides some tips to improve your physical health despite the challenges of shift work, overtime, irregular mealtimes, and the demands you face from your off-duty responsibilities (e.g., spouse, kids, home projects).

Your overall wellness also depends on your cognitive, emotional, social, and spiritual functioning. Chapters 2 and 3 offer specific suggestions that will help you keep your thoughts and emotions from negatively impacting your well-being. Chapter 4 addresses the importance of a healthy off-duty social life and provides you with recommendations to nurture your relationships and stay involved in your community. In Chapter 5, we discuss the important role that spirituality plays in your wellness. We're not talking about religion per se. Instead, this involves taking steps to continually remember your "purpose," nurture your spiritual self, and remain spiritually grounded, which are vital when it comes to insulating yourself from the most soul-wrenching aspects of policing.

Part II tackles your personal integrity and professional ethical commitments. Police work exposes you to numerous moral risks. Many of these risks are operational, but some of them are organizational. We won't ask you to directly buck your agency's culture, but your well-being depends on you staying true to your values. In this section, we discuss the threats to your ethics and offer specific suggestions that will help you to avoid the negative consequences of these risks. The chapters in this section are intended to make you think about aspects of your job that you may not have spent much time considering. These topics tend to subtly erode officers' ethical commitment, so we've provided specific strategies for you to use to maintain your integrity despite the challenges.

Chapter 6 introduces the concept of the "noble cause," which is the reason most officers get into policing in the first place—namely, a commitment to protecting and serving the public. Unfortunately, devotion to the noble cause can lead to unethical behavior as officers try any means to achieve their honorable ends. The chapter provides suggestions and encouragement to maintain your commitment to the noble cause without compromising your integrity.

Chapter 7 emphasizes the benefit of maintaining a guardian spirit of policing. This is in stark contrast to the warrior mentality that seems to breed "us versus them" thinking. Much of that originates from your academy training and is supported by field training officers (FTOs) when you hit the streets. As you progress in your career, the ungrateful and disrespectful people you encounter every day reinforce the "us versus them" perspective. Nevertheless, your well-being suffers from this viewpoint, so the chapter suggests ways to avoid moral disengagement, practice tactical empathy, and recommit to the guardian spirit. This is about what it takes for you to prevent issues such as burnout and remain motivated and healthy.

In Chapter 8, you'll learn about moral distress and ethical exhaustion, which are common outcomes for police officers. The chapter offers suggestions to recalibrate your moral compass, avoid pressures from peers and supervisors, maintain your integrity, and combat moral distress and ethical exhaustion.

The final section of the book, Part III, centers on your resilience. Resilience relates to your ability to continue to thrive despite adversity. Let's face it, police officers experience adversity. However, rather than only dealing with difficulties after they happen, resilient officers are better prepared to handle adversity before it happens and are more capable of coping with it after it does. In this section, we offer specific strategies that will protect officers from some of the routine stresses of the job. We also provide techniques for officers to successfully cope with critical incidents, as well as with traumatic and emotionally draining events. This section takes a broader view of resilience and asks you to make time for self-compassion. We provide a road map for officers to assess your personal and professional goals throughout the career cycle and offer suggestions for you to embrace the changes that occur during your career. We also introduce you to the field of positive psychology. Unlike the stereotype that psychology only focuses on problems or symptoms, positive psychology promotes people's strengths.

Optimal health and well-being depend on optimal growth, which depends on the extent to which you develop skills necessary to stay resilient. Chapter 9 introduces you to the concept of stress inoculation. Like medical vaccinations that keep you from developing physical diseases, stress inoculation can keep you safe from some psychological difficulties.

In Chapter 10, we discuss resilience and how to avoid the toll that constant exposure to human suffering can take on officers' well-being. The chapter offers strategies to grow through adversity, especially challenges associated with your exposure to traumatic incidents.

Chapter 11 talks about self-compassion and introduces you to positive psychology. The chapter presents the importance of focusing on your personal strengths to boost resilience and successfully cope with adversity. In these chapters, you will learn a variety of important techniques that will enhance your basic wellness program and improve your ability to stay healthy.

HOW TO USE THIS BOOK

You may be inclined to view this book as a menu from which you pick what you feel like doing in the moment. That would be like starting to eat better or hitting the gym a little more vigorously only after gaining a few pounds. We hope that you won't do this with what we've provided in this book. Instead, we want you to begin to view your health and wellness the same as you would any other tactical skill. It takes a lot of effort to become proficient and considerable commitment to keep your skills sharp. As with firearms and defensive tactics, your POWER comes from the dedication to learn, strengthen, and continually practice these skills. Your combined efforts will include wellness skills, ethics strategies, and resilience techniques. Rest assured, though, that we are not talking about adding a lot to your already crowded schedule. To borrow a common phrase, we show you how to work smarter, not harder, when it comes to staying healthy.

Several times in the book, we offer the option to write something down, either in a paper journal or a note-keeping app. If you want to write but don't like staring at a blank page, visit the Resource Library tab on this book's website (https://www.apa.org/pubs/books/the-power-manual) and download the POWER Manual Journal Pages.

We created these to summarize key lessons from each chapter and provide a bit of structure to your writing time. You can download the full PDF, hole-punch it, and write in the spaces provided, or you can just choose one exercise you like and print off that page multiple times. Take what is helpful and leave the rest.

We should mention that optimal POWER occurs when police executives are as committed to officers' wellness as the officers themselves. Although this book is intended for use by individuals in law enforcement, all three authors have been working for years with law enforcement agencies to adopt a culture of wellness. Such a culture would reevaluate how officers are hired, trained, supervised, promoted, and disciplined, with a focus on their long-term health and well-being. The agency would encourage officers to maintain balance, reinforce ethical commitments, provide psychological assistance when needed to officers and their family members, and actively support officers' wellness activities. Although our efforts continue to advance at what might be considered a snail's pace, these small steps are making significant progress.

We are not naive. Police officers cannot wait for their employer to adopt a culture of wellness or do what we know would facilitate officers' health. Therefore, it is up to you to take good care of yourself. At the same time, you are the future detectives, sergeants, lieutenants, and even police chiefs and sheriffs. Although you may one day be the executive who promotes a culture of wellness in your agency, you can make a difference now in helping to spread a culture of wellness by leading by example.

We also understand that you are busy. There are occasions when you literally don't have enough time to finish a meal. As you read this book, you may say that you don't have time to do the strategies that we are suggesting. We get it. However, if you sprained an ankle during a foot pursuit and the doctor recommended physical therapy to assist your recovery, you would, hopefully, make the time to properly and thoroughly rehab the injury. The exercises presented throughout this book will help prevent a variety of not uncommon psychological injuries that police officers experience. Just as important, these techniques will help you recover faster from any psychological difficulties you may face. So, we hope you will carve out some time here and there during your busy schedule to learn these techniques. After practicing them for a while, they will become second nature, and you will just automatically make time to do them. When that happens, you've achieved a healthier lifestyle.

We can tell you what works, but it's up to you to put these techniques to use. The good news is that any small step you take toward your wellness is a step in the right direction. Every effort counts. Just making the conscious decision to do something for your personal and professional benefit is, in itself, beneficial.

Despite the operational and organizational challenges to your wellness, we hope you will recognize the vital importance of maintaining your POWER. No matter the obstacles, you can learn the skills that will enable you to enjoy a long and productive career. Although you are ultimately responsible for your own health, you are not alone. You have the support of peers, family, and friends in these efforts. In addition, you will find our contact information at the back of the book; send us an email if you have any questions or would like additional resources. Perhaps the most important aspect of your POWER is to be proactive. Don't wait until you start noticing a crack in the armor. The skills outlined in this book are like body armor for your mind and soul. It only works when you wear it.

I

WELLNESS

CHAPTER I

PHYSICAL HEALTH

Let's start with the basics. Being a cop is a physical job. Just wearing the gear and getting in and out of a cruiser all day puts strain on your body. When you add enforcement actions, accidents and injuries, and the physical toll of stress, it makes sense that policing is one of the most "dangerous" occupations in America.[1] Maintaining your physical health is important for numerous reasons. On the one hand, being fit and healthy keeps you operationally ready to handle the tough stuff that you will encounter. And staying fit and healthy will make it less likely that you will be injured when the tough stuff happens. On the other hand, being in good physical shape means that you are able to recover faster and more completely if you do get injured (even a sprained ankle during a foot pursuit).

There are four main components to your physical wellness: (a) exercise, (b) nutrition, (c) sleep, and (d) avoiding self-medication. You already may be committed to maintaining your physical health, so this chapter provides a review and maybe some new tips that you can try. For many police officers, however, physical fitness has become a lower priority among all the other responsibilities they have in their lives. If this is the case for you, we hope that you will rethink that and that this chapter will motivate you to improve your physical health. We cover some of the basics, but we also want to provide you with some new ways to get healthier. Sometimes you just have to get a little creative.

Officer Mike

 When my daughter became old enough to sit in a child seat on the back of a bicycle, my wife and I would often bike-ride with her. Well, actually, I wanted a little more of a challenge, so my wife would ride the bike with my daughter on the back and I would jog alongside. We would have conversations about family, local and world events, our jobs, and so on. We would ride for quite some time and usually end up at a park or Dairy Queen, where my daughter could have a treat. When our daughter became mobile, my wife and I would climb the playground equipment with her, chase her around the park, and just have fun. We improved our relationship as a family and exercised at the same time.

STEP 1. EXERCISE AND PHYSICAL ACTIVITY

Exercise and physical activity are extremely important for an officer's overall health and wellness. This step is designed for those of you who do not currently have a well-balanced program of cardiovascular and weight resistance training. If you currently have such a program, please feel free to move on to the next step. That said, even the fittest cops may learn something new.

Many officers think they have to join a gym or purchase expensive home equipment to implement an exercise program. Moreover, they feel they must dedicate 1 or 2 hours multiple days a week and—if they don't have that time—they simply ignore exercise completely. However, it does not have to be like that. Officers can exercise on and off duty for short periods to gain positive outcomes. The rule of thumb here is that something is better than nothing. According to the World Health Organization,[2] those who partake in regular physical activity at sufficient levels not only improve muscular, bone, and cardiorespiratory fitness but also reduce their risk of heart disease, stroke, diabetes, certain types of cancer, anxiety, and depression. Remember that you don't have to be the fittest person to become fitter, and you don't have to be the healthiest person to become healthier. Do the best you can with the time you have. Also, if you are not familiar with exercise basics, consider hiring a personal trainer for a few sessions who can give you a program that you can do on your own.

Caution: Before beginning any exercise program, please consult your physician. All officers should have an annual physical and abide by the recommendations of their doctor. Monitor yourself during exercise for signs of overexertion (dizziness, nausea, shortness of breath, reduced sweating, chest pain, abnormal muscle or joint pain). Finally, if you feel that something doesn't seem normal during exercise, use your common sense and seek medical assistance. Nobody understands you better than you do.

Warm-Up

Depending on the intensity, it may be important to warm up first. The more intense your workout, the more important it is to warm up beforehand to help prevent injury. If you are planning to take an easy walk or perform another such low-intensity workout, it is usually not as crucial to warm up. Warming up simply means performing body movements that include the body parts you plan to exercise. If you plan to do sprints, it is important to warm up your legs. For example, you might start by walking, then jogging, and then stretching your leg muscles. By doing so, when you build up to sprinting, you are less likely to become injured. Likewise, if you are planning intense upper body exercises, it is a good idea to perform upper body movements incorporating the muscles to be used, such as push-ups, pull-ups, arm rotations, and trunk twists.

A simple warm-up begins at the neck area and works down the body. Spend about 30 seconds on each warm-up exercise. If necessary, you can take a few seconds between exercises. This warm-up takes 5 minutes on average:

- neck rotation
- shoulder shrugs
- arm circles
- arm extension and flexion
- trunk rotation
- leg lifts
- jog on the spot

Weight Resistance Training

As mentioned earlier, if you are already an avid weight lifter, feel free to skip this part. However, if you are a novice or even planning weight resistance training for the first time, the information presented in this section will be important. And if you've never done much resistance training before, consider consulting a personal trainer to get you started with a personalized plan designed just for you. Some basic rules of thumb are extremely important here. It is important to work all the major muscle groups in your body to prevent imbalances that could lead to serious issues as you age. Think of it like this: If I work my upper body, I need to work my lower body; if I do a pull exercise, I need to do a push exercise; if I perform an arm curl, I need to perform an arm extension; if I work my abdominal muscles, I need to work my back muscles. Simply put, you must work the opposing muscles to keep your body balanced.

One interesting fact about gaining muscular strength is that your muscles don't get stronger while you are working them. They get stronger after your workout, when you are resting. When you perform weight resistance exercises, this causes microtrauma to the muscles; in other words, it damages them. However, the body is a fantastic machine: When you are resting after your workout, your body overcompensates for that stress and gets stronger. Therefore, it is necessary to rest after weight training. In summary, the first rule of thumb is not to place the same stress on your muscles 2 days in a row.

The second weight training rule of thumb is that all movements should feel natural. For example, if you are placing yourself in an awkward position, such as doing a lat pull-down exercise behind your neck, avoid that exercise. Performing a lat pull-down exercise by pulling the weight to your chest feels much more natural. Avoid anything that feels like an unnatural movement.

In summary, performing a full-body workout can be easy if you simplify the necessary movements. The basic movements include push exercises, pull exercises, lateral arm exercises, abdominal exercises, lower back exercises, leg push exercises, and calf exercises. The following are examples of exercises you can do on duty and off duty. If you need definitions of these terms or how to perform the exercises properly, please consult a personal trainer.

Push exercise

- push-ups (on duty)
- bench press (off duty)

Pull exercise

- standing rowing exercise with resistance band (on duty)
- seated row with weight machine or bent over rows with dumbbells (off duty)

Lateral arm exercise

- lateral arm raises with resistance band (on duty)
- lateral arm raises with dumbbells (off duty)

Abdominal exercise

- crunches or sit-ups (on and off duty)

Lower back

- opposite arm and leg lifts (on duty)
- hyperextension bench or deadlift (off duty)

Squat

- body weight squats (on duty)
- leg press (off duty)

Calf raises

- body weight calf raises (on duty)
- weighted calf raises on a machine (off duty)

Cardiovascular Training

Cardiovascular exercises are important for heart and lung health. The most common cardiovascular fitness exercise is running, but other exercises include cycling, swimming, and using a fitness machine, such as an elliptical trainer. Indeed, it could be any exercise that raises your heart rate for an extended period. All these exercises can be performed off duty. However, this doesn't mean you can't improve your cardiovascular fitness on duty. Simply getting out of your squad car and going for a walk will benefit your cardiovascular health. Try to get 20 to 30 minutes of cardiovascular exercise 3 days a week. To simplify the benefits of cardiovascular exercise, it is important to understand that varying your heart rate benefits you in different ways. For example, lower heart rates during exercise can burn fat, while a higher heart rate is beneficial aerobically (heart and lungs); and a high heart rate will work your body at its peak capacity.

Consider this simple comparison: If you are tackling a resisting subject or even involved in an all-out brawl, what is your body going through? Your heart rate is at peak capacity, and your breathing is extremely labored. And for how long does this struggle usually last? From my experience, it can be anywhere from a few seconds to up to 5 minutes. So, one suggestion is to find an exercise you enjoy and work yourself hard enough to raise your heart rate and ensure you are "sucking air," just as you would in a fight. Make that exercise last for 2 to 5 minutes, and do it twice a week to help get and keep you in fighting shape. You aren't just training here for wellness; you are training to be in good enough condition to win these battles.

To know whether you are raising your heart rate to a suitable level for your intended training, here is a basic rule of thumb. First, figure out your maximum heart rate by subtracting your age from 220. For example, if you are 30 years old, your maximum heart rate is 190, which would be your peak level. For an aerobic workout, you want to keep your heart rate lower than your peak for the duration of the 20- to 30-minute exercise. To achieve this, your heart rate should be somewhere between 55% and 85% of your maximum. Using the earlier example, if the individual's maximum heart rate is 190, the aerobic heart rate zone would be between 105 (190×0.55) and 162 (190×0.85). However, even more moderate exercising can raise your heart rate and still be beneficial by burning fat and calories.

Stretching Basics

Stretching improves your flexibility, which can help you avoid injury. It's a good idea to implement some stretching into your fitness

routine. Always warm up before stretching. The best time to stretch is after a workout when your body is at its warmest. Don't just stretch one or two muscle groups. It is important to stretch all your major muscle groups. Stretching should not be painful, but there should be some discomfort. Try to hold stretches for about 30 seconds, and ensure you are breathing normally. The following are some examples of stretches:

- upper body stretches
- core stretches
- lower body stretches

Cooldown

It is also important to cool down after your workout. The cooldown also reduces unnecessary strain on the body. The more intense the workout is, the more important it is to cool down. For example, if you have been running intensely, a walk would work as a suitable cooldown. However, the cooldown could be as simple as repeating the same movements as your warm-up.

Taking Advantage of Your Time to Exercise

You can burn calories and get in extra steps by getting out of your squad car and walking whenever you get the chance. An important part of community policing is making nonenforcement contacts. So why not get some exercise while learning more about your community and enhancing community trust? For example, get out on foot and visit local businesses, walk the parks during community events, and have some fun playing with children (shoot some baskets, throw a ball, or just hang out). Have a resistance band at work and perform some basic exercises when you get a break. You also might consider wearing a Fitbit to help you keep track of the amount of exercise you are getting.

You have many opportunities both on and off duty to be more physically active. It may not be an intense or lengthy workout, but something is better than nothing. If you enjoy it, you are more likely to do it. If you work out with others, you are more likely to enjoy it and also become more accountable. Whether it is running, jogging, playing basketball, playing tennis, walking, or engaging in another activity, do what you enjoy.

STEP 2. NUTRITION AND SUPPLEMENTS

You may be fanatical about what you eat. If you always treat your body like the temple that it is, you can skip this section. However, most of us do what we can to eat right but frequently grab something because it's convenient or fast. Unfortunately, much of what is convenient and fast isn't really healthy. The goal is to have some basic knowledge about nutrition so that you can make better choices. You don't have to be a nutritionist to understand the basics of proper dietary habits. You can improve your nutritional intake in several ways. However, you are not expected to have the perfect diet—"not so healthy foods" are fine in moderation. You still need to enjoy life! Just a few changes in your diet can make you feel better and help you become healthier. Fad diets are not recommended. Never follow a diet that eliminates important nutrients such as carbs or fats. Your body needs carbohydrates, protein, fats, minerals, vitamins, and water to function correctly.

Officer Mike

 On my days off, I would cook out on my grill or cook inside if the weather was bad. I would make enough food for my meals for the week. I would grill chicken, pork chops, fish, or turkey burgers. Then, I would make myself five meals to take to work with me throughout my work week. A sample meal would be chicken breast, Greek yogurt, nuts, broccoli, cauliflower, and blueberries. And I usually had a tuna pack or two in my BDU cargo pocket, just in case. Doing this prevented me from going through the fast-food drive-through, encouraged me to eat my food throughout the shift instead of all at once, and most important, kept me from eating a burger with boogers and snot mixed in (just in case an employee is anti-police). It also saved me a lot of money!

Nutrition Basics

We know that it is virtually impossible to eat the perfect diet, and that's not what we are suggesting. However, understanding some basics of nutrition and following them in principle is beneficial to your overall health. A good source is myplate.gov, which provides basic tips for healthier eating. The following image shows a breakdown of the recommended food categories on your plate.[3]

As you can see from this diagram, vegetables make up the largest portion, followed by grains, protein, fruits, and dairy. Other nutritional recommendations from myplate.gov include making sure that half your grains are whole grains, changing to low-fat or fat-free milk and dairy, and eating foods that are lower in saturated fat, sodium, and added sugars.

Check food labels to see what you are consuming. A number of us look at food labels to check calorie content but forget to look at the number of servings per container. The product may state "300 calories," but if there are five servings per container, you are consuming 1,500 calories if you eat the whole thing. Food labels also provide details on saturated fat, trans fat, sodium (e.g., disodium phosphate, baking soda, baking powder, monosodium glutamate, salt), and sugar products (e.g., corn syrup, barley malt

Food Proportions

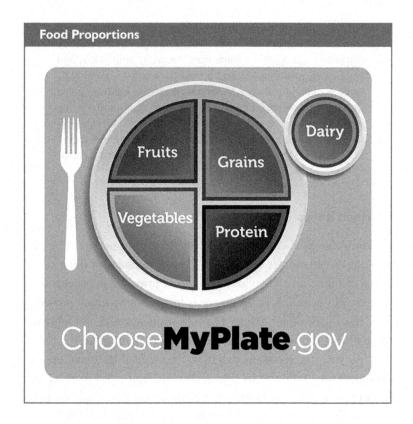

ChooseMyPlate.gov

syrup, rice syrup, glucose, fructose); you should try to limit your intake of these substances.

EATING OUT AT RESTAURANTS AND FAST-FOOD OUTLETS

Most of us enjoy eating out at a nice restaurant, and many have favorite fast-food restaurants. If you enjoy dining out, there is no issue with treating yourself once in a while. However, depending on fast food every day can have negative effects on your health. Here are a few suggestions you might try:

- Google your favorite restaurants and fast-food outlets and look at the nutrition values (calories, saturated fat content, and so on).
- Investigate alternatives at the same restaurant or fast-food joint to find something a little healthier.
- Select three things you'd be happy eating, and then pick the healthiest of the three. It may not be the healthiest thing on the menu, but it won't be the unhealthiest either.

PACK A LUNCH

So, if you are not eating out all the time, what are you doing for your meals? Many officers choose to pack meals at home to take to work. This is probably a healthier alternative to eating out, depending on what you pack, of course. Naturally, if you pack an entire container of cookies, chips, and pastries, it won't be healthier. That being said, there is nothing wrong with including some chocolate chip cookies

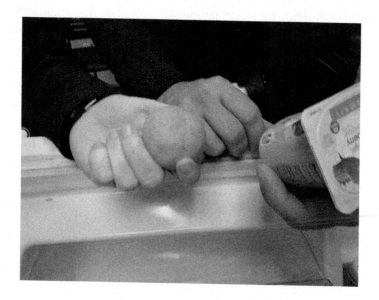

for a dessert option. A typical meal might include a sandwich, fresh veggies, some fruit, yogurt, and nuts.

Supplements

Taking supplements can be beneficial as long as we understand two things: (a) the best way to obtain your nutrients is through a healthy diet, and (b) many of us do not receive all the nutrients our body needs solely through our diet. So, certain supplements can benefit your health and can improve deficiencies in your diet. However, supplements *supplement* your diet; they do not replace it. If you think you need supplements, seek professional advice because taking unneeded supplements can cause harm rather than improve health. For example, some vitamins are fat soluble, and some are water soluble. Water-soluble vitamins, such as vitamin C, need constant replacement. However, fat-soluble vitamins, such as vitamin K, are stored in the body for longer periods and can build up to unhealthy levels, which will negatively impact your body. Other supplements can be harmful in certain contexts in certain people, including those used for weight loss, energy gain, bodybuilding, sleep, pain relief, heart health, and sexual enhancement, to name a few.[4] Therefore, seeking medical or professional advice before using supplements is crucial.

That being said, if you think that you would benefit from taking some supplements, after consulting your physician, here are a few that you might consider:

- a complete multivitamin
- omega-3-6-9 fatty acids blend (vegan if you want to avoid fish oil)
- vitamin B_{12}

- vitamin D_3
- high absorption CoQ10 (coenzyme Q10)
- acetyl-L-carnitine
- glucosamine with chondroitin for those with achy joints

Hydration

One of the more important aspects of your dietary health is hydration. It is often difficult for officers to drink enough water, although these days, most of you carry a good refillable water bottle on duty. Getting enough water is especially important if you are taking dietary supplements, if you drink alcohol or other diuretics, and because you are exercising regularly. Instead of grabbing a coffee or Super Big Gulp throughout your shift, fill up your water bottle and keep yourself hydrated. According to the USDA, men are recommended to drink 92 ounces of water per day and women 71 ounces per day. Given the activity level of most officers, consider drinking even more than that.

STEP 3. SLEEP

Sleep is an important part of being healthy. A lack of sleep can result in many negative effects, including fatigue, irritability, impaired concentration, and slower reaction times, which can result in critical mistakes when an officer may have to make a split-second decision. Sleep deprivation also contributes to a weakened immune system, depression, high blood pressure, and obesity. These outcomes will affect not only your health but also your work performance, compromising your own safety and that of your fellow officers and the public.

For many cops, a lack of sleep or poor-quality sleep is the norm. This is because of changing shifts, overtime, family responsibilities, and, yes, poor diet and a lack of regular exercise. Also, officers who have not established a comprehensive wellness program, like the one you will receive in this book, often have poor sleep hygiene because they worry excessively, are restless, and have not learned to control their stress level. You don't have to get caught up in figuring how much sleep is enough for you. However, try to pay attention to whether you get fatigued easily, feel like you need a nap, or have the problems mentioned earlier, such as irritability or poor concentration. If you have those symptoms, it may mean that you aren't getting enough sleep, but it could mean that you are not coping well with the stressors in your life—even if you are getting enough sleep!

If you struggle to get enough sleep or have poor-quality sleep, there are some strategies to improve your sleep hygiene. There is no single solution to obtaining good sleep, but many officers have found the following strategies to be effective:

- Darken the room.
- Do not have your phone, computer, or TV on during sleep (unless you are on call).
- Try keeping the room cool, somewhere between 65 and 68 degrees.
- Upgrade your mattress and pillow.
- Try a "white noise" machine or earplugs during sleep.
- Relax before bed—make sure there is time to wind down and do something relaxing, such as reading, listening to pleasant music, or taking a hot bath.
- If you find yourself lying awake for 30 minutes or more and are feeling anxious, you might try getting out of bed and doing something relaxing before returning.
- Try to go to sleep and wake up at the same time every day. Your work schedule may impact this, but some officers try to stick to this bedtime schedule even on their days off.

- A nap may be beneficial because any sleep is better than none, as long as it isn't near bedtime.
- Try to avoid nicotine, caffeine, and alcohol too close to your sleep time.
- Explain your work schedule to family and friends, showing them when you are available and when you do not want to be interrupted.
- Avoid eating large meals before going to bed.
- In the worst-case scenario, if you continue to have difficulty sleeping, see your physician, who may be able to prescribe something nonaddictive.

Although not intended specifically to benefit sleep, some of the most successful sleep strategies are presented later in the book. Breathing, relaxation exercises, and meditation can significantly improve the quality of your sleep.

STEP 4. EXERCISE, NUTRITION, AND SLEEP MONITORING

If you can monitor your exercise, nutrition, and sleep, you are more likely to recognize your strengths and weaknesses, which will, in turn, encourage you to reach your goals. The best way to begin monitoring these is using a fitness tracking device, such as a Fitbit. This device will highlight your progress in the following three important categories of wellness, as well as allow you to compete with yourself:

- monitoring your sleep, not only in terms of the total number of hours but also in terms of your REM, deep, and light sleep as well as awake time;
- tracking calories and nutrients by logging your food intake; and
- tracking your physical activities, heart rate, and calories burned, as well as logging specific exercises.

It's easy for officers to get distracted and begin to ignore their goals in these areas. A tracker app can remind you to pay attention, but if you are old-school, you can use a journal to log your sleep and wake times, your food and water intake, and your exercise patterns. The important part is to pay attention to how you are doing in these areas.

Note: We've provided an opportunity to write about your health habits and goals in the POWER Manual Journal Pages, which you may download from the Resource Library tab on this book's website (https://www.apa.org/pubs/books/the-power-manual).

STEP 5. MONITORING SELF-MEDICATION

Officer Mike

 I always found it ironic that so many officers would lack compassion for drug users. Officers would tell me that if someone is a heroin addict, the best outcome would be for them to just die. However, many officers self-medicate using alcohol. They literally drink themselves to sleep every night.

Police officers face many stressors that most of the general public never have to experience. Unfortunately, many cops use self-medication to relieve stress; turning to alcohol and other substances becomes a way to escape the pressures of the job. Self-medication can also take the form of compulsive gambling, shopping, gaming or online activity, overeating, and excessive use of caffeine, antacids, and other over-the-counter medicine. The most common form of self-medication for police officers remains the use of alcohol. The likely reason for this is that it is legal and easy to obtain.

Although consuming alcohol in moderation does not generally lead to problems, heavy use can affect officers' work, family, and life in general. Interestingly, some research indicates that moderate, regular alcohol consumption can be beneficial in regard to longevity.[5] According to health.gov,[6] moderate consumption is having one drink per day for women and one or two drinks per day for men. However, the guideline authors do not recommend taking up drinking alcohol if you currently do not drink. Unfortunately, it is not uncommon for officers to drink beyond moderation, and, again, this can impact their lives in a negative way.

Many officers who are heavy drinkers would not admit to drinking too much. They don't recognize how much it is affecting their work or family life. Ideally, officers will realize when it is time to seek help. But denial is not just a river in Egypt, as they say. If you step back and take stock of your use of alcohol and other forms of self-medication, ask yourself a few simple questions:

- Has anyone ever asked me to drink less?
- Do I need to drink more to feel the effects?
- Do I sometimes drink more than I intended?
- Do I sometimes have a strong urge to have a drink?
- Do I go days or even weeks between drinks, but when I do drink, I get really blitzed?

If you answered yes to any of these, you may be using alcohol (or something else) to self-medicate and could benefit from, at least, replacing alcohol (or other forms of self-medication) with the wellness strategies in this book. You also might consider talking with a counselor who has experience working with cops.

In addition, officers need to look out for one another and speak up if they think that a fellow officer is showing some problems associated with alcohol (or other forms of self-medication). You might be the first to notice that a colleague is smoking (or vaping) a lot more than usual or drinking way more coffee than he or she ever did in the past. Certainly, if you notice signs of a hangover or notice the smell of alcohol, which can linger the next day even when sober, it is imperative that you connect your colleague to peer support or other resources that are available to officers in your department. By saying or doing nothing, you are not doing your colleague any favors; the problem is likely to continue and get worse and could jeopardize everyone's safety.

Advice to officers:

- Don't be afraid to reach out. There are healthy alternatives to self-medication.
- Your friends and family care and will understand if you need and ask for help.
- Your fellow officers and department will understand if you need and ask for help. However, if you wait until after something bad happens, like a DUI, help will be available along with the appropriate discipline.

Resources are available for cops and their families:

- Drug and Alcohol Rehabs for Law Enforcement & First Responders
  https://www.addicted.org/drug-and-alcohol-rehabs-for-law-enforcement-first-responders.html
- Transformations Treatment Center, Substance Abuse & Mental Health
  https://helpforourheroes.com/who-we-serve/police-officers/
- New Beginnings Drug & Alcohol Rehabilitation
  https://www.newbeginningsdrugrehab.org/resources/rehab-for-police-officers/
- American Addiction Centers First Responder Lifeline
  https://americanaddictioncenters.org/law-enforcement

- Michael's House outpatient and residential treatment
  https://www.michaelshouse.com/blog/police-officers-and-drug-addiction/
- Banyan Treatment Centers
  https://www.banyantreatmentcenter.com/2020/06/01/cops-and-alcoholism/
- SAMHSA's National Helpline: 1-800-662-HELP (4357)

STEP 6. ONLY ONE PIECE OF THE LARGER PUZZLE

There are many reasons why being physically healthy is important. But many factors contribute to police officers being less than optimally healthy. Likewise, in addition to the suggestions presented in this chapter, we describe many strategies in the next several chapters that help make it easier for you to improve your physical health. You will find it is simpler to focus on your physical health when you simultaneously work on improving your social, cognitive, emotional, and spiritual health. We are, after all, focusing on the whole person here!

CHAPTER 2

COGNITIVE WELLNESS

Cognition is a fancy word for our mental processes. It encompasses perception, attention, memory, language, learning, problem solving, and decision making. When people refer to a lack of "wellness" in these areas, they're probably talking about neurological impairments or some sort of damage to the brain. However, there is another, more basic way to look at cognition. It's a term that refers to our thoughts, what we think about, and why we have those thoughts in our heads. A well-known quote by Abraham Maslow, a famous psychologist, is: "I can feel guilty about the past, apprehensive about the future, but only in the present can I act. The ability to be in the present moment is a major component of mental wellness."[1] We discuss this more in Chapter 9 when we give you some mindfulness strategies. However, in this chapter, we discuss why people have such a tough time staying in the present moment; it's not always easy to stop thinking about what already happened or what might happen next. Nevertheless, this ability is an important component of cognitive wellness.

Everyone, at one time or another, experiences a mental lapse. It could be a lack of concentration that leads to a careless error, forgetting something familiar such as someone's name or the date of a relative's birthday, having trouble coming up with a word that's on the tip of your tongue, or doing something after which you say,

"I can't believe I did that." Many factors contribute to these lapses, including lots of what we focus on throughout the book. For example, when you do not adequately manage your internal level of stress (see Chapter 9) or successfully resolve reactions to past traumas (Chapter 10), you may experience emotions (Chapter 3) that cause you to question your faith (Chapter 5) and your commitment to your job (Chapter 6). All these issues impact how well your mental processes are functioning. The challenge for police officers is to ensure that such normal mental lapses do not occur on duty in a manner that could lead to a bad outcome. But, regardless of the outcome, in Chapter 11, we provide some strategies that will help.

In this chapter, we won't be giving you tips to improve your memory or specific tools to maintain concentration. Instead, we give you some tools to help you prevent attitudes and expectations from interfering with your health and well-being. Specifically, there are common thinking errors that take a toll on your wellness. We show you how to identify and correct these errors. The chapter also provides some strategies to help you keep your attitudes and expectations rational and reasonable, which is a key component of cognitive wellness.

Some of this is a natural by-product of your police training. You've heard it a thousand times: "Hope for the best, but prepare for the worst." There are times on duty when this level of hyper-vigilance is not only helpful but also necessary. At the same time, there are many occasions on duty when staying in worst-case-scenario mode interferes with effective policing. And this is not a great attitude to have off duty, where worst-case thinking may do you more harm than good. So, another part of this chapter explores how you think about yourself and your role as a police officer. We give you some strategies to use so that you can remain balanced in this area.

To begin, though, we need to talk about rational and irrational thinking. The job is tough enough. Without knowing it, many officers make it far more difficult because they hang onto irrational thoughts. Besides potentially interfering with your job performance, these irrational thoughts can be toxic to your health, wellness, and relationships.

STEP 1. RATIONAL AND IRRATIONAL THINKING

We like to think of ourselves as rational. That means that we use facts and logic to decide what to think. But our brain produces thousands of thoughts every day. Even the most rational person would have to admit that some of those thoughts might be irrational. An irrational thought is something that we think is true without the objective evidence to support it or a thought that ignores the facts at hand and is, instead, based on our emotions or past experiences. This gets tricky. We learn from past experiences but cannot let them skew our perception in the moment, which might cause us to disregard contradictory evidence. In the simplest terms, whenever we jump to a wrong conclusion, we've been influenced by an irrational thought. This doesn't mean that we are an irrational person. It means that our actions, at times, stem from illogical or nonfactual thoughts. When this happens, let's just say that we committed a thinking error.

Off-Duty Exercise: Identifying Thinking Errors

There are some common thinking errors that everyone makes from time to time. When you understand these errors and how they impact you, it will become easier to avoid making them! We've compiled a list of 10 thinking errors.[2] Read through the list carefully and follow the instructions to write down some examples of each thinking error.

- *All-or-none thinking.* This is when you have a thought that lacks nuance. You see something (or yourself) as either completely good or bad. For example, after a meal at a pretty nice restaurant, although you loved every bite of your food, you give it only one star on Yelp because you think your server was rude.

  Write at least one example of this thinking error that you made on duty and one that you made off duty.

- *Overgeneralization.* This is when you have a thought based on one instance, which you generalize to a larger pattern. The larger pattern could be a blanket assessment of yourself or others without adequate evidence. For example, while working on Christmas and missing the holiday dinner with your family, you have the overgeneralized thought that you are a bad parent while ignoring all the great things you do for your kids. Or you think you are the greatest parent because, after missing the holiday dinner, you buy your kids some extravagant presents while ignoring all the other times you went out for beers with your friends instead of spending more quality time with your family.

  Write at least one example of this thinking error that you made on duty and one that you made off duty.

- *Disqualifying the positive.* This is when you have a thought after something good happens that it wasn't significant. For example, after receiving a commendation following letters from grateful citizens for exemplary service, you think it's no big deal, that it's just part of the job, and that you haven't done enough to stop more crimes.

Write at least one example of this thinking error that you made on duty and one that you made off duty.

- *Jumping to conclusions: Mind reading.* This is when you have a thought that you already know what someone else is thinking. For example, you respond to a robbery call and attempt to take a statement from the victim who makes a negative face at you. The errors would be (a) thinking that the facial expression was rude or (b) thinking that the victim doesn't like you. (Maybe the facial expression has nothing to do with you.)

  Write at least one example of this thinking error that you made on duty and one that you made off duty.

- *Catastrophizing or minimizing.* This is when you have a thought that magnifies or shrinks the meaning or importance of something instead of seeing things objectively. For example, after failing to include a key fact in one of your reports, such as the reporting party's address, for which your sergeant mildly reprimanded you, a catastrophizing thought would be "I'm a terrible cop," while a minimizing thought would be "That's a ticky-tack mistake not worth caring about."

  Write at least one example of a catastrophizing thinking error that you made on duty and one that you made off duty.

  Write at least one example of a minimizing thinking error that you made on duty and one that you made off duty.

- *Emotional reasoning.* This is when you have a thought that what you are feeling is a fact—for example, "It's the way I feel, so that has to be the truth!" Lots of cops make this thinking error all the time, but they attribute it to their "gut." For example, "I just know he's dirty. I can feel it," though there is a lack of evidence. Sometimes your experience leads you to this conclusion, but that would be a case of emotional-reasoning and jumping-to-conclusion thinking errors. Note that your hunch might end up being correct if the investigation uncovers enough evidence, but the thinking error could cause you to disregard disconfirming information. See the section on My-Side Bias.

  Write at least one example of an emotional reasoning thinking error that you made on duty and one that you made off duty.
- *Unreasonable expectations.* This is when you have a thought that you should or must do something even when the result is not completely within your control. Similarly, you can have a thought that someone else should or must do something. This thinking error sets you up to feel guilty if you don't do what you think you should have done and feel disappointed (or angry) if someone else doesn't do what you think they should have done. For example, you feel crushed (and embarrassed) when you fail a sergeant's exam after thinking that you absolutely must get that promotion. Likewise, if you think that everyone you encounter on duty should show you respect, you are setting yourself up to feel disappointed (and angry) quite often.

Write at least one example of an unreasonable expectation thinking error about yourself that you made on duty and one that you made off duty.

Write at least one example of an unreasonable expectation thinking error about someone else that you made on duty and one that you made off duty.

- *Personalization.* This is when you have a thought that you were completely responsible for something to which others contributed. For example, you blame yourself for losing a softball game because you made a costly error, but teammates also didn't do enough to win (e.g., one hit into a double play with a runner on third and only one out, one misplayed a catchable fly ball that went over his head, and one struck out to end the game).

  Write at least one example of this thinking error that you made on duty and one that you made off duty.

- *Hindsight bias.* This is when you beat yourself up over a thought that you have after the fact—for instance, "If only I knew then what I know now"—as though you would have acted differently then. For example, you respond to a person-in-distress call but get there too late. You think, "If only I'd have taken the other route, I would have avoided the traffic and could have made it there in time."

  Write at least one example of this thinking error that you made on duty and one that you made off duty.

- *Heaven's reward fallacy.* Like unreasonable expectations, this is when you have a thought that all your hard work will pay off in the end. In reality, sometimes your struggles are rewarded, and sometimes they aren't.

Maintaining this thinking error is an almost surefire way to end up frustrated and disappointed. For example, a homicide detective dedicates hundreds of hours to investigating a murder. This fallacy would result in an expectation of solving the case and intense disappointment when it remains unsolved.

Write at least one example of this thinking error that you made on duty and one that you made off duty.

You may have found that coming up with examples of some thinking errors was easier than for others. That is because different people are more prone to repeating some of the thinking errors than others. It is important for you to identify your "go-to" thinking errors. These are the thoughts that can zap your cognitive wellness.

Also, did you notice any patterns during this exercise? Do you tend to make thinking errors only in certain situations? Do you make more thinking errors around certain people than around other people? Whenever you realize that you've made a thinking error, add it to the list of examples that you started in the exercise. The goal here is for you to achieve greater self-awareness about these thinking errors. With greater self-awareness, you will begin to catch yourself in the act of making a thinking error and replace it with a rational thought in the moment. However, this takes some effort.

STEP 2. CORRECTING THINKING ERRORS

The various thinking errors increase your stress level. They also make it more likely that you will encounter some difficulties in your interactions with folks you encounter at work and in your relationships with those in your personal life, which increases your stress level even more. The good news is that you can take steps to correct these errors. This requires some repetition. Like an athlete in any sport, when you want to reduce the errors you make, you practice, practice, practice. Unlike athletes, however, try not to do this in one long session. Instead, it just takes a few minutes each day to learn how to replace a thinking error with a rational thought. Another famous psychologist, Albert Ellis, recommended spending about 10 minutes each day examining your thinking errors, as in the following exercise.[3] As you reduce the frequency of thinking errors, your cognitive wellness will improve.

Off-Duty Exercise

For each example of a thinking error you identified in the previous exercise, ask yourself a few questions. The answer to each question should be objective and unbiased, based on facts or verifiable evidence, and untainted by your opinion or emotions.

- Can I rationally support this thought?
- Is there any evidence to support this thought?
- Is there any evidence to refute this thought?
- How would I respond if my work (or home) partner told me this thought?

Answer the same questions whenever you add new examples of thinking errors to your list.

Example: Although rather self-explanatory, let's take the example from hindsight bias and answer these questions. "You respond to a person-in-distress call but get there too late. You think, 'If only I'd have taken the other route, I would have avoided the traffic and could have made it there in time.'" Your responses to the four questions might then be:

- No, I can't rationally support this thought.
- Well, my response time was slow because of the traffic, so yes, there is evidence.
- I guess that the traffic could have been just as bad if I had taken an alternate route.
- I would have said something like, "Don't be an idiot. He was very old. No matter how fast you got there, CPR would not likely have kept that massive heart attack from killing him."

There will be times when you do this exercise and discover that your thought was not a thinking error. In such moments, you've identified room for improvement because you did not perform up to your potential. When that happens, it's important to identify why and to take steps to avoid having the same outcome in the future. It's a great way to learn and progress. Nevertheless, thinking errors get in the way. They take you off your game and increase the chances that you will make a mistake. Hopefully, you see the importance of identifying and correcting thinking errors, which will help you make less of them.

STEP 3. MENTAL PREPARATION

For a long time, police training has mistakenly fostered the notion that cops are like soldiers going into battle. This is not a good analogy, in part because, historically, soldiers return to base camp after a battle and regroup until new orders are received. A better analogy than the soldier reference is that great cops are like world-class athletes competing at the highest level. Like athletes, police officers have to be ready to face everything they encounter and perform at their best despite various adversities. Of course, athletes and police officers have to have the physical skills. You won't go far if you are barely squeaking by with your perishable skills, so you need to work hard to improve in those areas. But assuming you are more than capable physically, it takes a lot more than that to excel. Like athletes, for you to perform at your peak, you need the proper mental preparation. Cognitive wellness ensures that you will have the right mindset to use your physical skills when you need them.

Most officers receive aspects of mental preparation in the academy. This usually occurs in defensive tactics and arrest and control learning domains. The idea is that you always have to be mentally prepared for an armed confrontation. This is important for officer safety and survival, but it is not the only aspect of mental preparation that you should use. Another aspect of mental preparation is that you are able to stay locked in, focused on the task at hand, even when doing the more mundane aspects of the job.

There are techniques that will help you to prepare mentally for every aspect of your job. Preparation starts with your mindset as you head to work each day. Are you approaching your shift with confidence and enthusiasm, or is something on your mind that could distract you? Mindfulness techniques (see Chapter 9) will help whenever you find your concentration slipping because of a distracting thought. Another technique to remove off-duty distracting thoughts is to develop some preshift rituals. You may have some without knowing it, but the key is to use those rituals to clear your mind of unnecessary baggage you are bringing to work with you. Athletes do this all the time—a batter before a pitch, a basketball player before a free throw, and a golfer before a putt. They don't do all those movements, tics, and twitches for the fun of it; they are clearing their minds and getting themselves in their optimal stress zone (see Chapter 9) to reach peak performance. Likewise, use the time when you are putting on your gear, loading your vehicle, and heading to preshift roll call to get your mind right for the shift ahead.

In addition, officers can stay mentally prepared for peak performance throughout each shift. When receiving a call for service, the first step, mentally, is to avoid a thinking error. You could let down your guard or, conversely, unnecessarily escalate the situation if you get the call and think, "I've been to that location a bunch of times before—here we go again," "Oh, it's just another one of these calls—no big deal," or "Boy, I am really sick of these calls." Instead, go through a mental checklist of how you will tactically approach the scene with contingency plans if things are not exactly what you expected. As important, you can remind yourself what sort of demeanor you want to project when you get there. This is where you maintain control of your mindset rather than allowing the situation to control you. Afterward, no matter how that call was resolved, you have to demonstrate excellent mental preparation for the next call. This means wiping the slate clean so that you aren't carrying any mental baggage with you from call to call. For example, a batter will never get a hit if he is dwelling on an error he made in the previous inning or the strikeout in his last at bat. That's where those prepitch rituals come in to help focus on the next pitch rather than on any lingering distracting thoughts. This can be accomplished with some breathing and relaxation exercises (see Chapter 9), as well as with some rituals of your own. One of Officer Mike's officers relayed the following:

> I had the hardest time letting go after a call. No matter what happened, good or bad, I would keep thinking about it. I wasn't second-guessing. I just would replay the events in my mind. By the end of the shift, I was exhausted. I was spending too much

mental energy on stuff that was over and done with. We were at Code 7 one day, and I was talking about an earlier call. One of the guys starts laughing and says, "Why think about that when we'll have plenty more to deal with tonight?" It got me to realize that there is a time and place to rehash, to review how I did, to keep improving. But that time is not during my shift! It wasn't easy to break the habit, but I started just repeating to myself, "Move on," and eventually, it worked.

STEP 4. ATTITUDE AND OPTIMISM

An important part of your mental preparation is your attitude. This does not refer to the specific thoughts running through your mind. It reflects your general state of mind or disposition. It doesn't take long for many police officers to start getting cynical. According to Merriam-Webster, a *cynical* person is "contemptuously distrustful of human nature and motives."[4] In simple terms, the cynic not only expects the worst from everyone but also does so with contempt (i.e., with scorn, disdain, and disrespect). You may think that you have to distrust everyone's motives. Maybe your academy training even instilled that thought. However, such thinking falls under the overgeneralization thinking error and can be detrimental to your health. Therefore, it is imperative for your cognitive wellness to cultivate some more realistic thoughts about people.

Let's start with the distrust. While you are on duty, it is important for you to stay vigilant and, in the least, curious about others' intentions. In fact, when you maintain a curious attitude rather than a distrustful approach, you are more likely to receive greater compliance because you will come across as more open-minded. In fact, not everyone should be distrusted, even if most of your daily contacts are with people who may not be honest with you. Nevertheless, let's say that there are times when you do not trust the person with whom you are dealing. You can be distrustful without disrespect;

in other words, you can question someone's motives without being cynical. This is an important attitude to nurture because once you get cynical, it is hard to leave that sort of thinking at work.

Do you find yourself questioning everyone's motives when you are off duty? Has this way of thinking infested how you interact with your kids, spouse, and friends, or is it reserved for strangers? We address this more in the next section, but for now, just ask yourself whether you've let cynical thinking impact your off-duty relationships. It's a good barometer of your cognitive health when you can confidently say that you leave the distrustful cop mentality at work.

Some police officers mistakenly think that they will be gullible or easily duped if they drop the cynicism. That is a mistake because you are capable of having different thoughts at the same time. You can be guarded but hopeful that your distrust is unwarranted. Also, you can compartmentalize somewhat to ensure that your skeptical thoughts about others' motives remain at work. Why is this important? We go into it in depth in Chapter 11, but there are many benefits to your health and wellness when you can develop more positive attitudes, which is not easy when you work in law enforcement!

By now, you may be assuming that we are going to tell you that you should try to be more optimistic. You'd be only partially right. First, optimism can help you to prevent the development of burnout[5] and may protect you against some stress reactions.[6] But let's go a little deeper. Take the proverbial 8-ounce glass containing 4 ounces of water. What do you have? As the saying goes, the pessimist says the glass is half empty, while the optimist sees it as half full. Well, they are both right. It's half a glass of water. The first thing to determine has nothing to do with your attitude. How much water do you need? To swallow a vitamin pill, you have more than enough water. If your radiator is empty, you don't have nearly enough water to get your car back on the road. So, how you think about a situation can only take you so far. You have to be able to objectively assess the situation to determine the necessary course of action.

This is where your attitude is crucial. Your mindset when assessing a situation can determine the outcome and, in some cases, save your life. The pessimist and the cynic are more likely to interpret the situation as direr than it may be. A realistic optimist will be more inclined to maintain a bit of hopefulness. It's not that the optimism deludes you to think that everything will turn out rosy. Rather, the person who has a more hopeful outlook will think that he or she is capable of getting through the ordeal. One of Officer Mike's officers relayed the following:

> After it was over, I heard from a lot of cops who told me they did the same thing. It's one of those stories we're told in the academy, but I didn't pay it too much attention. I guess it sunk in, though, and I'm glad it did. Bottom line, I got shot. It didn't matter that I had on my vest. The bullet ended up in my side, broke a couple ribs, and punctured a lung. All I can tell you is I never for a second thought I was going to die. I kept saying to myself I'll make it, even though I couldn't breathe good. I refused to have a single negative thought. I don't know how close I was to dying, but I'm pretty sure I would have if I let myself think I was going to.

There are a lot of websites that tell you how to increase your optimism. Some are better than others, but most are probably written by people who don't know what it's like to be a cop. As we said, the goal is not to convince yourself that everything will always turn out fine, because we know that's not going to happen. It's important, though, for your cognitive wellness not to think that everything will always turn to shit. The attitude adjustment about which we're talking is more of a fine-tuning than an overhaul. A more positive attitude on duty may help you in the heat of the moment, and it can also help get you through a shift.

One technique for developing a more positive state of mind is simply to maintain a future orientation. Although your immediate thoughts should remain focused in the moment, as we mentioned at the beginning of this chapter, we're talking here about your overall mindset or worldview. Rather than staying mired in so much of the negativity that you see on duty, a positive mindset about your future can improve your attitude. We discuss some specific techniques for this in Chapter 4, but one strategy is to schedule vacations. Even if you don't go anywhere, you can look forward to knowing that you will use the generous benefits that your job provides by getting a break from work. Moreover, some officers keep a positive mindset by occasionally imagining how much fun they will have enjoying their retirement benefits, even if retirement is many years away.

Another component of your attitude has to do with self-efficacy. Do you believe in your ability to accomplish what you set out to do? This doesn't mean that outside factors won't influence

an outcome, but a critical component of your cognitive wellness is having the confidence to achieve your objectives. You can remind yourself with a common adage of 10 two-letter words: **If it is to be, it is up to me.** Not to be confused with the cognitive error of personalization, this represents a core belief in yourself that helps you take the reins during tough times. However, just like optimism cannot ignore reality, neither can self-efficacy. Thinking that you can accomplish your goals when you lack the skills to do so is just false bravado. Therefore, a positive attitude and self-efficacy benefit from your realistic self-awareness. What are your strengths and weaknesses? In what areas would you benefit from increased training, more education, and regular practice? High self-efficacy includes the notion that you are capable of seeing areas that would benefit from some improvement and then doing whatever it takes to improve.

STEP 5. THE BADGE DOES NOT DEFINE ME

One way to avoid getting too cynical is to stay well-rounded. A thought, which is central to your identity, is how you answer the question "Who am I?" This relates to your cognitive wellness because your health depends on how balanced you can be in all areas of your life. We all wear multiple hats and fulfill various roles. Your job is usually a core component of your identity, but you are also husband or wife, mother or father, son or daughter, friend, and so on. Some people include their hobbies and recreational activities when defining themselves: runner, gym rat, amateur chef, surfer, and so forth. We discuss some strategies to stay balanced in Chapter 4, but in this section, we establish the foundation for why having a well-rounded view of yourself is so important. The balance is essential because if something goes amiss in one area of your life—for example, a divorce—you will have a tougher time cognitively coping with the change if your identity revolved around your marriage. It will still be challenging but easier to get through when your identity emphasizes all of your roles.

Officer Mike

 When I first became a police officer, I quickly realized how much everyone else defined me as "the police." Family get-togethers, activities with friends outside of policing, and conversations with the general public always involved some type of police talk: "Mike, I got stopped for speeding, and I was only going five miles per hour over the speed limit"; "Look out the window—there goes a cop, driving around, wasting my tax dollars"; "The police are never there when you need them"; and "Do I have to wear shoes when I drive?" It didn't take long before I started to see myself as Officer Mike. Then I really had to remember to take off my cop hat and put on my dad hat when I was home with my kids. With my friends, I wanted to talk about anything other than policing, such as movies; television shows; my Cubs, Bulls, and Bears; local community issues; world news; family; hobbies; and so on. I'm so much more than "the police."

Many police officers lose their balance. Sometimes this is their own fault—they don't work to live; they live for work. They think about nothing but the badge. Other times, however, our family and friends are responsible for this imbalance because when they see us, all they see is the badge. However, when officers' identities revolve around work, it is more likely that there will be setbacks in other roles, such as a spouse who feels left out, kids who feel abandoned, or noncop friends and other family members who feel ignored. It becomes a vicious cycle because those setbacks lead to greater imbalance. Some cops are okay with that imbalance—at least for a while. Their only friends are other cops; their recreational activities are cop oriented, such as shooting competitions; they vacation with their cop friends; their community involvement is cop related, such as coaching a PAL basketball team. You get the idea.

Now, what happens when that officer is injured or nears retirement? There will come a time when a police officer will no longer be a police officer. Hopefully, you will have a long and successful career and retire with your health intact. But some officers get injured and are no longer able to work in law enforcement. Same with retirement. Many officers feel a huge void when they can no longer put on the uniform. It is an agonizing realization when they defined themselves by their badge and were not well balanced cognitively.

Preparing for retirement can take many forms. Many officers find other professional interests related to police work, such as teaching criminal justice at their local community college, training recruit officers at a nearby police academy, serving as an accident investigator for an insurance company, and performing background checks for private businesses and/or governmental agencies. However, these post-law-enforcement jobs do not come with police powers and can cause those whose identity revolved around the badge some real discomfort unless they made room to think of themselves as someone other than a police officer. Other officers prepare for a second career outside the field of law enforcement, including becoming a fitness trainer or starting a business unrelated to policing (e.g., real estate, computer science, politics, construction). Such officers develop an outside interest and are proactive in preparing for this next chapter in their lives while still working as a cop, which helps promote cognitive balance. This might involve taking classes or obtaining a degree or certification and laying the groundwork for a well-rounded post-law-enforcement life.

Expanding how you think of yourself can make you a better cop. For one thing, staying balanced means not putting all your ego eggs in one basket. Officers who are well balanced are less likely to be badge heavy when dealing with the public. When your identity is related as much to your roles as husband or wife, son or daughter, friend, and community member as it is to your role as police officer, people tend to relate to you better. When people relate to you better, it's easier to do your job. It is not difficult to begin non-law-enforcement conversations with your community members. Think about your outside interests. Which sports teams do you root for (maybe even your local high school teams)? What music do you listen to, what television shows do you watch, what are your favorite movies, what are your hobbies, and so on? Talking to people you encounter on duty about these topics is a way for your community members to get to know you as a person, not just a police officer. It shows your humanity. It demonstrates that you have commonalities that may not have been realized. Officers can get to know community members on a more personal level, and community members can get to know officers on a more personal level. This is hugely helpful for gaining the trust of the community, as well as enhancing police legitimacy. It is a win-win for the police and the community. Just as important, it is an active, on-duty way for you to remain balanced.

STEP 6. MY-SIDE BIAS

Officer Mike

 When I first started as a trainer at the academy, I began working on my doctorate. One professor discussed confirmation bias, which helped me obtain a better understanding not only of myself but also of those in my world who had differing opinions. The professor made us read information that we did not believe, talk with people who had differing opinions, and write about the facts. Since then, I watch news from different sources, read information, pay attention to social media, and have open conversations based on ideas that differ from mine. Of course, we are encouraged to continue to pay attention to those media that are in line with our beliefs. However, I have become more objective in forming opinions. But, as Nike says, "there is no finish line."

We all have assumptions, biases, and stereotypes, and it doesn't make us bad people; it makes us human. Think about it this way. I am a Chicago Cubs fan, and I'm watching a game against the St. Louis Cardinals when Javier Baez hits the ball deep to the shortstop. There is a close play at first base. They call him out. I start screaming, seeing that he was obviously safe. At the same time, somewhere else, a Cardinals fan is saying that he was obviously out. The play is under review. Wow, so "obvious" to both of us. We both can't be right.

Consciously and unconsciously, we tend to seek out information with which we already agree, believe information that matches our beliefs, have friends who share our attitudes, and follow social media that aligns with our opinions and ideas. Conversely, we are likely to ignore or discard information that doesn't match our beliefs and distance ourselves from anyone who does not share our views. This creates a strong belief that "I am right because I think I'm right." But we can't always be right, and people with differing views and opinions can be right—at least partially.

Our view or opinion of something can be based on things that are factually incorrect. Therefore, we need to understand that what we think is right could actually be wrong, no matter how strongly we believe it. When officers handle calls, they gather facts and make decisions based on those facts. The person with whom the officer is interacting may disregard the facts, especially under emotional circumstances. At the same time, we have to realize that the same thing can happen to cops. We have to fight against only seeing what we believe because we could be wrong.

Everyone can unwittingly have blinders on from time to time. This is when you become narrow-minded and can lose sight of the big picture, which can have extremely negative results in police work. Officers may become prematurely convinced that a particular individual is responsible for a crime. It is common to look for evidence to build the case and perhaps, unintentionally, ignore evidence that could lead to another suspect. Adding to this is the pressure to make an arrest, especially on a high-profile case. Unfortunately, wearing the blinders can result in a wrongful conviction because those involved at the next step (court system) can suffer from this same phenomenon.[7] Because this is rooted deep in our brains, it is difficult to see things more objectively and take proactive steps. It is thus important to recognize that we all have assumptions, biases, and stereotypes. Accepting this is a significant first step toward reducing my-side bias.

To grow as a person, it is essential to understand differing views, gain empathy toward others, and listen to people with different views. Be curious about where someone else is coming from. We increase our empathy when we are willing to put ourselves in someone else's shoes. The more we understand our my-side biases and the differing views of others, the more capable we become of providing effective policing to diverse communities.

STEP 7. THE VALUE OF WRITING

Writing is a fantastic, effective stress management strategy. It is a purely cognitive release, even though what you write about might be quite emotional. It is important to write about both positive and negative experiences. When you write about good things happening in your life, you will remind yourself that not everything is as bad as it may seem. When you write about negative things going on, you can symbolically get them "out of your system."[8] This helps you to understand yourself better by linking your thoughts, emotions, and behavior. Writing is a safe way to release what is spinning around in your head, sort out your thoughts, and develop an action plan if you decide to do something about any of the things that are on your mind. You never have to share what you write with anyone. And the writing does not have to have any purpose other than to put on paper (or type on the computer) the things you're thinking about.

Off-Duty Exercise

- Schedule a time to write every day. If you can't swing every day, write at least 3 days per week.
- If you are concerned about privacy, create a password-protected file on your computer or tablet. Some officers prefer using the old school tools of pen and paper. For that matter, if you are tired of writing so much, you can express your thoughts into a voice recorder.
- Set a timer for 10 minutes. No matter what, keep writing for the whole time (i.e., don't even answer a phone call). And even if you are in the middle of a thought, stop when the timer goes off. In this way, you train yourself that you control these thoughts; they do not control you.
- If you have trouble getting a thought out of your head during a shift, tell yourself that you will write about it later during your writing time—jot a note about the thought so that you won't forget what was bothering you.
- Don't worry about grammar or punctuation; you are not writing a police report or scholarly article. This is just you writing to yourself.
- Write whatever comes to mind. There are no restrictions here. If you want to write specifically about one of the steps you're working on, you can download writing prompts related to each chapter from the Resource

Library tab on this book's website (https://www.apa.org/
pubs/books/the-power-manual).

- It's a good idea to keep what you write. Many officers look
  back at earlier writings, especially during stressful times,
  to remind themselves that things can get better. It's also a
  good way to monitor yourself, your thoughts, and your
  attitude to catch any negative changes you may experience.

Officer Mike

 I have always enjoyed writing, but I had lost the habit of writing solely for myself. When I began collaborating on this manual, we decided to include stories from my 36 years in law enforcement as an officer and at the police academy. Writing about my experiences became therapeutic, so I began writing about my dad's life. He passed away over a year ago and was a great father. I did this initially to ensure his legacy lived on, especially for my mother, who was still alive. I miss him, but writing about all the great times we had has been constructive. When I began writing, I realized the extent to which he influenced my life in so many positive ways. I had taken his guidance for granted. The writing helped me to reflect on all my experiences in childhood and adulthood where my father had such an impact. He was not perfect, but no one is. Reflecting on the positive interactions and experiences made me realize that although my children are now grown up, I can still have a positive impact on their lives. And this will continue with my grandchildren, too. I'm not sure I would have reached this place if I hadn't started writing.

Your cognitive wellness, like other areas of your health, requires
some active effort on your part. Some of this involves modifying the
way you think about certain things. Some of it depends on creating

an attitude that helps you stay more positive while working in a career that has so much negativity. A lot of your cognitive wellness hinges on your willingness to look objectively at your skills and weaknesses and actively work on improving those deficiencies. And there are some cognitive steps you can take, such as writing, to reduce your stress level. However, these efforts alone will only go so far. As we discuss in the next chapter, your cognitive wellness is inseparable from your emotional wellness and vice versa.

CHAPTER 3

EMOTIONAL WELLNESS

Officer Mike

 I'll never forget the time animal control was not in service, and we had to handle animal calls and complaints for our shift. I was dispatched to the area of Bradley Street and Franklin Road to try to locate a small white poodle that had run away from its owner, who lived in the nearby condos.[1] Great! It was zero degrees, windy, and snowy, and I was looking for a white poodle. I remember heading south on Franklin Road and getting about one quarter mile out of town when I saw what looked like either a poodle or a large snowball moving around in the empty field on the other side of the ditch. I walked into the field and grabbed the tiny poodle. I put the dog in the front seat and turned on the heat. As I reversed my squad car to head back to town, I noticed an elderly woman, bundled up, walking along the roadway. I pulled over and got out of my squad car. She looked in the car and said something I will never forget: "Thank God, you found her! She's all I have since my husband died." We went to her condo and ate cookies and drank coffee, and I had the opportunity to learn all the great things about her husband's legacy. It meant just as much to me as it did to her. It reinforced why I had chosen this career.

No matter how stoic you think you can or should be, police work is an emotionally demanding career. At one time or another, every officer will experience every single human emotion. Without going deeply into the science, the emotional roller coaster of policing can take a toll on your health. This has to do with your cortisol levels (google it to learn more about how stress hormones affect and can disrupt entire systems in your body). Therefore, your overall health depends quite a bit on the extent to which you are able to maintain emotional wellness, which includes learning how to regulate your emotions effectively. In this chapter, we give you some strategies that you can use to keep emotionally fit. However, before getting to the good stuff, we have to provide a foundation so that everyone is on the same page. This is important because most people, including many cops, don't understand much about their emotions.

STEP 1. UNDERSTANDING AND IDENTIFYING EMOTIONS

First, let's clear up something. There is no such thing as a bad or negative emotion. We may not like how we're feeling, but the emotion is what it is. Instead of thinking about emotions as good/positive or bad/negative, it is much more productive to consider emotions on only two dimensions: *desirability* and *intensity*. For example, most people want to feel happy, but it may be overwhelming to feel elated (happy with more intensity) for extended periods. Likewise, few people want to feel sad, scared, or mad, and even fewer people would want more intensity of those less-desirable emotions, namely, grief, terror, and rage. Every emotion can be plotted on a graph like the one shown in the Emotion Chart, although for our examples, we've only listed a few core emotions.

Of course, the placement on the graph depends on the emotions that are more or less desirable to you. Not everyone will place the emotions in the same order on the desirability axis.

Emotion Chart

Intense

terror	grief	rage		elated
frantic	hurt	irate		joyous
scared	**sad**	**angry**		**happy**
insecure	somber	upset		grateful

Unwanted ──────────────┼────────── Wanted

uneasy	lost	annoyed		satisfied
worried	moody	uptight		glad
timid	blue	irritated		content
unsure	upset	touchy		mellow

Weak

Second, it's important to be articulate about your various emotions. You have to have the words to know where to put your emotions on the graph. The Emotion Chart contains four basic feelings plus examples of different levels of intensity of these feelings, but there are so many more emotions that we feel all the time. Think of expert snow skiers. They have many words to describe the type of snow on which they'll be skiing. This knowledge is important to help them prepare for the conditions on a given day on the slopes. Likewise, it's essential to have the words to label our feelings if we want to learn how to manage and regulate our emotions.

Unfortunately, many of us weren't taught the words for our emotions by our parents, so we never developed a sophisticated emotion vocabulary. Parents typically do a great job teaching their children words for objects and even abstract concepts, such as sharing and friendship. They also are successful at teaching their children about shared perceptual experiences, such as colors; for example, parents can't know for sure that what they see as "blue" is the same as what their child sees when they are teaching them the word for the color of the sky. Conversely, parents are generally not as proficient at teaching their young children to put the proper word on the emotion that they are feeling.

That leaves many of us ill equipped. We may feel something in the moment but lack a label for it, which causes us to feel other emotions such as confusion, anxiety, or frustration. It would be like trying to order a burger at a restaurant without knowing the name for that delicious sandwich. Eventually, you may get the server to understand that you want some beef between a bun with some cheese, tomato, lettuce, and onion, but you will both be frustrated during the process. As you increase your emotion vocabulary, you will become more of an expert about your own emotional experiences. A good place to start is one of the many free emotion charts that you can find online.

Off-Duty Exercise: Identifying Emotions

Use the Emotion Chart provided here, or if you want to explore a greater variety of emotions, print one of the online charts, which can be found when you google "emotion chart for adults." If you look online, you'll see some are quite basic, while others display an extensive list of feelings.

Look over the emotions.

1. Put a check mark next to each emotion that you recognize feeling from time to time.
2. Put an X next to the emotions that you can't easily recall feeling.
3. Make a list of the emotions marked with an X.
4. For each emotion on your list, imagine a situation that would leave you feeling that emotion.

5. For an emotion that you can't foresee feeling, head to a dictionary. Read the definitions and see whether you can visualize yourself feeling that emotion. Make note of the context that could evoke that emotion.

6. Every so often, go back to the chart to see whether you can change some Xs to check marks.

7. By doing this, you will expand your emotion vocabulary and mentally prepare yourself to feel some of the emotions with which you previously weren't so familiar.

The third aspect of understanding emotions involves the intensity level. We generally feel okay with a certain level of emotional intensity and get uncomfortable quite quickly when the emotions get too intense. Think of it as a thermostat. Some people don't mind living in triple-digit climates, although most of us prefer a more moderate environment. It's the same with emotions. This is related, in part, to one's culture. People from certain cultures tend to be more restrained and experience emotions at lower levels of intensity, while other cultures are known for people who are more passionate with all their feelings.

It also is significantly influenced by the family in which you were raised. Some families are loud and comfortable with intense displays of emotion, including affection and anger. Other families have a much lower thermostat and rarely show much intensity. Think of the challenges that arise when the partners in a marriage have their thermostats set differently. This may have been what attracted them to each other initially. For example, she was drawn to his passionate personality, and he was attracted to how steady and stable she was. They didn't understand this and eventually divorced because he started thinking she was a cold-hearted robot, and she began to see him as a raving lunatic.

It is important to understand where your emotional thermostat is set. We tend to avoid the emotions that occur above our comfort level. However, we should know what they are and how to identify them so that we can effectively manage them once we feel them. One reason so many people have difficulty coping with a critical or traumatic incident is that the event forces us to feel emotions that are far more intense than where the thermostat is set. To avoid feeling these undesirable and uncomfortably intense emotions, we shut down. We turn the thermostat even lower. The unwanted consequence of trying to avoid feeling the intense undesirable emotions is that the thermostat is now set too low to feel the more intense desirable emotions. As Alfred, Lord Tennyson wrote in an 1850 poem, "'Tis better to have loved and lost than never to have loved at all." In simple terms, unless you are willing to feel grief, you'll never be able to feel joy. One of Officer Mike's officers recounted the following story:

> My most embarrassing moment as a cop was also my very saddest moment. One of our younger officers was in a foot pursuit and got shot by the fleeing perp. After shift, a group of us went to the hospital and waited for some news following his surgery. The doctor came out, told us that our guy wasn't going to make it, and turned to walk away. Just then, I noticed that the doc had some toilet paper on his shoe. I couldn't help myself. I burst out laughing. I tried to choke it back, but the more I fought it, the more I couldn't stop laughing and just had to get out of there. This bothered me so much that I eventually went to our department shrink. He helped me understand that the situation intensified all my emotions, that something stupid seemed hysterically funny only because I was feeling such intense grief in that moment.

The goal is to get more comfortable feeling all our emotions, even the intense and undesirable ones. For that to happen, however, we need to understand another important distinction about our emotions.

STEP 2. EMOTIONAL EXPERIENCE VERSUS EMOTIONAL EXPRESSION

It becomes difficult to get comfortable with all your emotions if you believe that bad things will happen when you express your feelings—or at least some of them. The trick is to understand that there is a big difference between what you feel and how you express those feelings. Your emotional experience is what you feel. This has nothing to do with whether you decide to express those feelings or, if you do, how you express them. As we said, there is no such thing as a bad emotion. However, how you express your emotions can be effective, productive, and healthy, or your emotional expression can be destructive, unproductive, and unhealthy. To put it bluntly, no one has died from the sadness experienced after getting dumped by a romantic partner. Conversely, many people have died from how they chose to express that pain. For many people, the distinction between emotional experience and expression is a novel concept because they wrongly assume that there is a direct correlation between a feeling and how it is expressed.

If we take another brief detour back to childhood, it is pretty easy to see where some of the confusion surrounding our emotions originated. Young children express their emotions as they feel them. They have to be taught that the feeling can be expressed in different ways, some good and some not so good. Parents, unfortunately, often respond only to the expression rather than to the underlying emotional experience, which leaves us mistakenly thinking that our feeling is the same as how we expressed it. Let's look at two scenarios:

- Four-year-old Jason is playing with his favorite new toy. His older sister, Julie, walks by and takes the toy from him. Jason starts crying. Is he sad? Is he mad? It's up to the parents to help him understand his feelings, teach him the names of his emotions, and help him develop effective ways to express them.
  (a) The kids' mother hears the crying and says, "Jason, stop crying. Don't be such a baby." Jason is not helped to understand what he's feeling and learns, instead, that his unnamed and unidentified emotion is bad, and crying isn't an acceptable way to express it.
  (b) A better parenting response would be, "Jason, I'm sure that you are upset that Julie took your toy. I would be upset, too. But crying isn't going to get your toy back. Why don't you tell Julie that it makes you mad when she takes your toy and ask her to give it back?" The feeling is validated, and the child is given an effective way to express the emotion.
- Five-year-old Julie ignored her younger brother's request to return his favorite toy. When he started to take it from her, she punched him in the arm. Was she angry? Was she jealous that he had a new toy, but she didn't? It's up to the parents to help her understand her feelings, teach her the names of her emotions, and, in this case, also effectively respond to how she expressed her feelings.
  (a) The kids' mother sees what happened and says, "Julie, don't hit Jason. That's not ladylike." Julie is not helped to understand what she's feeling and learns, instead, that it isn't acceptable to feel angry.
  (b) A better parenting response would be, "Julie, it looks like you are upset that Jason got a new toy. It's okay that you

are upset, but it's not okay to hit. So, you have a time-out. If you are still feeling upset, you can punch your pillow." The feeling is validated, and the child learns that certain emotional expressions are acceptable and others will result in some discipline.

The goals are to be able to verbalize the feeling, which requires having a label for the emotion, and to have some safe outlets to express it. In the scenario, Jason may not have gotten the toy back when he told his sister how he felt and asked for it back. That would have led to other feelings, such as disappointment, frustration, and exasperation, especially if this was Julie's frequent MO. Jason would need additional outlets to express those additional feelings. A tough lesson here is that we may not have things turn out the way we want even though we can identify our feelings and constructively express them.

As important as it is to be able to identify all your emotional experiences, it is equally important to have a large repertoire of safe, healthy outlets to express your feelings. You probably know people who yell when they're mad, but they also yell when they're sad or scared or frustrated or annoyed. Similarly, there are people who cry when they are sad, but they also cry when they are mad or disappointed or happy. Your emotional wellness will improve if you develop a variety of constructive ways to express your emotions. Here are two of Officer Mike's:

Officer Mike

 One of the best ways for me to vent was through kicking and punching a heavy bag. My anger would eventually disappear out of pure exhaustion. I also knew that this method of venting would improve my physical condition.

Officer Mike

 In the late 1990s, I was called in early to help look for a missing 5-year-old girl. When I arrived at the station, I was assigned a geographic area for the search. I looked everywhere a little girl would hide; I knocked on every door, asking questions while waiting for someone to radio to me that she had been found. No such luck. It wasn't until months later that someone called dispatch, advising they had found the remains of a small child in a shallow grave behind their backyard. I arrived at the scene, and investigators arrived shortly after. Only her remains were left, but what made this seem more real was the fact that she was still wearing a white nightgown and was the same age as my little girl. When I finished my part of the investigation, I drove home and went into my daughter's room, where she was sleeping. I picked her up, held her in my arms, cried, and realized how thankful I was that my baby was fine. In that moment, crying really helped. It alleviated my sadness over that murdered girl, as well as my fear for my own daughter's safety and the helplessness I felt about keeping her safe.

Perhaps the healthiest way to express your emotions is to verbalize them. Of course, there is an art to this, and expressing your feelings in the moment you experience them may not be the most practical time to do so (we explain more about that later in this chapter). You also can articulate your emotions by writing them down. Again, the objective is to identify what you are feeling and release the emotions. You can do this any way you want, as long as (a) you do not hurt yourself (no punching walls), (b) you do not hurt someone else, and (c) you do not damage anything (again, no punching walls). Try, however, to have the emotional expression match the emotional experience in some way.

Off-Duty Exercise: Emotional Expression

Revisit the Emotion Chart from the earlier exercise.

1. For each emotion with a check mark, write down two or three ways that you could constructively express the feeling.
2. Decide whether you could use each emotional expression in the moment or whether you would have to wait to express the feeling later.
3. If the emotion comes up while you are off duty, it will be beneficial to develop some polite, assertive (i.e., non-aggressive) ways to express the emotion in the moment.
4. On or off duty, however, you may notice that the majority of your ideas will work only later when you are alone. And, certainly, in many on-duty situations, it would not be prudent to express the way you feel, even if you do so in a constructive, polite manner.

STEP 3. VENTING

In addition to the assortment of constructive ways to express all your emotions, it is important to have one or two go-to outlets to vent emotions, especially feelings such as anger and frustration. This is not so easy for many people who were raised to think that expressing anger and frustration is bad. For that matter, many people were taught that even feeling anger is wrong, which is rough because it is a natural human emotion. They repress the feelings, bottle them up, and hope they just go away. Unfortunately, this won't work. There are techniques that help in the moment, such as breathing and relaxation strategies, which are presented later in this book. But as anger and frustration build without a constructive outlet, they eventually will come out at inopportune times in ways that can be quite detrimental. As long as you do so constructively, it is a critical part of your emotional wellness to embrace the rage and safely release it! The most important part of the safety aspect is that you do the venting alone. A key note, however, is that venting should not be confused with complaining. Venting is a healthy release, while complaining just roils the emotions and keeps them festering.

When we teach this to groups of cops, there is always a little uncomfortable laughter because this exercise addresses feelings that are above some folks' thermostats. Like a teakettle, everyone needs a release valve to blow off steam regularly. Unlike a teakettle, however, you don't want to wait until you are boiling to do some venting. In fact, making time to vent is one of the first components of emotion regulation. This is because it is easier to keep your cool in a volatile situation when you regularly and safely release your emotions and never allow them to build up.

There are many venting strategies that safely release your emotional intensity. Officer Mike mentioned working out with a heavy bag, which is an excellent technique. Some people claim that running is their go-to strategy. This is a great exercise for your physical wellness and can be a good way to sort out your thoughts for your cognitive wellness. However, running isn't always a great way to vent your emotional intensity. It may tire you out so that you don't feel as bothered by the emotions, but it is a passive strategy that by itself doesn't directly release your emotions. In fact, other people find that the undesirable emotions get more intense while running because they are stewing in them rather than releasing them. However, some officers have found that an excellent release while running is to give off a loud yell every few hundred yards; the shout releases any pent-up feelings and nagging thoughts.

Sometimes someone does something that upsets you and that person becomes the target of your anger or frustration. You may have learned excellent communication skills, can avoid unnecessary escalations and confrontations, and know when it might be best to hold your tongue, as they say. Even if you talk it over and resolve whatever happened, there still may be residual emotions. That's why it is important to have a venting strategy or two and make some time to release the emotions constructively—that is, don't let them build up.

In many cases, however, there is nothing to resolve because the source of your anger is a superior, a citizen, an attorney, a politician, a community leader, and so forth. It may not be appropriate or even possible to communicate your emotions directly to that person, but it is perfectly acceptable to vent your feelings by yourself while thinking about what they did to upset you. It also is important to remember that you can have an intense emotion about what someone did, which causes you to think some pretty terrible things, but this does not mean that you would ever consider doing anything terrible to retaliate or that you would want something bad to happen to them. Venting allows you to release those feelings and let go of any associated "terrible" thoughts.

The following is a list of strategies that can be used to vent anger and frustration safely. Each of the activities was reported to be the venting strategy of choice by a police officer. Some of the techniques involve physical exertion, but others are more cerebral. Some will sound quite reasonable to you, while others may seem really out there. Also, some of the venting strategies help you focus your release according to the source of your anger or frustration, while others are more general. Not all the strategies listed will work for each person, so you may need to try some trial and error here to find the best outlets for you. Remember to wear proper safety equipment (e.g., gloves, goggles) when doing some of these:

- punch or kick a heavy bag
- punch a speed bag
- chop wood
- smash rocks
- throw glass bottles into a recycling bin
- hit a mattress with a baseball bat
- stick pins into a voodoo doll
- scream into a pillow
- tear paper that is heading to the trash into tiny pieces
- make Play-Doh antagonists and then smash them
- write (but don't send) a hostile letter
- stomp or squish some bubble wrap
- blast a song like Black Sabbath's "Iron Man," and sing along as loudly as you can
- hold a racquetball in each hand and squeeze them repeatedly
- buy a "giant stress ball" (several varieties are available from Amazon) to punch, squeeze, pull, and squish

Off-Duty Activity: Venting

If you already have a go-to strategy for venting, this will be easy. Otherwise, review the list of venting activities and pick one that sounds like it could work for you as a viable release valve. When you begin venting, it may seem awkward or uncomfortable at first. Fight through the discomfort and keep doing it. However, if one strategy just doesn't feel right, try another. The more you practice venting, the more natural and comfortable it will become. And it won't take long after regularly making time to vent for you to notice feeling a lot less angry or frustrated throughout your day. You'll see fairly quickly how well this works!

- Schedule time on your calendar to vent. Try to book 5 minutes for yourself to vent at least 3 or 4 days per week, but every day is ideal.
- For each vent session, set a timer for 5 minutes. Make sure that you will not be interrupted—don't even answer the phone if it rings during these 5 minutes.
- Do the activity until the timer goes off. It may be hard to sustain the venting that long for some activities, although others will feel like you are just getting started and don't want to stop when the timer goes off.
- It is important to use the entire 5 minutes. In this way, you are training yourself that you control the release of your emotions; your emotions do not control you. For example, if you were writing a letter but weren't finished, stop after 5 minutes and return to it during your next vent session. At that time, you might continue where you left off, or if those feelings no longer need a release, you can move on to something else.
- When you have vent sessions scheduled, if something happens during a shift that leaves you with some unexpressed emotions, make a note (mentally or jot it down) that those are the feelings that you will vent during your next session.

STEP 4. EMOTIONAL LABOR

One of the reasons regular vent sessions are important is that police officers can become exhausted and burned out due to the emotional labor required on the job. In a nutshell, *emotional labor* is the effort you expend when you have to display emotions to the public that are quite different from the emotions that you are actually feeling.[2,3] This happens when you have to suppress the emotions you are feeling in the moment to accomplish your task. For example, when citing a motorist who is trying to wrangle out of a citation, it may take some effort to hide the annoyance you feel so that you don't end up saying something that provokes them to file a complaint against you. On a regular basis, officers hide their true emotions to convey a professional demeanor. This is especially true in your work at critical and traumatic incidents, such as the one described earlier by Officer Mike, and when you have to stay professional around truly despicable people, such as pedophiles. At the same time, it is emotionally demanding to constantly display a strong command presence even when you are not feeling your best. Officers frequently have to seek compliance by conveying feelings of confidence and cannot show any fear even when feeling afraid, which, by the way, is also a natural emotion.

We refer to the skill of remaining professional no matter what your underlying emotions are as *tactical empathy*.[4] In Chapter 7, we provide suggestions for using tactical empathy, but for now, it is important to focus on how exhausting it can be to constantly try to suppress how you are feeling in the moment. Most officers understand how easily their tone of voice, body language, and badge-heavy demeanor can escalate an already volatile encounter. Those are signs that emotions are not being adequately regulated and may be getting in the way of effective police work. When using empathy and respect tactically, you cannot let your true feelings show. If you sound or act the way you feel, such as sarcastic or degrading, it unnecessarily escalates the encounter.

Knowledge here is power. Understand the negative impact of emotional labor. You know that there are times when you deserve an Academy Award because the emotions you show are so far from how you really feel. Take steps to prevent the performance from wearing you down and burning you out. One technique is to vent every day, as described earlier. While venting, you may even find that it is helpful to think about the people to whom you showed excellent tactical empathy and respect despite feeling just the opposite. We discuss some additional emotional wellness exercises later in this chapter that can help offset the emotional labor you expend on the job.

STEP 5. ORIGIN OF EMOTIONS

Another emotional wellness strategy is to understand where your emotions originate. Without going into the various psychological theories, the easiest way to view this is that your emotions come from your thoughts. We revisit this a bit in Chapter 9. You have little control over your emotions, but you have tremendous control over your thoughts. Therefore, as you learn to control your thoughts, you will be more effective at regulating your emotions. Let's illustrate this with a simple off-duty example.

You are driving down the highway with your family to visit your in-laws. In your rearview mirror, you notice a car weaving through traffic at an excessive speed. He gets too close, zips around, and cuts you off before speeding away.

Most people in this situation get pissed off to some level or another, which can lead to some cursing, honking, head shaking, grumbling, and so forth. Other people shrug it off without much of an emotional reaction at all. What's the difference? The same event leads different people to different emotional reactions.

The difference between the emotional reactions is the intervening thought. We can't know why that motorist was driving like that. So, like a blank canvas, we put whatever thought we choose onto the event. Those who swear, honk, or flipped the middle finger most likely thought the driver was a rude asshole who is endangering the public; such a thought naturally evokes feelings of anger. However, some people think quite differently, shrugging it off as if it wasn't worth the energy to get mad—they might think, for example, "There are a lot of terrible drivers out there. I can't take it personally."

Now, imagine the same event. This time, however, instead of thinking that the driver is an asshole, what emotion would you feel if you knew that he was driving that way because his house was on fire or his child was just hit by a bus? He is still endangering the public, but maybe has a better reason for driving like a maniac than just being a jerk. When you don't know the facts, you will have a thought that may or may not be correct. In this situation, would you rather stay calm and shrug it off or let the ambiguous situation leave you pissed off because of how you interpreted it? For your emotional wellness, the better answer is to train yourself to interpret uncertain events in ways that leave you feeling calmer and more in control.

You can use this thought-changing technique to manage your emotions at work, as well. It's easy to get impatient or annoyed with people, especially if you think that they are being noncompliant, purposefully antagonistic, or outwardly rude. For that matter, when an arrestee tries to fight you, it can be difficult not to take it personally and think, "This dude is trying to hurt me!" When you have these thoughts, your emotions will intensify, which could cause you to lose control. Instead, it is important that you insulate yourself from what people say or do to you. If you train yourself to think that they are having a worse day than you and are taking out on you whatever crap is going on in their life, without taking it personally, you will be able to effectively manage your emotions and stay better focused on the task at hand. In other words, it's up to you to prevent your emotions from interfering with your training by maintaining thoughts, such as

- I trust my training to get me through this safely.
- It's okay if I don't have all the answers.
- I can't help everyone who calls for service; I can only do my best.
- I will survive if something bad happens.
- I never take this stuff personally.

STEP 6. TEMPERAMENT AND MOOD

Another component of your emotional wellness involves your temperament. In plain terms, this is your disposition or general way of reacting to people and situations. You know people who are usually calm and pleasant, others who are typically irritable or churlish, and many who fall somewhere in between. It used to be pretty common to label people as a Type A or Type B personality. The Type A person is competitive, ambitious, and frequently aggressive. Type B personalities are more laid back and easygoing but can procrastinate and seem lackadaisical. These personality types don't involve your emotions. However, there also are Type C and Type D personalities that do relate more to one's emotional temperament. Type C personalities are meeker and more serious. The Type D person tends to worry and feel gloomy or angry. Why is this important? Research shows that the Type D emotional disposition is associated with heart disease,[5] which, if you tend to be gloomy or angry, may be a good reason to get motivated to improve your outlook.

Regardless of general temperament, your mood can fluctuate. Even the crankiest person will laugh from time to time. That tells us that there is potential for people whose disposition leans toward the gloomy or grumpy. For your overall emotional wellness, it is important to use strategies that help you to maintain a pleasant, hopeful mood. We know that may be easier said than done because there is so much that you encounter every day that is unpleasant. And we're not suggesting that you should always feel cheerful dealing with what you face at work. However, you get to choose how much of that unpleasantness will contaminate your mood and negatively impact your health.

This is not a new concept. In 1937, the song "Whistle While You Work" came out in Disney's *Snow White and the Seven Dwarfs*. The idea was that singing, humming, or whistling makes you feel

more pleasant while doing something tedious. Some science has even supported the idea that you can improve your mood regardless of the situation. In one study, researchers covertly got participants to smile by holding a pen between their teeth. The results showed that "the act of smiling can trick your mind into being more positive, simply by moving your facial muscles."[6] This means that if you remind yourself to smile even when you are not feeling happy, it will, nevertheless, help you feel more pleasant. Perhaps even more important, when you are feeling somewhat down, don't wait for something to come along to lift your spirits. You can do it for yourself. This shows that you have more control over your mood than you may realize.

STEP 7. THE ROLE OF HUMOR

A great way to stay emotionally balanced in the midst of all the negativity at work is to make time each week for some humor. Although cops are famous for crude humor and making jokes at inappropriate times (about which you have to be extremely careful now that everyone has a video camera handy), humor is a way to increase the emotional intensity on the desirable side of the Emotion Chart shown earlier in the chapter. Laughter can be the best medicine! If you want more proof of this, google Norman Cousins, who used laughter to help treat a medical disease.

There are probably lots of things that bring a smile to your face or elicit a little chuckle. It's good to allow yourself to feel amused as often as you can. But what makes you really laugh out loud? Try to figure this out. What are your top five favorite funny movies? Who are your favorite stand-up comedians? The things that make you laugh may not be what someone else finds funny. For Norman Cousins, it was Marx Brothers' movies and reruns of the television show *Candid Camera*. If nothing readily comes to mind, YouTube is a great place to discover some videos that can get you laughing. By the way, if you tend to watch dramas or scary movies or play violent video games, try to wean yourself off them. Trade those in for the stuff that makes you laugh or at least brings a smile to your face.

Off-Duty Exercise: Laughter

- Download or bookmark at least five to 10 short videos or clips from movies that make you laugh every time you view them.
- Carve out some time each week for some belly laughs (i.e., deep, sustained laughter).
- Ideally, every day find time to watch a brief video that you downloaded.
- Watch, laugh, repeat.

STEP 8. TALKING ABOUT YOUR EMOTIONS

Besides venting and writing to release emotions before they get intrusively intense, an important component of emotional wellness is your ability to talk about your feelings. This is, ideally, with your spouse or, if you are single, your closest friend, which we discuss more in the next chapter. Talking about your emotions is a way for you to keep cognitive control of your feelings and examine the thoughts that may have caused them. By doing this regularly, you will identify patterns that lead to your emotional reactions. You will become more aware of what pushes your buttons. The process also helps normalize all your emotions, including the undesirable feelings. Unlike a typical conversation, when you talk about your feelings in this context, the listener is supposed to offer support and validation without any suggestions. The goal is for you to hear yourself describing your emotions, get comfortable sharing your feelings with your partner, and reinforce that there is a reliable person from whom you obtain emotional support. If you establish this as a routine when your emotions are of mild intensity, you will be less likely to isolate yourself when your emotions get uncomfortably intense. At that point, you may have to do some venting first, but afterward, you will be ready to talk about your feelings.

Off-Duty Exercise: Daily Questions

1. Make time every day to talk about your emotions. If you are single, find someone with whom you can do this activity. It could be before bed, during a meal, or if all else fails, over the telephone. Most of the emotions you'll mention won't be intense unless you responded to some challenging calls that day. You may need to keep track during the day about what you plan to share.

2. Have your partner ask you, "What happened today that left you feeling happy?"

   Your response should take the format: "When _____ [the event] happened, I thought _____, which made me happy." On some days, nothing might have made you happy, so you have to describe a happy feeling of less intensity, such as amused or pleased or fine—for example, "When a kid gave me a thumbs-up today, I thought it was a nice gesture, which made me feel satisfied with what I'd done."

3. Have your partner ask you, "What happened today that left you feeling sad?"

   For example, "I saw a dead cat in the road. I thought of the kids who will find out that their pet was killed, which made me sad."

4. Have your partner ask you, "What happened today that left you feeling scared?"

   For example, "I was in the elevator at the courthouse, and it lurched. I thought it was broken, which made me a little uneasy."

5. Have your partner ask you, "What happened today that left you feeling angry?"

   For example, "When my sergeant told me to revise a report, I thought he was singling me out, which made me aggravated."

BONUS: You can take turns with each of the emotions. After you share your feeling, have your partner share his or hers. In this way, in addition to getting comfortable receiving emotional support, you will train yourself to get better at providing emotional support.

Note: This exercise is included in the POWER Manual Journal Pages, available for download from the Resource Library tab on this book's website (https://www.apa.org/pubs/books/the-power-manual).

This exercise creates a process. Many officers find that when something terrible happens, they don't have to wait to be asked to share their feelings. One of Officer Mike's officers shared the following:

When I first learned about this daily question activity, I thought it was pretty lame. But I gave it a try. It became a habit, but lots of days, we just laughed because there wasn't really anything that made me happy or angry. Sure, stuff happens a lot that stirred up some fear, like every time I have to stop a vehicle with heavily tinted windows. Same with sad because every day I see something that is sad. Lots of days, I'm saying the same thing I said last week or yesterday. But one of my buddies, only 3 years older than me, dropped dead of a heart attack. That night, I went home and said, "You won't believe what happened. Doug died. I'm just devastated." It felt good to have someone not from work to talk to.

There's no doubt that your emotional wellness is critically important to your overall health. In this chapter, we provided some important tools to keep you emotionally healthy. But there's a lot more you can do. For example, there has been considerable research that points to the importance of emotional intelligence (EI). High EI is equated with improved wellness and enhanced police performance.[7] Perhaps your agency contracted with someone to provide training on EI, which typically focuses on awareness of your emotions, effective management of your emotions, keen awareness of the emotions of others, and the ability to use emotions to manage your interactions with others successfully. Whether or not your agency is making an effort to boost your EI, we recommend that you consider doing this on your own through reading, workshops, or even with the assistance of a life coach or psychologist.

Your emotions occur through your interactions and ongoing relationships with others. For this reason, your emotional wellness cannot be improved alone. Although many interactions with others while on duty may evoke undesirable emotions, try to pay attention to work-related interactions that bring on desirable feelings, such as contentment, pride, friendliness, and warmheartedness. At times, your close relationships can cause some undesirable emotions, but most of the time, these are the source of your most intense desirable emotions. Finding ways to nurture those relationships to increase the amount of time and intensity of your desirable emotions will hopefully become a top priority. We explore this more in the next chapter.

CHAPTER 4

SOCIAL WELLNESS

As many philosophers and scientists have said, humans are social animals.[1] Our health depends on positive affiliations with others. In this chapter, we focus on two important words in that last sentence, *positive affiliations*, and explain how you can take steps to improve your social wellness. Not surprisingly, an early warning sign of someone's distress is that they begin to isolate themselves from friends and family. Conversely, a way to combat distress is to stay connected to others and maintain healthy social and recreational outlets. This is easier to do if you continue to practice the strategies in the previous three chapters. For example, if you are not coping well with your emotions, you may lose interest in recreational activities and prefer not to "burden" your friends and family with your less-than cheerful mood. However, it is precisely when you are having some challenges that your friends and family can help you, which is why it's important to develop and maintain positive affiliations and a well-rounded social life.

Before we begin, there are a couple of rather touchy subjects that need to be mentioned. First, because this chapter is about the importance of social relationships, if you are an introvert, a loner, or even a total hermit, you might not immediately connect with our emphasis on activities to do with other people. We don't want or expect you to change your personality. However, were you always that way, or have you slowly become more reclusive over the years? Especially in the latter case, improving your social wellness is critically important to your overall health. But even if you've always been a loner, you can improve your health and well-being by having one or two close friends with whom you can share some of these wellness suggestions.

Second, in this chapter, we emphasize family and present activities to share with your spouse or significant other. We understand that not everyone is in a committed relationship, not everyone has family living nearby, and not everyone has close relationships with their parents and/or siblings. For that matter, there are plenty of folks who are in committed relationships that are not fulfilling; for a variety of reasons, you and your partner may not have a close connection. If you fall into one of these categories, you can substitute a close friend with whom you can build your social wellness and adapt our suggestions accordingly. At the same time, if you are in a less than effective or less than emotionally supportive committed relationship, what we offer here is aspirational. Although not meant as any sort of marriage counseling, our strategies might improve the intimacy in your relationship, which will definitely boost your social wellness.

STEP 1. FAMILY AND FRIENDSHIPS

Officer Mike

 As a working cop, I limited my overtime. It was important to me to spend time with my family and friends. I also saw how cops who regularly took overtime could get burned out, sometimes working 15 to 20 days in a row. Not only would I limit my overtime but I would also take comp time rather than pay, which would build up even more days to be off for family and friends. I knew I would have to budget accordingly, but the extra time off was more valuable than the money.

Your social wellness starts with friends and family. If you are married or in a committed romantic relationship, that person is your life partner. Ideally, you will be closer to them than to anyone else in the world, including your work partner. Lots of cops say that they don't like to bring work home, but that's a cop-out. Either there are some "issues" in that relationship (get some good marriage counseling to learn better communication skills), or you are avoiding dealing with some issues at work by not wanting to talk about what's going on (get some good marriage counseling to learn better communication skills). Your social wellness will improve as you improve your ability to open up and be vulnerable with your life partner, as will their ability to open up and be vulnerable with you. This is what breeds intimacy, and emotional intimacy is an important component of your social wellness.

Off-Duty Activities With Your Spouse or Partner

- No matter how chaotic your lives get, plan a date night once per week. It can be staying in with a movie or a romantic dinner or going out for something you both enjoy. One tip is to alternate who picks the activity. If you didn't choose it and it's not something you would have picked, try not to grumble. Enjoy it because it's a chance to spend some time together, and next week you get to choose.
- Once per month, make the date night something a bit more special, such as a dinner or movie out. Again, you can alternate who picks.

- Once per quarter, use a date night for an overnighter. Get someone to watch the kids if you have them. It can be a nice hotel with a spa where you can get a couples' massage, a quaint B&B, or the Motel 6 down by the highway. Just get a night together away from home. Again, you can alternate who picks to avoid any arguments about where you're going to go.

Note: Journal pages for you to download and use to record your ideas for social wellness are available from the Resource Library tab on this book's website (https://www.apa.org/pubs/books/the-power-manual).

If you have children, another central component of your social wellness is to thoroughly embrace your role as a parent. Being an active and involved parent helps your life to stay balanced. It's just as important for you to be in their lives as it is for them to have you involved in their life. Go to their school functions (e.g., back-to-school night, parent–teacher conferences, carnivals, holiday assemblies). As much as your work schedule permits, attend their recitals, athletic events, and anything that is significant to them. For some of these events, take a vacation day if you have to.

Off-Duty Activities With Your Children and Family

- At least once per month, plan an event to do alone with your kids, and make sure to follow through. Leave the other parent at home to do whatever they want. This doesn't have to cost money. It could be a special hike or a day fishing, skating, or rock climbing. Make it something that your kids like to do. If you have more than one and they have different interests, alternate months so that each will get to do something they like. No grumbling from the other one(s) who will eventually get their chance to pick. It doesn't matter how old your kids are. The activities will change, but even when they are grown, make time to get together for something fun to do with each other.

- At least once per quarter, plan an event that is a little more special, such as going to an amusement park or a ball game. This can be with or without their other parent. Again, if everyone has different interests, alternate who gets to choose.

- At least once per month, plan a special outing for the whole family. This can be free, such as a trip to the beach if you live close by, or it can cost some money, such as a night at the movies. Try not to settle for just dinner at a local restaurant, but it could include a meal if your budget can afford it.

- If you are a single parent, things get hectic, and it's easy to forget to have fun. Do your best to infuse some fun when your kids are with you (assuming some form of shared custody). If they are with you full time, schedule some fun as mentioned in the items just listed.

Off-Duty Activity for Vacation Time

Use your vacation time for something other than finishing home projects. The vacation does not have to be extravagant. It could be camping or borrowing someone's timeshare somewhere. It could be visiting extended family. The important point is to go somewhere to enjoy some time away from home.

- Plan a week away with your spouse or partner without the kids if you have someone to watch them (e.g., parents or in-laws).
- Plan a week away with the whole family.
- If you are a single parent, have fun planning vacations with your kids, as well as planning surprise vacations when the kids don't know in advance where you're going.

Tip: If your children are involved in many activities, such as sports, scouts, or band, pay for trip insurance in case something comes up that they can't miss. Better yet, plan your vacations around those activities, if you can.

One of the hidden benefits of all this scheduling is that it puts social activities with your spouse and kids on your calendar as far out as you can preplan them. This gives you something to look forward to, which can be a great stress reliever when things get rough at work. You want to try as much as possible to keep these appointments. That means only a true emergency would cause you to cancel something you've planned to do with your family. If you do have to scratch an event, reschedule it for as soon as possible. Not only does this help you maintain balance in your life but it also shows your family how important they are to you. After all, nothing, including your job, is more important to your kids and family than you are.

Family Gatherings

The extended family can be a source of stress. Many cops come from troubled families and are no longer close with their parents or siblings. Other cops had good childhoods but are now, as adults, closer to some family members than others. In other words, family reunions, if they even happen, may not be a lot of fun. When you add in some issues with in-laws, it may seem easier just to keep your distance from the extended family. However, there is value in nurturing your relationships with your extended family and in-laws or, at least, with some of them. Ideally, your extended family keeps you connected to your history. They keep you humble but also are so proud of you. Regardless of how rough things get at work, your family has your back and loves you no matter what; they will always see you as the hero you are.

So, make time to stay in touch with your family members who don't live near you. Try to find ways to see them and not just during the holidays, which can be stressful enough (and you may have to work anyway). If some of your family members live nearby, make time to get together at least every other month or more frequently. By the way, when you are with the extended family, some of them may want to hear about your work or discuss the current climate of policing. Do your best not to engage! Have some clever ways to evade those conversations, such as "I left my badge at home," "Let's just enjoy these burgers," or "My therapist said I'm not supposed to talk about police work when I'm off duty."

Officer Mike

 Holidays and birthdays are crucial gatherings for my family. When I became a police officer, my family realized that I often had to work during these important family gatherings.

Throughout my career, my family (mom, dad, wife, sister, children) would make every effort to ensure I was part of these events. For example, our Thanksgiving celebration might not always be on Thanksgiving Day, Christmas might not be on Christmas Day, and birthday parties might not be on the actual birthday. They made these modifications for me so I could be part of the celebrations. I have always appreciated my family making this sacrifice.

"Flavors" of Friends

Friendships are another important part of your social wellness. Your friendships, however, come in two flavors: cops and noncops. It's important that you have a balanced diet that contains both flavors. But it's not a coincidence that this paragraph comes last in this section. Unless you are single and without children, your friendships shouldn't take priority over your relationships with your family. Friendships, for those with families, complete your social wellness picture. They can provide an occasional break from family responsibilities and work stresses. Maybe you play on a softball team or enjoy golfing with a few buddies. Maybe you are in a serious fantasy football league. Your friendships can provide a great recreational outlet for you. Try to have some recreational activity that you do with friends regularly, at least once or twice per month. However, when your priorities are straight, some of these activities have to be curtailed when you have kids because you don't want to miss out on time with them.

It's also important that you have a friend in whom you can confide. This requires a delicate balance. Your spouse or partner is, ideally, your go-to confidante. It's not cool if you share things with a friend but keep your spouse in the dark only to have them find out later. Your spouse hopefully understands that you share some things with your friend about stresses in your family. You can benefit from the objective ear of a supportive friend.

Of course, when it comes to some of your recreational activities, such as golfing or skiing or scuba diving, it wouldn't hurt to do these activities with your spouse to improve the quality of that relationship; time together builds intimacy. It may be a sign of some trouble in the relationship when you look for things to do with your friends instead of spending time with your spouse or say that you sometimes need a break from the family. Many cops with families stop hanging out with their single friends and start getting together with married friends as couples or as families with their friends who also have kids.

Let's revisit the idea of two flavors of friends. It's pretty reasonable that you will become close friends with some of the officers with whom you work. Some cops keep those friendships at work because they don't want their off-duty time to remind them of work. Other cops socialize with their work friends, play on a rec sports team together, and even vacation together. The key is to make sure that when you socialize with cops, there is minimal cop talk (which can alienate spouses anyway). You need balance in your life for your social wellness, but if your social life is dominated by friendships with other cops and all you do is cop stuff, then you are not balanced.

One way to ensure some balance is to have friends who are not in law enforcement. In many cases, this happens naturally by socializing with your spouse's friends (assuming your spouse isn't a cop). Many officers remain close with the friends they had before law enforcement. Some of those old friends may not be supportive of police, so weed them out. Most will be proud of you, even if they don't exactly understand everything you deal with. That's what makes it hard for many officers to keep friendships with those not in law enforcement and, frankly, what leads to many law enforcement divorces. The officer says, "They just can't relate to what I have to deal with." So, instead of working to improve the relationship or friendship, they withdraw and gravitate to other cops. The result is a dangerous lack of balance that leads to a lack of social wellness. Not all your friends have to relate to what you have to deal with! Not all your friends have to be your closest confidante. Some of these friends are just for having fun with. Let's be honest, do you relate to everything all your noncop friends have to deal with in their jobs?

If you are not in a serious relationship or do not have children, your friends can provide the support of a surrogate family. As just mentioned, you ideally have friends of both flavors. But, even if all your friends are cops because, for example, you moved away from where you grew up and don't know many people who aren't in law enforcement, the goal is for you to maintain social balance. That means that you don't live law enforcement 24/7. Even if all your friends are cops who are serving as your surrogate family, make sure that you develop a variety of recreational activities and that your social life is not dominated by cop stuff.

At the same time, it wouldn't hurt to cultivate friendships with some noncops. To do that, you have to see yourself as more than the badge. Most officers have interests and hobbies outside of law enforcement, whether in sports, music, carpentry, or construction. It's not uncommon for officers whose only friendships are with other cops to spend less time with those hobbies and interests. Instead, you might connect with people outside of law enforcement who share those interests and hobbies. The challenge, and what seems to inhibit many officers from doing this, is that they are worried about developing friendships with noncops who might be antagonistic to law enforcement or engage in illegal activity. Nevertheless, this should not deter you from attempting to develop new friendships.

Officer Mike

 Martial arts is not only an important recreational activity for me but also an escape from my police identity. We have martial arts in common, yet we are police officers, accountants, chiropractors, construction workers, and factory workers. This commonality, as well as our differences, brings us together in such a magnificent way.

STEP 2. RECREATION

Officer Mike

 Whenever my oldest son visits from Chicago and the weather is nice (and sometimes when it is not), we always take the time to play catch with the baseball. We are not only active but, during this playtime, we also have some of our greatest conversations. It might even be about my awesome 40-miles-per-hour knuckleball.

Another component of your social wellness is to have some favorite recreational activities that you do just for fun. Some of these are seasonal, such as skiing, which you look forward to and plan for even during the off season. Some take place regularly throughout the year, while others are more like special, fun "rituals" you do around the holidays (e.g., picking out a Christmas tree or driving through the neighborhoods with the extravagant Christmas lights). One thing for certain, though, is that recreation is a personal preference. No one can tell you how to have fun. Instead, here are some steps for you to take so you remember to make the time to recreate:

1. Make a list of your favorite activities.
2. Add to that list some bucket list activities that you always wanted to do but haven't yet.
3. Add to that list your spouse or life partner's favorite activities and some from their bucket list. For that matter, add to the list your kids' favorite activities. Amend the list as necessary as interests change and as you check some of the items off the list.
4. Calculate the financial investment for each activity on the newly expanded list:
   - What equipment will you need to purchase?
   - What is the cost of joining the team or group?
   - What is the cost of the necessary equipment, gear, clothing, and footwear?
   - How much are those season tickets?
5. Create a calendar to schedule when you will do the activities and with whom (alone or with spouse, kids, family, or friend).
6. For the bucket list activities, prioritize them and see when you can add them to the calendar.
7. For activities that will take place in the distant future, plan to review your list a couple of times per year. For example, how well are you saving money for something big, such as an anniversary cruise? Plan, save, and review.

8. Turn down overtime if you have something already planned.
9. Make sure to use your vacation time. And plan to put in for it as early as you can if you want to lock in the leave. However, it's always a good idea to be as flexible as possible when making your vacation plans.

STEP 3. COMMUNITY INVOLVEMENT

It is important for police officers to be involved in their community, both on duty and off duty. There are two components to this. If you live in the community in which you work, you will cover both at the same time. However, if you live in a community other than the one you work in, your off-duty community involvement will probably mostly be in the community in which you live. And there are significant benefits of volunteering some of your time in the community in which you work even if you don't live there, such as participating at local church events, attending youth sports activities, and going to street fairs where you can meet the locals without worrying about enforcement actions. Community involvement offers both personal and professional benefits. One of Officer Mike's colleagues related the following story:

> I was up for promotion. I didn't get it. When I asked for some feedback, they said I didn't have enough on my resume that showed volunteer activity in the community. I don't really know if that was it or if it was just a bullshit excuse for passing me over, but I went home and told my kids that they were going to have a new coach on their basketball and soccer teams. I didn't know squat about soccer, but it didn't matter. The following year, I went into the promotional interview and told them that I appreciated their feedback last time and spent over 500 hours volunteering for two youth sports teams in my community. I got the promotion. And I had a blast with my kids.

The more you can get involved in your community, the better you will feel about your role as a citizen as well as your role as a police officer. One obvious advantage of community involvement is the feeling of "belonging" you get when others don't just see you as a cop but also see you as a regular member of the community. Moreover, there are many professional advantages to community involvement for officers, including

- showing less cynicism toward the community members you serve;
- developing strong relationships, which, in turn, promote community policing, creating important partnerships to address and solve community issues and problems;
- having a better understanding of the community and its needs;
- becoming more multiculturally competent;
- having greater respect for and empathy toward community members (i.e., reducing the "us-against-them" mentality);
- finding commonality with community members, such as rooting for the same sports team and liking the same music and food;
- increasing overall job satisfaction;
- increasing officer and citizen safety; and
- raising motivation to solve community issues and improve the quality of life for everyone in the community.

Perhaps most important of all is that you can focus your off-duty community involvement on having some fun. It may take some effort, but it could be easier than you think. Here are some suggestions for community involvement while on duty and off duty. If you are racing from call to call on duty, consider some of these during your "lunch." Also, when you work at night, you will have to postpone these until you have a shift change.

On-Duty Exercise

- Stop by a youth center, Boys and Girls Club, or YMCA. Play some games or just get to know them by hanging out.
- Get out of your car as often as possible while patrolling and make nonenforcement contacts. It is nice to chat with citizens when it is not a traffic stop or call for service.
- Walk your beat and go into each business. Ask workers and owners whether they have any concerns or simply chat for a while.
- Walk the parks during youth and adult sporting events and just be a fan.

Officer Mike

 When I was a patrolman on second shift, I would report to work at 3:00 p.m. and work the school zones. Afterward, if I wasn't busy on a call, I would stop by the afterschool center and hang out with the kids. Many of these youth were living in poverty and had little guidance. I loved hanging out with them as a police officer, person, and mentor. When I became a sergeant on second shift, I told my officers that whoever was assigned the patrol beat of the afterschool center must, if not busy, stop by and see the kids. Most officers were hesitant, saying things like "I'm not a DARE officer" or "I'm not an SRO [school resource officer]." I told them that they only need to stay for 5 minutes and just hang out and play a game with the kids—play Connect Four, buy a bag of Doritos and share it with them, play basketball with the older kids. Within 2 weeks, my officers were staying until they received a call for service. What a great way to build relationships with the community and gain trust.

Off-Duty Exercise

- Volunteer at a soup kitchen, deliver meals to seniors, work the pancake breakfast at a church, and so forth.
- Coach a youth sports team or get on the board of a local youth sports league.
- Organize a team with fellow officers to participate in charity events. It is great optics, and you will be raising money for a worthy cause.

Officer Mike

 Some of the best memories of my police career involved the things officers did together off duty. Two memories of getting together for charities stand out in particular. For "Cop on Top," we gathered on the roof of a Dunkin' Donuts and hung out all day. For the infamous "Polar Bear Plunge," we all dove into a lake together in winter, as a team, for charity. It sucked, but it sucked as a team. Both events raised money for Special Olympics, a cause that the police have been contributing to for years. Everyone who participated was reminded (even if implicitly) of why they chose this honorable career.

Your social wellness may require you to leave your comfort zone from time to time. But once you achieve balance in this area, there will be no looking back. This becomes especially important as you near retirement. After you've left police work, a well-rounded social life, which you began to develop while you were still working, means that there won't be such a large void to fill. You just keep engaging in all those hobbies, interests, and volunteer activities. Of course, then you'll have even more time to have even more fun!

CHAPTER 5

SPIRITUAL WELLNESS

Your spiritual health depends on your ability to remain committed to your values. Although there are many insidious ways policing can lead officers to question or even to compromise their principles, in this chapter, we focus on strategies to help you stay true to your core beliefs. This steadfast devotion to the things that matter most to you establishes a critical foundation, which is necessary for you to maintain your integrity (and which we address more directly in later chapters).

From our experience, however, when we start talking about values, integrity, and spirituality, many officers want to tune out. This may be because religion is one of those "off-limits" topics. However, when we mention spirituality, we are not referring to religion. Our focus is on something much more than whether or not you consider yourself religious. Spirituality helps give your life meaning, which is why having a well-articulated value system is important. In addition, more recently, there has been increased attention to the importance of spirituality for police officers to manage stress and boost resilience.[1, 2] This chapter emphasizes the importance of spirituality as a crucial component of your overall health and well-being. Let's dive into some strategies to stay spiritually healthy.

STEP 1. MISSION STATEMENT

One way for people to remain professionally ethical is to understand, articulate, and stay true to one's core values,[3] and staying
ethical is an important component of your spiritual wellness. The
first step is to write a personal and professional **mission statement**.
This is the anchor to your spiritual health. It contains the guiding
principles you aspire to and the broad objectives you establish for
your behavior. If you've never done this before, no matter where you

are in your career, give it some thought and write your mission statement. If you wrote one some time ago, take a look and see whether your goals are still the same.

To help you get started, think about and answer the following questions:

- What do you aim to accomplish in your day-to-day activities that will allow you to look in the mirror and feel proud of yourself?
- What goals and values distinguish you from others?
- What reputation do you want to have among people who matter most to you?
- What kind of person do you aspire to be?

The textbox shows you an example of a mission statement written by one of Officer Mike's trainees.

Sample Mission Statement

- I provide quality service, where honesty and integrity guide my decisions.
- I maintain a personal and professional balance between team and self, work and pleasure, accountability and compassion, and dependence and interdependence.
- I seek situations that encourage my innovation and creativity and will inspire others to develop those traits.
- I aspire to always be a good role model to colleagues and the public.

Note: From the Resource Library tab on this book's website (https://www.apa.org/pubs/books/the-power-manual) you can download a blank form (on which you can write your mission statement) as well as journal pages (for you to explore your core values and purposes).

On-Duty Activity

Before each shift, take out your mission statement and read it to yourself. When you start work each day by reminding yourself what kind of cop you are, you've developed a healthy habit!

Off-Duty Activity

Schedule a regular time to review your mission statement, such as once per quarter or at the start of each shift change. Put it on your calendar. Try to review the mission statement roughly four times per year. During each review, you are going to answer a few questions. The goal of the activity is to determine how well you are living up to your mission statement and identify factors that may be interfering with your performance. And don't think only about how well you exhibit your values at work; how well are you living up to your values at home, too? At each mission statement review, ask yourself these questions:

- How am I living up to my guiding principles?
- Where have I fallen a little short of my guiding principles?
- Have I allowed outside influences to negatively affect me?
- What will I do to recommit to my guiding principles and get back on track?

Note: You can find a blank mission statement form and more spiritual wellness exercises in the Resource Library tab on this book's website (https://www.apa.org/pubs/books/the-power-manual).

Answering these questions can make you aware of any "mission drift" that may have started. Identify whether you have begun to stray from what is most important to you, and try to figure out why this is happening. If you recognize that you have been reacting to things that are out of your control, you can begin to refocus on what you can control and make the necessary improvements.

STEP 2. YOUR CORE VALUES

Get specific about what is most important to you with a **values exercise**. Take 15 to 20 blank index cards. On each card, write a single word that represents one of your core values. If you've never thought about this before, it may be helpful to write down 25 to 30 values so that you can review the cards and then whittle them down to a final list of your top 10 to 15 values. If you have done something like this before, take some time to reevaluate whether those are still your most important values or whether one or more others are now more important to you; make the necessary additions and subtractions. You want to end up with a list of traits and standards that are most meaningful to you and that best define your ideal self. The words you write on these cards will become the characteristics that help you live up to your mission statement. Next, spread the cards out and determine the order you want to put them in based on how critically important each value is to your core sense of identity. This is how you see yourself and how you want to be seen by others. When you have the cards prioritized, write the words on a single card that you will keep by your bed. The textbox gives you an example of a list of **core values** written by one of Officer Mike's recruits.

> ## Sample List of Core Values
>
> | | |
> |---|---|
> | Ethical | Compassionate |
> | Courageous | Adventurous |
> | Trustworthy | Loving husband and father |
> | Respectful | Happy, optimistic |
> | Loyal | Fair-minded |

Use this only to get a rough idea; it's important to come up with your own list of values that describe the kind of person you are and strive to be.

Off-Duty Activity

Each day, before going to sleep, do a **5-minute values check-in.** Take a look at your core values list and ask yourself the following questions with regard to your values:

- What went well today?
- What did not go so well?
- What, if anything, could I have done differently?
- What changes will I make to do a better job being the kind of person I want to be?

This is not intended to be a deep, soul-searching endeavor. It's just a way for you to take a couple of minutes to think about your behavior that day. And this is not just about how you did at work but how well you lived up to your values at home, too.

On-Duty Activity

When you are at work, try to notice when other people (fellow officers and other department employees, as well as members of the public) demonstrate your core values. Look for examples of those values in action. At the same time, make a mental note when you see someone showing a lack of those values, which is a good way to remind yourself what kind of person you do not want to be! Make it a habit to start paying closer attention to the good and the bad role models you encounter throughout the day, and it will be easier to stay on the core values path you've created for yourself.

STEP 3. PURPOSE AND MEANING

Now that you've dropped your spiritual anchor and developed some good habits to stay committed to your values, it's time to direct some attention to the bigger picture. Your life has **purpose and meaning**. It's easy to get bogged down by all the BS in your agency, your community, and the world. Now and then, you may even feel as if you are in a rut. However, your spiritual wellness depends on your ability to transcend the daily grind and maintain some hope and faith. If you already have a strong sense of spirituality, this makes complete sense to you. If this is something that is missing in your life, you may ask, "Hope and faith in what?" Although we'd like you to answer this for yourself, here are a few ideas for you to consider that Officer Mike's trainees came up with:

- I have faith in my courage and confidence.
- My faith in something bigger keeps me grounded and humble.
- My faith prevents my fears from getting the best of me.
- Things happen for reasons that I may not understand, but hardships help me improve.

Off-Duty Activity

The challenge that we all face is staying committed to our purpose despite the obstacles. When was the last time that you thought about why you wanted to be a cop in the first place? Take a few minutes to write down your answer. Then answer the question as though today was the first time you ever thought about it. What's the same, and what's different between the two answers? The textbox shows you one of Officer Mike's officer's answers.

Sample Purpose Statement

Why I wanted to be a cop (then)	Why I want to be a cop (now)
To help people	Steady job with benefits and retirement
To give back to the community	Good amount of paid vacation time
To make a difference	What else would I do?
"Serve and protect"—really!	
Get crooks off the street	

Lots of things cause cops to lose faith in their purpose. Mostly this comes from thoughts such as "Nothing I do matters" and "Why bother when no one appreciates us." However, regardless of all the factors that are out of your control, your spiritual wellness depends on your ability to recommit to your purpose—in ways within your control.

On-Duty Activity

Without overthinking this, look for small ways that you do fulfill your purpose. Jot down these wins and make note of any setbacks. These can be what you think about each night during your off-duty **5-minute values check-in**. One of Officer Mike's officers wrote what's mentioned in the next textbox after a shift one night. This activity refocuses your attention on your own behavior and helps you avoid being overly reactive to the behavior of others.

Sample Recommitment Statement

Three people today actually said "thank you."
It was a slow night, but I hooked up a DUI who blew a .12. Glad I got him before he hurt someone.
Got a hostile look from the clerk at 7-Eleven but made an effort to smile and be friendly to him anyway.
I could have been nicer to a lady I stopped for rolling a stop sign.
I decided to put in for FTO. I could be a good training officer.

STEP 4. INNER CONTENTMENT

As you continue to find ways to live up to your core values and recommit to your purpose, the final step to achieve spiritual health is to reach a sense of **inner contentment**. We are not striving for the elusive (and probably impossible) "inner peace" that yoga masters brag about. Keeping the peace is one thing, but cops are just not likely to ever feel inner peace. We can, however, become healthier by achieving inner contentment. The goal is to find ways to stay connected with something "bigger" and avoid what the philosophers refer to as an *existential crisis*, when a person begins to question the very meaning of their life. Once feelings of boredom or disillusionment creep in, this existential crisis has been found to even increase aggressive tendencies.[4] Although it is a far more complex problem with a variety of causes, many police suicides involve officers who are in existential distress. There are steps, however, that officers can take to attain inner contentment.

Let's talk about ways for this to happen. Some of these strategies may sound a bit weird, and a few of them could feel a little awkward when you first give them a try. We encourage you to push past those initial feelings, and these activities will, in a short time, improve how you cope with some of the challenges in your life. The strategies to accomplish inner contentment fall into two categories: internal and external.

External Activities for Inner Contentment

It's pretty easy to get mired in day-to-day crap, but the world has a lot more to offer. When you achieve more balance in your life, you will actively seek opportunities to experience parts of the world that you may not pay much attention to or get to experience often because of the demands of your job and, more broadly, your personal life.

On-Duty Activity

As often as possible, stop to notice the sunrise or sunset. Step back from the smell left over in your backseat from the junkie who puked as you drove him to jail and consider that the world is vast and not entirely vomit ridden. But, seriously, find small ways to pay attention to natural beauty in the midst of all the human ugliness you encounter on the job every day.

Off-Duty Activity

In that regard, use some of your vacation time for an actual trip to somewhere that surrounds you in nature's beauty. Instead of spending every vacation in long lines at amusement parks or with your relatives, escape to somewhere that reminds you (and shows your spouse and kids) that there's a benefit to unplugging for a few days or weeks: Take a hike, explore the redwoods, smell fresh air, sit on the beach and just watch the waves.

For that matter, on a regular basis (e.g., a couple of times per month), find a spot near where you live that gets you back to (or closer to) nature. For these occasions, we recommend that this should be a solitary activity that gives you a little time alone. This won't be too difficult if you live anywhere outside of a big city. If you are in a city, you may have to get creative. Go to a dog park or feed pigeons in a park, or go to the roof and just watch the clouds or stars. Do something that helps remind you that the world is a lot bigger than your daily routine. You could even just watch episodes of *Seven Worlds, One Planet*, preferably on a large-screen HDTV, if that's the closest you can get to nature.[5] One officer wrote,

> This may sound crazy to you, but my spirituality is rooted in literal roots. I have an old oak tree that's on my property. It's survived tornadoes, drought, lightning storms—you name it. Who knows if it will be there forever, but I'm sure it will be here long after I'm gone. I look at it all the time. When I'm out cutting the grass or raking the leaves, I tell it that I'm thankful for it being here. Sometimes I even give it a hug. It reminds me that the world is full of things that don't give a crap about how many tickets I wrote this month.

Off-Duty Activity

In addition to nature, another way toward inner contentment is through exposure to the arts. You probably listen to music, maybe during workouts or while driving. Beyond motivating or distracting you, find some music to listen to that will rejuvenate you and emotionally move you.

Off-Duty Activity

Many officers make time to build things or tend a garden. When you see so much death and loss as part of your job, it helps in your off time to create something or bring something to life. Many officers enjoy woodworking; the process is a great distraction, and the result is often something that brings a sense of pride. The same can be said of gardening. One of Officer Mike's officers grew tomatoes and felt a great sense of accomplishment every time he sliced one up for a sandwich.

Internal Activities for Inner Contentment

We can't ignore one of the key components of inner contentment, namely, the "inner" part. This takes a little work because some of these strategies require practice. At the same time, this can motivate you. Inner contentment does not require anything from outside of you to achieve, which means you are in complete control over whether or not you attain it. It doesn't matter where you live, what challenges you face in your organization and your community, or what stressors you have at home. However, you will only learn some of these skills by taking advantage of the resources that we've listed because the specific training is beyond the scope of this book.

MEDITATION, BIOFEEDBACK, PROGRESSIVE MUSCLE RELAXATION

Each of these three activities has a goal of helping you achieve and maintain a better level of calmness. Each is a skill that, when learned, can be used to turn off racing thoughts, slow your heart rate, and return some control of your physiological reactions to your cognitive mind. Moreover, each provides you with a mechanism to tap into your spiritual side, spend a little time contemplating your purpose, and recharge your spiritual battery. However, because they have different styles, people tend to react differently to them. You have to find the one that you innately relate to best. Interestingly, these skills do more than just propel you toward inner contentment. These skills are used by elite athletes for performance enhancement because they give them tools to use during high-pressure moments so that their nerves don't cause them to choke. In Chapter 9, we guide you in learning and practicing these techniques, but for now, we'll give you an introduction to them. At the same time, although they are often used to promote relaxation, these strategies can also help you achieve a great sense of spiritual wellness.

Meditation. Meditation often works best for cops who describe themselves as religious or those who have a philosophical or spiritual way of thinking. There are many types of meditation, including some forms of yoga. Frankly, prayer can be meditation when you use it to connect with your higher power. Self-hypnosis can be considered a form of meditation, too, but it is usually used to kick a habit. You don't need someone to teach you how to meditate. You can read a book on it, watch a TED talk, or just make time to sit quietly for 15 minutes or so and clear your mind. Police officers who do this regularly (i.e., four or five times per week) report that they start feeling greater inner contentment after only a couple of months.

Biofeedback. Many police officers have found great benefits from meditation, but if it doesn't interest or appeal to you, you could consult a biofeedback practitioner to teach you this skill. Although it's usually used to help people manage physical problems, such as headaches, high blood pressure, and chronic pain, it also can be used to improve your sense of inner calm. It requires you to be hooked up to sensors that pay attention to your heart rate and/or blood pressure. You then learn, by monitoring your outputs, to make yourself more relaxed.

Progressive Muscle Relaxation. Progressive muscle relaxation is a skill that many police officers find more palatable than the other two techniques. It does not require machines like biofeedback does and is often viewed as more tangible than meditation. You learn the skill by sitting in a quiet room and focusing on breathing and gradually relaxing each muscle. Some officers consult a practitioner to guide them through this at least once. Other officers, instead, use recordings of a facilitator leading them through the exercise. Once learned, the relaxation techniques can be used on the job in many challenging moments, such as helping officers to de-escalate volatile situations, staying calm when feeling frustrated with a witness, or to avoid lashing out at a rude supervisor. But when you are off duty, this exercise helps you obtain a sense of complete calm. When you have attained that level of relaxation without any tension in your body, you can begin to think about your connection to something spiritual, something beyond your daily stresses.

Gratitude. The last internal strategy for inner contentment is gratitude. Just as it sounds, you need to pay some attention to what you are thankful for and to the people and things in your life that you appreciate. This is not complicated at all. Your inner contentment expands as you reduce (and hopefully eliminate) any feelings of bitterness. To do this, it is important to feel grateful. And you will feel grateful after you start expressing gratitude. Although we know that you can come up with your own ways of expressing gratitude, we will show you some activities that officers have said work for them.

Off-Duty Activity

In honor of all our brothers and sisters in blue who have died in the line of duty, be thankful each day that you are alive. Literally, when you wake up, say something to yourself, such as "I'm grateful for my life," or "I'm glad to have another day with my loved ones."

However, your inner contentment does not depend on feeling grateful only for the big, important things in your life. It grows by training yourself to appreciate small things that we often take for granted. Many officers start the day by reminding themselves of the little stuff in their life for which they are grateful. The textbox shows a gratitude list written by one of Officer Mike's recruits.

Sample Gratitude List

Hot coffee
The smell of bacon cooking
My daughter saying, "Hi Daddy!"
My wife's smile
The NFL RedZone
How green my grass is
Hummingbirds in my yard
Hot showers
My dog greeting me when I come in

In addition to reminding yourself to feel grateful for things that are easily ignored during your busy day, you can express gratitude to the people in your life who you appreciate. Tell the people you care about that you are glad they are in your life. Officers often say, after it's too late, "I wish I would have told him how much he meant to me." We don't often share our feelings like this, but this is a way to strengthen your spiritual wellness by doing something really simple. It doesn't matter how the person responds because the value here comes from you saying it, not from them hearing it.

If directly telling someone that you are grateful seems too difficult for you, another gratitude strategy is letter writing. Whether or not you ever mail (or email) the letter, from time to time (e.g., once a month), write a gratitude letter to someone and express your appreciation for how your life was impacted by that relationship. The person could be in your life now or from your past, including those who are no longer living. They might have been a grandparent, a middle school teacher, a high school coach, or that one FTO who saw some potential in you and convinced you not to quit when you doubted your ability to make it as a cop.

Your spiritual health, like the other areas of your wellness, requires some effort on your part to practice and keep doing the preventive activities that we've outlined in these last few chapters. Once you commit to being as healthy as possible, it won't be that difficult to make these on-duty and off-duty activities a routine part of your day. They will become good habits that you don't have to think much about—you just do them.

II

ETHICS

CHAPTER 6

COMMITMENT TO
THE NOBLE CAUSE

Police officers spend quite a bit of time learning the law in order to enforce it properly. Beyond statutes and the penal code, however, most officers have a pretty clear understanding of the difference between right and wrong. This is where the personal values discussed in the previous chapter come in and where we begin our focus on integrity and professional ethics. The challenge is that the line between right and wrong can easily become blurred if officers aren't careful.[1] There are times when doing the wrong thing may seem right, but this is exactly what gets some cops in career-ending trouble. The issue for us here, however, is that making a decision that officers know is wrong, despite their noble intentions, begins the slow deterioration of their physical and mental health. In this chapter, we offer strategies and suggestions to maintain your commitment to the noble cause and some that will help get you back on track if you do cross the line. This isn't a lecture about ethical decision making; that's between you and your conscience. Instead, we are focusing on how important it is for your overall health and wellness that you stay ethical.

Many people go into law enforcement in the first place because it is a noble profession. No matter how poorly some individual cops are portrayed in the news, on YouTube, or across social media, the profession remains one of the most respected and trusted in the United States and around the world. A large 2020 survey found police officer was ranked as the fifth most respected profession.[2] Unfortunately, police officers don't always make the best decisions. One explanation for why cops might do something wrong for the "right" reason is referred to as the *corruption of the noble cause*.[3] This is when cops decide that noble ends, such as getting a terrible person off the street, justify unethical and, in some cases, illegal means, such as fabricating details on an incident report. However, these moments do not happen in a vacuum and are sometimes embedded in the agency's culture.[4] Officers may feel internal urges or face external pressures, which can lead them to act unethically.

After an internal affairs (IA) investigation regarding unnecessary force, one of Officer Mike's officers said the following:

> I knew it was wrong. I'm not going to pretend that I didn't. But we'd been hearing it from our sergeant for months that these [name of gang removed] were getting a lot more active around some schools, recruiting, harassing, and dealing. It just didn't seem like such a big deal at the time when we decided to teach a couple of them a lesson.

Besides the discipline that results when officers are found to be in violation of department policies or procedures, these experiences, as well as ones that never come to light or those that fall short of a disciplinary threshold, can push officers to doubt their values and leave some questioning the kind of person they are.

STEP 1. MORAL CODE

When you establish a well-defined moral code, it will be easier for you to stay committed to doing what you believe is right. In the last chapter, you were encouraged to list your core values. Here, we are taking that up a notch and focusing on personal integrity. In a nutshell, your moral code relates to how you treat all people regardless of the circumstances. Another way to look at this is that while your core values help you strive toward achieving your ideal self, your moral code establishes the standards for you to live by every day. Look at your list of core values. See how many of them relate to your integrity. In the example from Chapter 5, you will notice that six of Officer Mike's recruit's core values are related to his moral code: ethical, trustworthy, respectful, loyal, compassionate, and fairminded. He then turned those ideals into action statements related to a steadfast commitment to doing what he knows is right. The officer's moral code is shown in the following textbox.

Sample Moral Code

My Moral Code

I am honest in everything I do.
I go out of my way to help anyone in need.
I can be counted on during dangerous and stressful situations.
I stand up for underdogs.
I treat others with respect, patience, and fairness.

Note: You can download a blank form for My Moral Code and related journal prompts from the Resource Library tab on this book's website (https://www.apa.org/pubs/books/the-power-manual).

Off-Duty Activity

Take your list of core values and convert them into action statements, which will become your moral code. For example, ethical becomes "I am honest in everything I do," trustworthy becomes "I can be counted on during dangerous and stressful situations," and compassionate becomes "I go out of my way to help anyone in need."

Now that you've written out your moral code, next, ask yourself a few questions:

- How willing are you to stand up for what you know to be morally correct regardless of the consequences?
- What situations might you find yourself in that could make it difficult to stick to your principles?
- Is there anyone who ever pressures you to violate your principles?
- How have you felt after violating one of your moral standards?

No one is perfect. We all make mistakes now and then. The challenge is to learn from the mistakes and figure out ways to prevent them from happening again. However, the mistakes that will have the most detrimental impact on your health and wellness are violations of your moral code.

Off-Duty Activity

Take some time to write out a moral inventory. This is not what you may know happens during a 12-step recovery process; we are suggesting something here that is a lot less complicated. Just look at what you wrote for My Moral Code. Go through the list and write down specific examples when you did not perform how you said you would. Some of these examples might be incidents that you tend to dwell on or maybe even feel some guilt about. Some of them come to mind pretty easily when you think about it. And some may be events that you haven't thought about for some time, if ever.

Off-Duty Activity

Next, as objectively as you can, examine each incident you wrote down in your moral inventory. For each item, ask yourself:

- What were the circumstances when I failed to act in accordance with my moral code?
- Was I feeling pressure from a peer or supervisor to violate my principles?
- Did someone just push my button the wrong way, and I reacted by violating my principles?
- Had something happened at home that was weighing on me when I violated my principles?
- Was I preoccupied with a previous call or by something else that distracted me, which led me to violate my principles?

These two exercises show that adhering to your moral code isn't easy. You aren't a bad person for failing to live up to the moral standards you've set for yourself. On the one hand, it takes a lot of effort to perform your duties every day according to your moral code. And on the other hand, many factors may have contributed to your behavior. Nevertheless, when you violate your principles, it takes a direct toll on your health and wellness. This happens most destructively when officers see their actions as an indication that they aren't as good a person as they thought they were. The officer who was involved in the IA investigation mentioned earlier said the following:

> I had to ask myself, "What kind of person would do that?" I'd never done it before, and I never thought I ever would. I always looked down at guys who did that, but now am I that kind of cop? This whole thing really messed me up. My sleep went to shit. I lost weight, stopped working out, started drinking more. I could barely look my friends in the eye. My sergeant said it would blow over, that I should just accept the 2 weeks on the beach and forget it ever happened. Well, it didn't. I eventually went to talk to someone. I needed help getting over this.

STEP 2. MORAL COMPASS

Now that you've examined your behavior and identified times when you failed to live up to your moral standards, it's time to recalibrate the moral compass. This does not mean that you are going to lower your moral bar. It means that you are going to take the steps necessary to make sure that you will stay on the right ethical track. Your moral code establishes your guiding principles, but your moral compass directs you to follow those principles in your daily actions.

Off-Duty Activity

In the last activity, you identified some of your actions that did not meet your moral standards. Look over the incidents from the previous activity, and for each one, write an op plan. Ask yourself: If the same or a similar event occurs, what will I do differently to ensure that I am living up to my moral code? Visualize yourself blocking out the external pressures and ignoring the internal distractions so that you can act with honor and integrity.

On-Duty Activity

Knowing the right thing to do doesn't mean that you will automatically do the right thing. Start by paying closer attention to the behavior of your colleagues. Notice whenever someone does something that meets or even exceeds your moral standards. Usually, these are acts that don't get much attention from supervisors and rarely find their way to the media, although sometimes they lead to a commendation or Medal of Valor. If you are comfortable saying something, tell them that you were impressed by what they did. That gesture serves two purposes. The first is showing your colleague that someone appreciated their ethical behavior. The second is to remind you that doing what's right still matters. When you express your appreciation to your colleague or even just take note of their behavior, it reinforces the importance of adhering to your moral code.

Secondarily, pay attention when you see colleagues violating your moral standards. Regardless of whether that behavior strays from their moral code, it is an opportunity for you to notice how it feels to you when someone does something you believe is wrong. This is a helpful reminder for you to keep your moral compass pointed in the right direction. As a "bonus" activity, if you want to strengthen your commitment to your moral code, find a private moment to tell your colleague, in a nonthreatening way, that you did not appreciate their behavior, that you think it was wrong, and that you know they can do better.

Of course, if you see a clear violation of the law or department policy or procedure, you might consider what has been referred to as *active bystandership*[5] and report the misconduct. This can be tricky. On the one hand, intervening may seem to violate the core value of loyalty if you only are thinking about your colleague and not considering your loyalty to your oath, the organization, or the community. On the other hand, ignoring such an ethical or legal breach probably violates another of your core values, such as honesty. It requires some moral courage to intervene, but doing nothing may jeopardize your career and cause you to question the kind of person you are.

On-Duty Activity

Others are not often likely to notice or appreciate your moral actions. Start paying closer attention when you do something that represents your ethical principles. This may be quite minor but nevertheless deserves some positive reinforcement. Find a way to give yourself a metaphorical pat on the back. Similarly, don't ignore when you slip up. Figure out a way to fine yourself for falling short of your ethical principles. By paying closer attention to your own moral behavior, you will be keeping your moral compass well calibrated.

The following is an example of how one of Officer Mike's officers keeps her moral compass calibrated:

> We have a version of a gold star chart that we keep on the refrigerator. It's not for grades. It's for good citizenship at school and for doing good deeds. Whenever one of the kids gets enough of the stickers, I take them to their favorite restaurant, and they can order whatever they want.

When the kids were in middle school, we started a swear jar. It's in the kitchen. Whenever someone swears, they have to put a quarter in the jar. I noticed that the kids starting adding a quarter even when no one heard them say a bad word, and they told me that "a swear is a swear; even if no one hears it, you still said it."

That got me thinking about my own behavior at work. We always gripe that the only attention we get is when we do something wrong. So, I came up with the opposite of a swear jar. Whenever I catch myself doing a good deed, something from my moral code, I add $5 to a good deed jar. I will keep putting in $5 until I get enough to pay for a 90-minute sports massage at a local spa. They cost around $200, so that's 40 good deeds to get something that I really love and really need.

Now, if I catch myself doing something that goes against my moral code, I lose $5 from my good deed jar and have to give it to one of the homeless on my beat, which really ticks me off.

So far, it's been working pretty well. I've already had a few massages.

STEP 3. TEAMWORK

An aspect of noble cause corruption that doesn't get enough attention is teamwork. This can be viewed as everything from collaborating effectively with others to pulling your weight and not dragging down your colleagues or causing more work for them. It means putting your own interests aside and focusing on what's best for the group or organization. It reflects good teamwork, also, when you don't let conflicts or personal differences negatively impact the work.

When your behavior drifts away from your moral code, you are letting down all your brothers and sisters in blue. The unethical behavior of any cop stains all cops because it causes the community to lose trust and respect in their public servants. When it's because of the behavior of other officers, regardless of where they work, it makes life more difficult for you. And, likewise, your unethical behavior makes it more difficult for every other cop. In fact, it could be argued that you are failing in the core job competency of teamwork when you violate your moral standards.

Most likely, when you read the previous paragraph, you thought of times when police officers violated someone's rights, committed flagrant misconduct, or showed up on YouTube acting like an imbecile. The most infamous of these videos may cause your friends and family members to ask you why cops act that way, as though it's your job to defend everyone who wears a badge. Unfortunately, some of these behaviors lead people you encounter on the job to treat you a lot worse than if they hadn't recently been reminded on social media how some police officers sometimes mistreat some community members. These are pretty obvious examples of poor teamwork on the part of the officers who fail to live up to their moral code.

Off-Duty Activity

At the same time, teamwork involves many more small acts associated with your moral code. Using the example of Officer Mike's recruit's moral code at the beginning of this chapter, make a list of behaviors associated with his principles that demonstrate good teamwork. Specifically, focus on times when you

- went out of your way to help a colleague;
- backed up a colleague during a dangerous or stressful situation; and
- treated a colleague with respect, patience, and fairness, whether or not they deserved it.

Next, make a similar list of times when you failed to show good teamwork related to those same principles.

Finally, review your moral code and see whether your guiding principles include behaviors that reflect good teamwork. Make a list of your past behaviors associated with your principles that demonstrate good teamwork and a list of your past behaviors that you now see did not represent good teamwork.

On-Duty Activity

Make a conscious effort to be a good teammate. On each shift, find a way to help, support, respect, compliment, back up, and thank a colleague. After you do, jot down what you did so that you can go back later and remind yourself how well you are doing. It doesn't matter whether your efforts are reciprocated or whether they are even noticed. These actions are for you, regardless of how they are received. This is a way for you to keep your moral compass calibrated and live up to your moral code.

The bottom line in this chapter is that doing what you know is right isn't always easy. It takes effort to remain noble in this noble profession. Many factors can derail your efforts and lead you to act in ways contrary to your principles. In fact, there are many aspects of policing that we discuss in the next two chapters that can lead to a reduction in your integrity and ethical decision making—unless you take active measures to avoid this from happening. The activities outlined in this chapter lay the foundation to keep you committed to your moral code, which is essential for you to stay physically and mentally healthy. But, for now, we have two more questions for you to consider:

- Do you believe that being a good cop is more important than being a good person?
- How will you make sure that you can still be a good person while being an excellent cop?

CHAPTER 7

THE GUARDIAN SPIRIT OF POLICING

Over the past few years, you probably heard the debate about cops being warriors or guardians. In April 2015, the National Institute of Justice published one of their *New Perspectives in Policing* on just that topic.[1] The argument goes something like this. Policing, especially since the 9/11 terrorist attacks, has shifted more and more to a warrior mindset whereby officers are extensively (and primarily) trained to be prepared at all times for the worst. However, the warrior mindset, according to this argument, takes police officers away from their central mission of protecting and serving members of their community as guardians. Unlike a warrior who is always involved in battle, a guardian, according to the dictionary, is a person who is tasked with caring for other people and their property. Although guardians may at times be forced into a war-like confrontation, their motivation and primary sense of identity come from serving and protecting people in their community.

Interestingly, recent research found that academy training, which emphasizes the guardian approach, appears to reduce the use of deadly force.[2] In reality, however, today's police officers serve simultaneously as warriors, guardians, social workers, mental health therapists, drug and alcohol counselors, and surrogate parents and in numerous other roles. The issue here, at least for us, is not all the various, sometimes contradictory, responsibilities that you perform while on duty. The concern regarding your health and wellness revolves around the mindset that you have about your job. The **guardian spirit** connects you with your community. The warrior mindset alienates you from your community by establishing an *us-versus-them* attitude; essentially, this view sees anyone who isn't a cop as the enemy or, at least, as someone to be highly mistrusted until proven otherwise. Not surprisingly, the warrior mindset contributes significantly to a reduction in your overall well-being.

In this chapter, we emphasize ways for those of you who have the warrior mindset to establish, or regain, the guardian spirit without compromising your readiness for "combat." We're going to expand a bit on Teddy Roosevelt's famous saying, "Speak softly and carry a big stick." Actually, most of the chapter focuses on the speaking softly part. But, first, let's talk about the big stick. To move from warrior to guardian, officers have to have confidence that their training adequately prepared them for battle; they are supremely ready when the shit hits the fan. They have to trust their training, equipment, and fellow officers. Preferably, officers also trust their organization to have their backs and provide the necessary support and resources. However, even though it is not their primary mission, guardians will go to battle even when conditions are not ideal.

Police officers who are completely confident in their ability to go into combat can learn to "speak softly" when there is no imminent war to fight. This is the guardian spirit that will help to keep you healthy. It means that you don't feel the need to constantly exert authority because you are the one who always has the authority. Unlike the warrior who is amped up to fight, the guardian begins with defusing, rather than escalating, potentially volatile situations but is quite capable of responding appropriately to others' escalations when necessary. One of Officer Mike's commanders said the following:

> When I get a complaint from a citizen, I automatically assume it's about one of our insecure officers; they tend to be the most badge heavy. Doesn't matter—big or small, male or female—the officers who rarely, if ever, get a complaint are the ones who are friendly, smile a lot, and are always respectful, even when making an arrest. These are the officers who are confident that they can take care of themselves. They are in shape. Many practice martial arts. They aren't always looking over their shoulder in fear.

Off-Duty Activity

Take a few minutes to answer the following questions.

- How confident are you in your defensive tactics and arrest and control skills?
- In what situations might you not be as confident?
- What steps will you take to improve these skills and gain more confidence?

On-Duty Activity

Make a mental note when you see colleagues demonstrating the guardian spirit. Pay attention to how that behavior is received by the public. Similarly, make a mental note when you see colleagues foregoing this and acting with a warrior mindset. How are those behaviors received by the public?

STEP 1. FIGHTING MORAL DISENGAGEMENT

To maintain the guardian spirit, it is important for officers to eliminate the us-versus-them view that permeates many law enforcement agencies. This is far easier said than done, but we'll give you some strategies that will help. We're focusing on your health, which means that these strategies will work for you even if most of your colleagues continue to view members of your community as "them."

First, we have to understand and fight against moral disengagement. Without getting too academic, *moral disengagement* is a comprehensive theory[3] that, in part, explains how people are capable of distancing themselves emotionally and ethically from others. For example, police officers may "bend rules" not because they are corrupt cops but because they succumb to mechanisms of moral disengagement, which lead to such misconduct.[4] The theory describes how people acquire the view that others are not part of "us" but are seen as "them." Specifically, moral disengagement leads people to dehumanize others and blame them for their own misfortune.

At some level, soldiers need to morally disengage to do what has to be done in combat. For police officers, though, moral disengagement perpetuates an unhealthy warrior mindset. Unfortunately, there are many aspects of routine police work that foster moral disengagement.[5] It's sometimes emotionally simpler to dehumanize or blame people who are experiencing homelessness, crime victims, or those living in deplorable conditions than it is to feel empathy for them. So, while emotional disengagement may make it easier to do your job, it also erodes your humanity, and that is not good for your long-term health. You may see the dilemma here and think that it would be best to stay morally disengaged if it helps make the job more tolerable. Unfortunately, that is a short-term strategy that will cost you in the long run. Instead, when you implement a comprehensive wellness program, which we presented in the wellness chapters of the book (Chapters 1–5), taking steps to fight against moral disengagement will not be detrimental. In fact, it will help you maintain a guardian spirit, which promotes your well-being.

The guardian spirit does not oblige you to start overflowing with empathy for everyone you encounter on the job. We aren't suggesting that you like every criminal you arrest, every motorist you cite, or every annoying complainant. The guardian spirit merely requires you to remember that every person you encounter on the job is, in fact, a fellow human being.

Officer Mike heard this from one of his officers:

> There was an old dude who I got so sick of driving to detox. He was one of those drunks who would tie one on and start going in and out of businesses on my beat. I'd show up after someone called to complain. There wasn't anything to do; he lived on the streets somewhere, for crying out loud. After the third or fourth time, I would get pretty rude with him, which would just piss him off. One time, as we headed to detox, I said something about the Sox. He tells me he was a kid at Comiskey for Game 1 in 1959 against LA when Ted Kluszewski hits two out. From then on, every time I ran into him, drunk or not, he sees me, and we tell each other how much we hate the Dodgers.

On-Duty Activity

Find some common ground with people you encounter. First, try it in your mind by connecting on some level. For example, when taking a statement from a victim who may not seem sympathetic, ask yourself whether the same thing could have happened to your parents or another relative. When a motorist you stop is disrespectful, tell yourself that he's having a worse day than you, that she just lost her job, or that his kids are sick. It doesn't matter why the person is being disrespectful, and there is no point in reacting to their rudeness. You can do your job safely and effectively (maybe even more effectively) when you maintain your composure and your compassion.

On-Duty Activity

Phase 2 of finding some common ground happens when you make an effort to talk to people you encounter on the job about anything other than your police business. The guardian spirit thrives when you feel connected to people, even those who are different from you. Like Officer Mike's colleague who talked baseball on the way to detox, you and the guy you just arrested might like the same sports team or listen to the same music. Try this when there's room for some small talk, such as while you're waiting for your sergeant to arrive at the scene or after you've taken a victim's or witness's statement. If you are lucky enough to have some time between calls for service, instead of meeting up at a park to talk with fellow cops, take the opportunity to talk to some of the folks hanging out in the park. You may have to let them know that you just want to chat and that it's not a consensual stop. Remember, they aren't likely to think that they have anything in common with you. The more skilled you become at connecting with those who, on the surface, seem most dissimilar to you, the more you can avoid becoming unhealthfully cynical.

STEP 2. TACTICAL EMPATHY

Although common ground conversations occur best when you have time to just talk to people, a technique that will help you act like a guardian during enforcement actions, even if you are holding on to the warrior mindset, is *tactical empathy*,[6] which we touched on in Chapter 3. It is imperative for police officers to learn not to take everything said to them so personally. When someone you engage with shows a lack of respect or even becomes verbally abusive, it is not always easy to respond with respect and empathy. Arrestees, particularly, can be rude to the arresting officer. It is not uncommon for arrestees to yell, cuss, and degrade an officer. Many act as though they are intentionally provoking the officer to retaliate.

The key factor is to understand the meaning behind the arrestee's language. In actuality, the arrestee is unlikely to be angry with you and probably has nothing against you personally. Your arrestee is more likely just angry at the situation, about what happened before your arrival, and even at him- or herself. Once you recognize that a verbal attack is not personal, you are less likely to act out of frustration and more likely to use tactical communication skills. These are tactical because they help you accomplish your mission in the most effective way possible.

Empathy phrases show respect toward the individual. You don't need to feel empathy or respect for the person when using these phrases. This is a tactic and strategy to gain cooperation and compliance and to prevent unnecessary escalations.

Off-Duty Activity

Practice tactical empathy phrases with friends and family. Rehearsing these phrases off duty will make it easier to use them on duty. Examples of empathy phrases include the following:

- I can see where you are coming from . . .
- I want to understand that . . .

- I can appreciate what you are saying . . .
- I can see you are upset. I would be too . . .

On-Duty Activity

Use the tactical empathy phrases as much as you can. You can use them with colleagues and supervisors, too, to facilitate cooperative conversations. When you are dealing with individuals who are angry and noncompliant, you can begin with a deflection phrase and explain what's in it for them. For example,

- Sir, I can understand where you are coming from, but if I can take a look at your ID, I can get you on your way a lot sooner.
- Sir, I can see you are upset, and I get it, but right now, all we have is a minor warrant to take care of. If you don't comply, unfortunately, you will have additional charges, like resisting arrest. I'm sure you don't want that, and I don't want that for you.
- Ma'am, I can see you are upset. I probably would be too if someone had called the police on me, but I just need to step inside and make sure everyone is okay. Unfortunately, I can't leave until I do that.

Note: You can find journal pages with this and other related exercises in the Resource Library tab on this book's website (https://www.apa.org/pubs/books/the-power-manual).

In many cases, your tone of voice is even more important than the words being spoken because the subject is reacting to the emotions in your voice even before the meaning of your words registers. It is important for the person to feel that you are sincere, which is determined by your tone and your nonverbal communication. Nonverbal communication, as you know, includes your body language and facial expression. It also involves making eye contact (don't forget to remove your sunglasses). Pay attention, too, to your body positioning and try to avoid an overly defensive posture, which may cause the other person to feel unnecessarily threatened. When you are calm, pleasant, and reassuring, even during a volatile encounter, subjects are far more likely to remain cooperative. Certainly, it is easier to do this when you are skilled at finding some common ground.

STEP 3. THE ROLE OF DISCRETION

An important component of good police work is the appropriate use of discretion. When it comes to infractions and low-level misdemeanors, you are typically given a fair amount of enforcement leeway. This, however, can be a double-edged sword. First, your guardian spirit comes through in your use of leniency; it's a way to show compassion and an understanding of the various hardships that others are experiencing. Officers with the guardian spirit realize that not all people who break the law should receive the most punitive outcome; you consider the context and the possibility of mitigating circumstances in your use of discretion.

At the same time, the use of discretion may not always be dispensed fairly. One could argue that officers tend to be more lenient toward those who are viewed as "us" than to individuals who are thought of as "them." Certainly, whether or not the perception is accurate, many members of economically disadvantaged communities do not feel as though they receive the same level of leniency as those living in more affluent communities. However, officers with the guardian spirit recognize the humanity in everyone, regardless of their zip code, including lawbreakers.

Nevertheless, when using discretion, it helps to have some insight and a willingness to be self-reflective to be fair-minded. More pointedly, officers with a guardian spirit are impartial when it comes to their use of discretion. In other words, your decision to be lenient or not should be determined by the nature of the situation rather than by the nature of the offender. You might even consider your use of discretion as an objectivity test.

Off-Duty Activity

Schedule some time to reflect on your use of discretion. Take out a notepad and make two columns. In the first column, write down as many incidents as you can remember when you decided to be lenient. In the second column, write down situations when you used discretion and chose to take a harder line. Next, look over your lists, and try to identify any patterns.

- Are there certain people with whom you tend to be lenient?
- Are there certain people with whom you tend to be stricter and more uncompromising?
- Are there calls in which you feel more compassion regardless of who's involved?
- Are there calls in which you tend to be quite stringent regardless of who's involved?
- Can you identify reasons why you were lenient or strict in those various situations?

After completing this exercise, one officer reflected:

> I never would have believed it until Officer Mike had us look at this. I found that I just don't cite a mother with kids in the car. Always a warning. Car doesn't matter. Offense doesn't matter. Race doesn't matter. Her demeanor doesn't matter. Maybe it's because I know how hard it was for my wife when our kids were still young with the car seats, booster seats, diaper bags, and stuff. I have to admit, though, that I am not always as lenient with dads who have kids in the car. No idea why not. This exercise forced me to look at this. I'll think more about it next time.

The goal is to be evenhanded with your use of discretion because you don't want anyone to accuse you of bias. It is defensible, even if you are asked about it on the stand, when you are able to say, "Whenever I encounter [this type of situation], I give the person the benefit of the doubt and send them on their way with a warning." Similarly, "Regardless of the offender, whenever I encounter [this type of situation], they are either getting cited or going to jail."

On-Duty Activity

Be consistently fair with your use of discretion. From the previous off-duty activity, you recognize the situations in which you tend to be lenient and those in which you are more by the book. Now, in every encounter where you could use discretion, determine before your decision why you will or will not be lenient. Ask yourself one simple question: Is it the situation, or is it the person? As long as your answer is "the situation," you know that you are acting without bias regardless of whether you end up being lenient or strict.

STEP 4. COMPASSION SATISFACTION

Manifesting your guardian spirit can make it easier to do your job by obtaining more compliance, more cooperation, and a lot less unnecessary escalation. However, feeling more compassion and using discretion and tactical empathy can lead to emotional exhaustion and burnout among police officers.[7] When you are emotionally drained, there is, unfortunately, also a tendency to become morally disengaged. Although the wellness tools offered earlier in the book will help you stay emotionally healthy, here, we focus on another strategy that specifically addresses this complex issue: compassion satisfaction. By engaging in activities that boost your compassion satisfaction, you can protect yourself from developing burnout and other emotional byproducts of this challenging profession.[8, 9]

Compassion satisfaction prevents the type of emotional exhaustion that officers may encounter when they implement the guardian spirit. Instead of only focusing on the crap you see on the job every day, the activities associated with compassion satisfaction encourage you to spend a little time focusing on the positive feelings you get from serving your community.

Off-Duty Activity

Review the mission statement that you wrote in Chapter 5. Add two or three more action statements to your mission, which reflect realistic expectations that you now have about your job. One of Officer Mike's officers added the following items to his:

> I understand that there are limits to what I am able to accomplish on the job.

> I accept that I will not be able to help or protect everyone.

On-Duty Activity

Like the activity in Chapter 5 when you identified how you fulfill your purpose, here is where you start paying attention to small victories. Look for opportunities to feel good about how you did your job regardless of the outcome, which is often out of your control. During your shift, make a mental note or, better yet, jot down each small victory. Fill in the blank throughout your shift: I felt good, positive, or effective when

_____.

On-Duty Activity

Don't ignore or downplay how it feels when you hit a home run on the job. It doesn't matter whether your supervisor notices. It doesn't matter whether you receive a commendation. It doesn't matter whether you are thanked by anyone for your service. This is 100% about how you feel about yourself every time you show what a great cop you are. You can still be humble while patting yourself on the back. Fill in the blank whenever you can: I felt great today when _____.

In addition to paying attention to the small victories and home runs, compassion satisfaction involves feelings of gratitude.[10] You can consider gratitude as one of the antidotes in your fight against burnout and compassion fatigue (which is addressed more thoroughly in Chapter 10). Remember what we talked about in Chapter 5 and the gratitude strategies presented there for your spiritual health. In addition to revisiting those exercises, there are two more activities you can do to increase compassion satisfaction.

On-Duty Activity

Despite all the negativity cops face in the media (social and otherwise) and from just doing their job, there are a lot of people out there who appreciate you. Start paying more attention to and keeping track of the signs that someone you encounter is grateful for what you do. Sometimes these are quite obvious, such as when a victim wants to give you a hug after you take their statement. Other times they are small indications of gratitude, such as a smile or handshake. It's important for you to remember that what you do matters. Here is an illustration of that idea:

> Officer Mike told me that I was getting cynical. After I looked it up, I had to admit that he was right. Here's how bad I was. Whenever I was getting lunch or at 7-Eleven and someone said, "Thank you for your service," I would nod, but inside I would just roll my eyes. So, I decided to change that. When someone said it, I would smile, I would thank them for thanking me, and I would shake their hand. It actually happened a lot more than I would have thought before I started paying attention to it.

Off-Duty Activity

Besides noticing how much you are appreciated by others, you deserve some self-gratitude. This is more than keeping track of your small victories and home runs. This transcends the specific highs and lows you experience on the job. Put a 5-minute entry in your calendar, scheduled to repeat every couple of weeks or so, for a moment of self-gratitude. Appreciate yourself and the effort you give to make your community a better place. Take some pride in how willing you are to face so many challenges, despite all the obstacles. This can be something you include in your journaling, or it can be a moment for you to just give yourself a pat on the back.

The guardian spirit of policing is an attitude that can keep you healthy. However, it is accompanied by some threats to your wellness, such as moral disengagement, emotional exhaustion, compassion fatigue, and burnout. Therefore, when you embrace the guardian spirit, it is imperative that you maintain a robust wellness program and practice the additional strategies outlined in this chapter. This becomes particularly important as we move to Chapter 8, where we discuss some additional moral risks of policing.

CHAPTER 8

MORAL DISTRESS AND ETHICAL EXHAUSTION

The previous two chapters helped you establish a foundation for maintaining your integrity and compassion while working in this demanding career. In this chapter, we address some external threats to your health and offer a few strategies that many police officers have found quite helpful. These are not threats to your physical safety; in fact, they are not often identified as common police stressors. Nevertheless, we describe some insidious challenges that officers routinely face, which can be extremely detrimental to your cognitive, emotional, and spiritual health.

The threats to your health discussed here are the result of moral distress and ethical exhaustion.[1] Unlike the emotional exhaustion mentioned in the last chapter, which can be a by-product of your compassion, *ethical exhaustion* happens when you feel helpless about making much of a positive impact with the work you are doing. It's as if no matter what you do, people's suffering continues, children are still abused and neglected, and the system keeps returning criminals to your streets. Likewise, *moral distress* stems from feelings of powerlessness when you can't do what you know should or could be done to improve things in your community.[2] For example, the various governmental agencies don't allocate enough resources, your department's executives tie your hands when it comes to some of their enforcement priorities, and you see that a few of your colleagues do not treat some of the members of your community in the way you know they should be treated.

Let's be honest here: Are there many feelings less welcome to cops, whose mission in life is to serve and protect, than helplessness and powerlessness? Unfortunately, these feelings are inevitable at various times during your law enforcement career. In this chapter, we identify some sources of these feelings of futility and offer strategies to help you overcome them. You may not be able to do much to avoid these feelings. However, there are steps that you can take so that they don't become detrimental to your health. Mostly, the key is to recognize them and understand where they originate.

STEP 1. COPING WITH EXTERNAL PRESSURES

The external pressures begin, for many, when you graduate from the academy and start your field training. It's pretty common for the new rookie to hear something like this from an old-timer: "Forget everything they taught in the academy, kid; things are different on the street." Hopefully, this didn't come from your FTO, which makes things even more uncomfortable. Nevertheless, it begins a process that often continues throughout your career. Sometimes the pressure is to do something that you think, or even know, is not right. Other times the pressure is not to do something that you think, or even know, is right. It can come from a supervisor. Sometimes it comes from your beat partner or other colleagues. At times, the organization itself enacts policies that leave you scratching your head because they just seem wrong. One of Officer Mike's officers said the following:

> I really couldn't believe it when they said that we were sup-
> posed to conduct homeless sweeps. These people have no place
> else to go. How is this part of our job? It's going to make things

a lot harder because, instead of having them fairly centralized, they are going to be all over the city now. It's not "just politics" when it affects what we have to do every day. I mean, how does this do anything to solve the problem?

Off-Duty Activity

One evening when you are doing some journaling, think about and write down the various external pressures you face that seem to make it more difficult to do your job. Identify the source: peer, supervisor, or organization. Next, although you may not have much power to stop some of the pressure, decide how you will feel and whether you will speak up when the pressure confronts you. Will you say something to a colleague or a supervisor when they want you to do something you know is wrong or not to do something you know is right? When it comes to the organization, make a mental plan to prepare yourself to handle a policy with which you disagree. The goal of this activity is to make you more aware of situations that may lead to feelings of powerlessness. Once you identify the sources of the feeling, although there may not be much that you can do about it, you can use the strategies presented in the wellness chapters (Chapters 1–5) to help you vent and reduce the impact of the powerlessness.

Another source of external pressure comes from your spouse, family, and noncop friends. Even though they may mean well, their concern for your safety may come across as nagging, which inevitably feels like pressure from them for you to do something (other than just reassure them). And if they do not fully understand the challenges you face on the job or your commitment to always doing the right thing, their pressure may take the form of disappointment or even disgust after seeing something they didn't like on the news or YouTube about how some cop somewhere did something to someone. These pressures have ended friendships, strained family relationships, and been the source of many divorces.

Off-Duty Activity

As in the previous activity, make an inventory of the pressures you feel from family and friends. Although some of this may be quite obvious, such as a "friend" who gives you crap about being a cop, you may not experience many of these as pressure. Nevertheless, they can leave you feeling somewhat helpless. For example, your kids may express intense fear about your safety, which nothing you say or do will alleviate.

After you identify the various pressures, develop a game plan. Will you tell your "friend" that you don't appreciate his comments or take steps to curtail the friendship? When it comes to your spouse, children, and other family members, if they express their concerns more and more regularly, it may be time to consult a qualified police psychologist to help you all find constructive ways to communicate.

Paradoxically, having your family's fears on your mind while you are working will likely make you less safe, so this really needs to be addressed. You want to be able to validate their feelings but get them to understand the pressure that their fears place on you. They may benefit from outlets for these fears other than constantly expressing them to you. If your department has a spouse auxiliary group whose members provide peer support, connect your spouse to them.

Another strategy that works for many families is for the spouse and children to begin writing about their concerns. Then schedule a time once a month or once a quarter for a family "talk" where you let them read what they wrote to you. Moreover, spouses and children whose fears for your safety are quite intense will benefit from a hiatus from the things that stoke those fears, such as police-related television shows and movies, as well as news, YouTube, and social media stories associated with law enforcement.

Also, you could develop some arrangements to reassure them while you are on duty (e.g., a text or call), though these can backfire when you are on an extended call, and they don't hear from you when they expected to. For your own health, however, despite how helpless you may feel about your loved one's fears, you will eventually have to accept that you are not responsible for their feelings. Counseling from a professional who is knowledgeable about stresses among police families might help with this.

STEP 2. CONFLICTING PRESSURES

There are times when you will confront conflicting pressures. You've heard the saying "caught between a rock and a hard place," and you've probably experienced the feeling at various times on the job. You strive for win-win outcomes, but sometimes you are faced with no-win situations. This is when the law, department policies, or an uncooperative victim leaves you with a moral dilemma. Doing nothing leaves you feeling powerless. But doing something may mean violating your moral code. Sitting here reading this, most officers will say that they would elect to do nothing. However, in the heat of the moment, we know that some cops would rather make an unethical decision than feel as though a crook is going to go unpunished. These officers avoid feeling powerless by choosing to do something unethical. Remember Officer Mike's officer from Chapter 6 who was investigated by IA for roughing up some gang members. That was a good example of conflicting pressures that led to a bad decision. It probably would have been better for everyone involved if they had learned how to better tolerate their feeling of powerlessness.

On-Duty Activity

Pay closer attention to the moral dilemmas that come up on the job. Make the time (on duty or off duty) to jot down the dilemmas and what you chose to do in the moment. The straightforward goal here is for you to become more aware of no-win situations that could elicit feelings of powerlessness and provoke you to do something unethical. This can be thought of as the downside of the discretion that we talked about in the last chapter. Would you rather do nothing and feel powerless or do something that could end up getting you in some trouble? Similarly, you could be faced with a moral dilemma in which doing nothing might get you in trouble, even though doing what you have to do may leave you feeling pretty rotten. For example, one officer said,

> Nobody likes DV calls. It tears me up to arrest someone when his kids are crying and screaming not to take away their dad. Most times, the asshole did something terrible, but sometimes it's not so black and white. More than once, I've asked myself what I should do. You got to do something, but there isn't always a good choice.

STEP 3. ACCEPTING YOUR LIMITATIONS, AKA SOMETIMES NOTHING CAN BE DONE

Despite your best efforts, there are times during your career when things don't turn out the way you would have liked them to. Organizationally, this might be a promotion you didn't get or a transfer to a specialized unit that wasn't approved. Such decisions are out of your control. However, these disappointments can lead some officers to become bitter and resentful and have prompted many to look for a job with another agency. In these situations, your challenge is not to allow your feelings to negatively impact how you do your job. You also might consider contacting a trusted superior to ask what you can do to make yourself more competitive for the next round of promotions. Focus on what you can control, and recommit yourself to the principles in your mission statement.

Conversely, many operational factors are out of your control and lead to the inevitable powerlessness that you will feel at various times on the job. While being the best cop you can be, you will encounter situations when, no matter what you do, nothing positive comes from your efforts. Similarly, there will be times when there just isn't anything that you could do to make a positive impact. It took one of Officer Mike's colleagues many years to understand this.

> I must have been on nearly 10 years when I finally figured out something they never taught us in the academy. Most of what I do every day amounts to squat. It's the opposite of what they tell you and what you see in the movies. Every now and then, it seems like I make a difference, actually help someone. For a long time, I would go home thinking, "What's the use?" Then, it hit me that serving and protecting is not the same thing as keeping everyone safe. I'd go nuts if that was the goal. We can only try our best and focus on the small wins.

Unfortunately, many officers who do not accept their limitations begin a downward spiral associated with moral distress and ethical exhaustion. Potentially destructive emotions intensify, such as betrayal and anger over the lack of resources and failures of the criminal justice system. Many officers start feeling guilt or shame because they couldn't do more to help. All of us are aware of the alarming rates of suicide among police officers. Although it is a complex problem caused by a variety of factors, and there are no easy solutions, we believe that these intense emotions play a significant role in the minds of many officers who choose to end their lives. After all, when that sense of futility gets too strong, it's hard not to be consumed by asking, "What's the use?"

Although this is similar to the suggestion about setting realistic expectations that we presented in Chapter 7, the emphasis here is on accepting your limitations and learning to tolerate the powerlessness and helplessness. Every officer is different when it comes to calls that evoke the most intense feelings of futility. Most cops abhor crimes against children and animals and are frustrated about not being able to do more to protect these innocent victims. However, there are many other situations that you encounter on a fairly regular basis that raise your futility meter.

On-Duty Activity

When you get a break during a shift, either between calls or during a meal, review the outcomes of each of the calls to which you responded so far that day. Ask yourself the following question: What might have happened if I hadn't been there? There may not have been a positive outcome, but try to think of the ways that things could have been worse if you hadn't shown up. For example, that driver who gave you a lot of shit after you stopped him for rolling a stop sign might have hit a kid on a bike if you hadn't pulled him over. This doesn't reset your futility meter to zero, but it will drop it down a few notches.

STEP 4. THE VALUE OF GRIEF

I remember the first dead body I saw on the job. It wasn't the same as the field trip to the morgue during the academy. Even though I've hunted all my life and have no problem with the blood and guts stuff, that first one has really stuck with me, and it wasn't that bad. It was a lady in her 70s who just died—heart attack, I guess. Her husband called it in, and we were first on scene. She looked fine, but he was crying hysterically. Over the years, I've seen so much worse: dead babies, horrible car wrecks, lots of homicides. For some reason, that first one really sticks with me, though.

One of the things that academies don't have time to cover is how officers' careers are impacted by their emotions. More recently, many agencies have begun to provide training in emotion regulation and emotional intelligence because these skills improve police performance.[3] However, you are pretty much on your own when it comes to learning how to cope with feelings such as anger, frustration, and sadness. These emotions, along with helplessness, powerlessness, and guilt, are easy to understand once you recognize that police work routinely exposes you to loss. Many of the losses you experience on the job are related to death. Most of these involve a call to which you responded. Some are, tragically, associated with the death of a fellow officer, either from an on-duty incident, suicide, an illness, or an off-duty accident.

Some of the losses that elicit intense, often intrusive emotions are not so easy to recognize, even though they can end up being detrimental to your health. These losses are associated with a loss of support and a loss of your identity. For some officers, a transfer or getting a new supervisor can lead to a host of uncomfortable feelings because you no longer have your primary source of support on which to rely. Similarly, as you get older or experience an on-duty injury, you may start feeling like you are not the same cop you once were. Some officers experience this as a loss of identity. For example, one officer said,

> It's not something I like to talk about, and there aren't too many people who know it, but there was a time I was pretty close to eating my gun. It wasn't one thing that led me to it or one thing that kept me from doing it. The only way I can explain it is I felt dead inside. There was nothing but death all around me on the job, and then a couple friends died. I had to go on TRD [temporary restricted duty] because of a back injury and didn't know if they'd ever let me back on patrol. I was totally lost. I wasn't me anymore. There was nothing I could do other than just end it. I still don't know why I didn't. So, I swallowed my pride instead of my gun and went and saw our department shrink. I went for a full year. I can't say what worked, but it did, and I'm glad I'm still here.

No matter how well you practice the stress management strategies provided earlier in this book, you will encounter a variety of uncomfortable, often intense emotions throughout your career. These are normal responses to the various losses that you experience on and off duty. The one tool at your disposal to cope most effectively with these losses is called *grief work*. Many people, including a lot of cops, would prefer to "just move on" after a loss. They don't recognize that this is an ineffective strategy that invariably makes things worse. The losses keep piling up until they can smother you—unless you actively work to address them when they happen.

Grief work, however, is a powerful tool that will enable you to endure these losses without significant damage to your health. Although there are many approaches to handling loss, including consultation with a professional bereavement counselor when your own efforts do not seem to be providing enough relief, we are going to give you some basics that you can use following losses. At the same time, there is no single path to recover from a loss; different officers find some strategies more helpful than others. You have to develop and then use the plan that you've found works best for you. Nevertheless, many officers have found it productive to follow these activities.

Grief Work Activities

- Acknowledge the loss. Don't sweep any loss under the proverbial rug. Tell your significant other about what happened, describe your sense of loss, and explain the emotions you are feeling. If you are single, do this with a trusted friend. In the least, write it down in a journal.
- Embrace your humanity. A loss may force you to confront your mortality. For some young officers who feel invincible, the death of a colleague or loved one bursts their immortality illusion. After each loss, take a step back and appreciate that you are still alive. Take extra good care of your health with fitness and nutrition, even though you may not feel motivated to do so. And be careful to avoid self-medicating; alcohol will just intensify the painful emotions.
- Connect with loved ones. Despite what may be intense feelings of grief and a desire to isolate from others, it's especially important after a loss to reach out to those closest to you for support. They may not fully appreciate what you are going through, but you don't need to try to make them understand. They aren't there to fix anything; they are just there to love you.
- Connect with others who've been there. Some of your fellow officers have experienced similar losses. They may or may not have felt the same way you feel, but it will help you to know that there are people who completely understand what it's like to go through what you are experiencing. At the same time, there are some losses that you directly share with some

colleagues. You were at the same gruesome accident with multiple fatalities. No one who wasn't there could exactly imagine the horror you witnessed. After these incidents, it's important to debrief your emotions together. These debriefings are an important step toward processing your intense feelings and not bottling them up.

- Drop the tough guy act. Even if you are not that bothered by most on-duty tragedies anymore because you've pretty much seen it all, there will be losses from time to time that hit home and can knock you for a loop. It is not a good idea to act like these incidents are just business as usual. When you ignore the intense emotions from one of these losses, you are more likely to make a mistake or get yourself in some trouble because the emotions may be clouding your judgment. You have vacation days for a reason. Take a day or two off after one of these significant losses.

- Practice spiritual wellness strategies. It's especially important following a loss to increase the frequency and intensity of the strategies presented in Chapter 5. In fact, because loss is inevitable in police work, it is vital for you to establish these skills early in your career; without them already in place, it is more difficult to learn them for the first time following a loss.

- Strengthen your resilience. Resilient officers cope best following any loss. The next several chapters will provide you with numerous strategies to boost your resilience.

Note: A download for your journal related to the grief work activities is available in the Resource Library tab on this book's website (https://www.apa.org/pubs/books/the-power-manual).

The moral risks of policing are quite real and can be harmful to officers' health and well-being. These risks stem from organizational, operational, and your own internal pressures to fight crime and serve your community. The pressures lead many officers to violate their moral code, which results in unethical decisions. Aspects of the job often make it easier to compromise your integrity by dehumanizing those you swore to protect. Much of this is a natural by-product of moral distress and ethical exhaustion. Officers who feel overwhelmed by powerlessness and helplessness are simply not capable of being effective cops.

There are steps that you can take to prevent yourself from falling into this abyss. The activities presented in the last three chapters can help you maintain your integrity, compassion, and commitment to always doing the right thing. Although you and your fellow officers have chosen a career that brings you face to face with the worst of society, you have control over whether you will retain your humanity. This takes dedication to practice the strategies we've presented so far throughout the book. And perhaps most important, it takes a willingness to become more resilient. In the next three chapters, we show you how you can sustain positive personal growth throughout your law enforcement career.

III

RESILIENCE

CHAPTER 9

STRESS INOCULATION

In this chapter, we provide you with some practical information about stress and stress management skills. Our aim is to guide you with strategies designed to help you become less reactive and more tolerant of many stressful situations that you routinely encounter on the job. The chapter contains many proven exercises. Try them and determine which work best for you. But like the wellness exercises described earlier, you may not experience immediate results; you need to practice, stick with them, and incorporate them into your overall wellness regimen. As we remind you, preparing to cope with the stress of police work is no different than preparing to compete in the Olympics. It takes a combination of intense commitment to succeed, the dedication to keep pushing despite distractions and setbacks, a willingness to incorporate the latest scientific training advancements, and a team of supportive coaches (that's us in this metaphor).

STEP 1. UNDERSTANDING THE NATURE OF STRESS

Officer Mike

 It sure takes a lot of training to become a cop, and it can be stressful—first, the weeks at the academy, then the field training, and then the probationary period. Completing field training was a great feeling. I was finally there. On my first day on solo patrol, I was so excited about being on my own. I felt proud of myself after all the hoops I had jumped through. But what was my first day like? It was exciting but one of the most stressful days of my life.

Stress is a necessary part of life. It is the internal way our mind and body react to external situations, which are referred to as *stressors* (i.e., the things that cause our stress). Because it is internal, we have quite a bit of control over our level of stress. However, it takes a lot of practice of some highly effective techniques to learn how to control that internal level of stress. Conversely, we often have little control over the external stressors that impact us and to which we have to react. Moreover, we are usually juggling numerous stressors, such as relationships, health, finances, and job concerns, at the same time. The more stressors you face, the more important it is to learn how to manage your internal level of stress successfully.

Interestingly, the term *stress* was initially developed by engineers as a way to measure the pressure that certain materials can sustain over time. Like those materials, the human body and mind experience internal stress when under external pressure, and as happens with machines, the pressure on the human body can have negative consequences. One of the earliest scientists to delve into the relationship between stress and illness was Hans Selye.[1] Since then, there has been a lot of research on stress and health, including the damage that too much stress can cause police officers.[2] However, stress is not always bad. In fact, we need a certain amount of stress to function at our peak level of performance. Although the topic is far more complex than we make it here,[3] Selye identified two major types of stress: *eustress*, which is positive stress; and *distress*, which is negative stress that interferes with performance. Eustress is, essentially, the necessary amount of internal energy required to function in various settings. Without enough of this good stress, you could end up, literally, asleep at the wheel. Distress is an overwhelming and potentially detrimental type of internal energy. In sports, it's called a choke; too much of that distress and your performance falls off dramatically from your peak level. As you can see in the following stress–performance graph, the relationship between stress and performance has an inverted-U shape.

You function at your maximum level when you maintain your internal level of stress in the optimal zone. As an officer, your performance suffers with too little or too much of that internal energy. When there is too little, you may become complacent, drop your guard, and jeopardize your (or someone else's) safety. When there is too much distress, you are prone to significant errors that may leave you saying afterward, "I can't believe I did that." During these times, your actions are more likely to violate procedures by

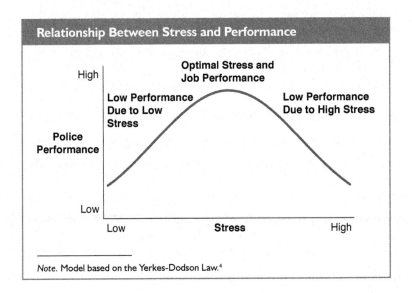

Relationship Between Stress and Performance

High — **Optimal Stress and Job Performance**

Low Performance Due to Low Stress

Low Performance Due to High Stress

Police Performance

Low

Low   **Stress**   High

Note. Model based on the Yerkes-Dodson Law.[4]

which you were trained and/or organizational policies that you usually have no problem following.

When exposed to an extreme stressor, the body goes through all sorts of immediate reactions, including the very real fight-flight-or-freeze stress response.[5] Your heart races, you start to sweat, and breathing becomes irregular. Police training hopefully kicks in so that officers do not freeze or flee. They remain committed to protecting and serving, even when confronted with extreme stressors. However, we've all seen examples of officers not performing effectively under pressure. When you understand the relationship between stress and performance, it's pretty clear that this is because those officers were not adequately managing their internal level of energy.

This is where the good news comes in. You can learn techniques to maintain the internal level of energy in your optimal stress zone so that you perform at your peak during slow times (i.e., never drop your guard) and especially when you are under pressure (i.e., no choking). As we said in Chapter 2, in many ways, effective police work requires the stress management skills of a world-class athlete who trains to always be able to compete, mentally and physically, at their highest level.

STEP 2. DEVELOPING HEALTHY STRESS MANAGEMENT SKILLS

We are going to give you different strategies that you can incorporate on duty and off duty to help you manage stress in ways that do not negatively affect your health, wellness, or job performance. First, however, we have to mention that everyone develops their own ways to handle stress. Some of these are more effective than others, and some are not healthy at all, no matter how much you've come to rely on them (e.g., tobacco use, excessive alcohol consumption, as well as isolation and avoidance).

Off-Duty Activity

Take a look at how you tend to react to a particularly stressful call or after a distressing day. What are your go-to stress management skills? Do you have any coping strategies that could be considered bad habits? Make a list of your healthy stress management strategies and your less healthy ones.

If you have developed unhealthy strategies to deal with the stressors in your life, we'd like you to consider the alternative tools we give you in this chapter. Once you start practicing these new skills, it would be great if you decided to cut back or replace those unhealthy outlets with the healthier strategies.

If you already rely on healthy coping strategies, the suggestions in this chapter will strengthen your ability to fend off the negative impacts of external stressors. The most important places to start when it comes to healthy stress management skills are all the suggestions outlined in the wellness chapters of this book (Chapters 1–5). Beyond those, however, stress inoculation provides additional techniques for you to remain in your optimal stress zone. It will be up to you to determine what works best for you. Try them out, practice, and select the most effective techniques.

Before jumping in and practicing the stress management techniques in this chapter, refer to the figure of the stress thermometer as a way to learn more about your stress management needs. Identify calls and situations to which you respond that, for you, are mildly or moderately stressful. Next, identify calls and situations that are the most stressful for you. This knowledge helps you prepare for how you may react to a given situation. Those that are low on the thermometer may require you to "amp up" to stay

Cops Stress Thermometer

100:	Highest stress that you ever felt.
90:	Extremely stressed: extreme fight, flight, or freeze response
80:	Very stressed: cannot concentrate
70:	Quite stressed: interference with performance
50:	Moderate stress: you are uncomfortable, but you can still perform
30:	Mild stress: no interference on performance
20:	Minimal stress
10:	Alert and awake: you concentrate well
0:	Totally relaxed

Note. From *Concurrent Treatment of PTSD and Substance Use Disorders Using Prolonged Exposure (COPE): Patient Workbook* (p. 146), by S. E. Back, E. B. Foa, T. K. Killeen, K. L. Mills, M. Teesson, B. D. Cotton, K. M. Carroll, and K. T. Brady, 2014, Oxford University Press. Adapted with permission.

in your optimal stress zone, whereas those at the top will require you to master these strategies to get back down into your optimal stress zone.

STEP 3. COGNITIVE CONTROL TECHNIQUES

In this section, we introduce you to the principles of cognitive behavior therapy (CBT).[6] We are not sending you to therapy or asking you to do therapy on yourself. Rather, we think it's useful to know about how CBT works because it provides skills that will prevent you from getting too distressed in the moment. Ultimately, this strategy optimizes your functioning because it keeps you in control of the reactions that can lead you out of your optimal stress zone. Overall, the philosophy of CBT says that our actions stem from a combination of our thoughts, emotions, and awareness of physical (i.e., bodily) reactions. Likewise, different objects, places, and people are associated with different thoughts and memories. Those thoughts are interconnected with certain emotions and physical reactions, as well as with patterns of behavior.

That being said, our internal level of stress becomes less than optimal when several things happen: (a) irrational thoughts can trigger unwanted or undesirable emotions that, for example, can make us unnecessarily or more intensely angry, scared, or frustrated; (b) we misinterpret a physical reaction, such as thinking that a situation is more dangerous than it is when our heart starts racing; and (c) certain levels of certain emotions (e.g., anger) cause us to think that we have to react in a certain way. The goals of this approach to stress management are to ensure that our thoughts are rational, we don't misinterpret our physical reactions, and we accept our emotional experiences without necessarily having to express those feelings in the moment.

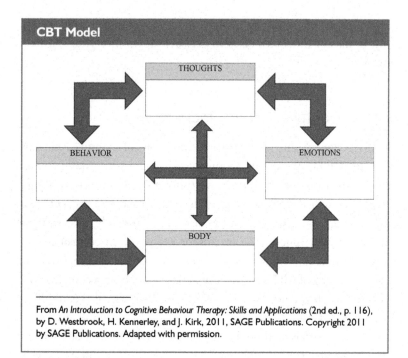

CBT Model

From *An Introduction to Cognitive Behaviour Therapy: Skills and Applications* (2nd ed., p. 116), by D. Westbrook, H. Kennerley, and J. Kirk, 2011, SAGE Publications. Copyright 2011 by SAGE Publications. Adapted with permission.

The above figure is a visual representation of the CBT model. The chart shows the interconnected relationship between your thoughts, emotions, awareness of bodily reactions, and your behavior.

Let's revisit Officer Mike's first day on solo patrol, mentioned at the beginning of this chapter, to highlight each component of the CBT model. His thoughts (see the top of the chart) were

> It feels so good to be finished with field training, and finally, I'm on solo patrol. Dang, I'm on solo patrol! I hope I know what to do. I hope I can find the address where I am dispatched. I need to have some self-initiated activity. I'll find something,

even if it means running some radar. Once it gets dark, there will be traffic stops for having a headlight or taillight out.

He described his behaviors (left side of the chart) this way:

> I did my squad car check. I have everything I need, and all equipment is functioning properly. I wasn't dispatched to any hot calls, mostly service calls. However, I found my way around and knew my geography. I made a few traffic stops for various violations writing a couple of tickets and a couple of warning tickets. Everyone I interacted with was very compliant and understanding.

Officer Mike's emotions went something like this:

> I'm feeling kind of anxious, in both a positive and negative way at the same time. I'm looking for some self-initiated activity making me hypervigilant. I felt much better after my first call— I found the address—and my first traffic stop went just like when I was with my FTO. But still a bit anxious the entire shift.

He reflected on what his body felt like too:

> As soon as I drove off the lot for solo patrol, it was very exciting, but I was a bit nervous. I didn't check my pulse, but I bet my resting heart rate was about 100 bpm. As the shift went on, I became more relaxed (but not completely), more confident, and the only time my heart rate went up again was my first couple of calls I was dispatched to and my first couple of solo traffic stops.

How were Officer Mike's thoughts connected to his emotions? How did his behavior and body sensations reflect his emotions? How might his fast heart rate have affected his thoughts, emotions, or behavior if it had continued the entire shift?

Choose a day, good or bad, that you'd like to revisit using the CBT model. What were your thoughts? In what ways did your emotions, your behavior, or the state of your body mirror your thoughts? Write it down. Feel free to use the blank CBT chart provided in the book to help you get a clear breakdown of how these components of your experience are connected.

Note: More blank charts are available for download from the Resource Library tab on this book's website (https://www.apa.org/pubs/books/the-power-manual).

We next present some practical scenarios that will help you better conceptualize the CBT perspective and appreciate its applications for your health and wellness. An irrational thought, which can snowball over time, is likely to trigger more intense unwanted or undesired emotions, which can lead to negative health reactions, as well as problematic behaviors. The idea here is that when you are able to monitor your thinking and replace those irrational thoughts, you will be able to prevent yourself from experiencing unwanted or undesired emotions, which often have a toxic impact on your physical reactions and behavior.

Off-Duty Activity

Remember, in Chapter 2, we presented a list of common irrational thoughts called *thinking errors*. Please review the list you made in Chapter 2 of your common thinking errors. (If you didn't make a list then, make one now.) Look over the list and identify which of those irrational thoughts may be causing you some unnecessary distress in various parts of your life (e.g., at work, in relationships).

As you may have noticed, we do not refer to "negative" thoughts or "negative" emotions. Instead, we call them irrational thoughts and unwanted or undesirable emotions. This is because many negative thoughts or negative emotions are not necessarily bad or inappropriate. Negative thoughts and emotions are expected when a family member is sick, or your supervisor does not recognize your great work during a difficult call. However, irrational thoughts are the ones that do not correspond to reality ("I am a bad cop because I messed up the call") and then trigger those unwanted or undesirable emotions. In addition, extremely intense emotions (coming from a bunch of irrational thoughts) can also be problematic. For example, extreme bravado can cause you to feel invincible, which could lead to a lack of situational awareness.

STEP 4. RECOGNIZING IRRATIONAL THOUGHTS (A REFRESHER COURSE FROM CHAPTER 2)

A core component of CBT is an understanding of the role of irrational thoughts in fueling the intensity of our emotions and guiding our behavior. Remember, an irrational thought is something that we think to be true even when reality does not support it. We can believe something is a fact despite a lack of supporting evidence, which is the basis of faith. However, sometimes we are sure about something while ignoring the facts because we are convinced that what we think to be true is the actual truth. Other times, the truth is uncertain, or a situation is ambiguous. Nevertheless, rather than thinking, "I need to know more before deciding what to think," we may come to a premature, unsupported conclusion. That unsupported conclusion could turn out to be true, but it may be just as likely that it is an irrational thought. Unfortunately, irrational thoughts often arouse unnecessarily intense undesirable emotions and, worse, cause us to act in ways that can lead to bad outcomes.

Doing the exercises from Chapter 2 is a good way to monitor our thoughts to determine whether they are rational and correct those that are irrational. Moreover, CBT trains us to recognize the mechanisms of how we think, feel, and act. These skills allow us to have better emotion regulation because as we eliminate irrational thoughts, we are dealing with facts, accepting ambiguity, and remaining comfortably in our optimal stress zone. Let's look at a couple of scenarios.

Scenario 1

Imagine that you are at home lying in bed. It is after midnight, and the rest of the family is sleeping. All of a sudden, you hear a creaky noise near your front door. What is your immediate thought? How do you react? Perhaps you think that someone is trying to break into your residence. What is your emotional reaction? Perhaps you feel some level of nervousness, which would be totally understandable! Or maybe you become instantly pissed off that someone dares to burgle your home. How does your body react? You probably notice tension somewhere in your body, such as your chest, shoulders, and legs. Also, in your mind, you probably go into tactical mode. That leads you to act: You start approaching the door while holding your weapon. Then, in the dim light, you see your nephew coming into the house. Your oldest son gave him a key because he was going to spend the night at your house. What are your thoughts, emotions, and bodily reactions at that moment? Are you relieved that you kept your cool and didn't shoot the "intruder"? Do you start yelling at the nephew or your son who neglected to tell you about their plan? How quickly are you able to calm down and get to sleep?

The important point in this scenario is identifying the thoughts you had when you first heard the noise. It was ambiguous. Your actions were based on your thoughts, which stemmed from an interpretation of your emotions in the moment and attention to your physical alertness. Were the thoughts rational or irrational? Even a rational thought ("Sounds like someone is trying to break in") can lead to emotions and physical reactions that produce an irrational thought ("Someone is trying to kill my family"). Past experience contributes to whether you act rationally in the moment. If you were aware of a rash of break-ins in the neighborhood, it might have led to a different outcome because you were primed to shoot an intruder. However, if you had a rodent problem at your house, you may have assumed that the noise was from a roof rat and stayed in bed, which would have been a problem if the noise was not from your nephew but a burglar. Your thoughts, based on past experiences, can shape your behavior by causing you to (a) ignore the facts at hand or (b) not gather enough facts before taking action.

Scenario 2

You are about to start your shift. After the line-up, as the lieutenant walks by you, you say, "Good morning, 'Lt,'" but she completely ignores you. What's the first thing that goes through your mind? Do you automatically think one of the following thoughts?

- "What did I do wrong?"
- "Why is 'Lt' having a bad day?"
- "Something big just happened; I better go 10-8 fast."
- "Maybe 'Lt' didn't hear me."

Now, think about what emotion and physical reaction you might experience from each of those different thoughts. Finally, ask yourself how you might act in response to each of those thoughts. Each thought could impact how your whole shift goes, so it's pretty important not to cling to a thought that could be irrational.

You can't always know for sure what is or isn't irrational. Maybe one of those thoughts is exactly why the lieutenant didn't respond to you, or maybe it was for a completely different reason.

You could spend the whole shift with a thought (rational or irrational) and the resulting unnecessarily intense emotions, which could significantly impact your behavior on duty. Or you could ask the lieutenant whether she heard you say good morning and why she didn't respond. This would give you the facts, which, if you did do something wrong, is likely to bug you the whole shift. Or you could let the whole thing go by telling yourself a thought that leaves you feeling calm and ready to perform at your peak during your shift (e.g., "No biggie. Let's assume she didn't hear me"). Until the lieutenant clearly tells you there is a problem, it does you no good to think something that negatively affects your internal level of stress.

STEP 5. PHYSIOLOGICAL CONTROL: BREATHING AND PROGRESSIVE MUSCLE RELAXATION

Officer Mike

 I began my martial arts career in high school in the late 1970s. The thing I loved most about class was sparring. I can remember having to sit correctly in "seiza" position on my knees and practicing breathing and imagery exercises. I sat there, thinking to myself, "This is stupid, I just want to spar! Come on, let's pad up!" It wasn't until I took a class in junior college that I learned the importance of what I was doing. In addition, hearing that so many professional athletes were practicing such techniques encouraged me to start to take this part of my martial arts training seriously. And at 57 years old, I am still competing, usually against competitors who are much younger than me.

When I retired from my PD and began teaching at the police academy, I noted the lack of a wellness course for recruit officers. At the time, it was not mandated by the state. However, I collaborated with a professor at the university, and we developed a wellness block of instruction. We included the important aspects of breathing exercises, meditation, and imagery into the curriculum. I knew many recruit officers would see this as unimportant, just as I did in high school when I began practicing martial arts. Therefore, to get buy-in, I realized we needed to change the name. I would call it "tactical breathing" or "combat breathing." This may sound weird, but it worked. They didn't care about empirical research on how this could lower the heart rate or reduce the stress hormones in the body. They wanted to know that it would make them think more clearly and give them more situational awareness.

As your internal level of tension increases beyond your optimal stress zone, two common physiological reactions are impaired breathing and muscle tension or even cramping. This is why breathing exercises and progressive muscle relaxation are central to most athletes' performance enhancement routines: They help you stay in, or get back into, your optimal stress zone. Once the technique is learned, you can develop little habits to keep you in the "zone" whenever the shit starts to hit the fan. Baseball players do this in the batter's box with prepitch rituals. Basketball players do this before a free throw. Sometimes it's as small as a deep breath accompanied by a quick visualization (see the next section). The result is that you maintain control of your internal level of tension. Before those little habits can work, however, you have to learn the techniques!

Breathing Exercises

You may be familiar with what Officer Mike called tactical breathing techniques. If you have been trained in tactical breathing, you may want to skip this section. If you are not familiar with them, breathing exercises train you to control some of your physiological reactions during distressing moments. They take some practice to master. When first learning these exercises, practice them at least four times per day. Once you have been doing them for several weeks, you may find yourself naturally breathing in ways that keep you in your optimal stress zone. Then, you can go into maintenance mode and practice the exercises just a couple of times per day. It's important to start by learning the breathing techniques in a quiet, undisturbed setting off duty.

Off-Duty Breathing Exercise 1

1. Find a comfortable position in a chair or lying down.
2. Breathe in through your nose for 2 to 3 seconds.
3. Hold your breath for 2 to 3 seconds.
4. Breathe out through your mouth for 2 to 3 seconds.
5. As you breathe out, say the word *relax* to yourself (or use another word that you prefer, such as *calm, focus, control, easy, center*). It's important to choose one word and use only this word every time.
6. Repeat for 2 to 3 minutes.

Off-Duty Breathing Exercise 2

1. Find a comfortable position in a chair or lying down.
2. Lightly place both hands on your stomach area just under your rib cage or on your chest, depending on what part of your body you prefer to focus your attention.
3. Take slow, deep breaths.
4. Hold each inhale for 2 to 3 seconds before you exhale.
5. As you breathe in and out, pay attention to the rise and fall of your stomach (or chest) by focusing on that part of your body.

6. As you exhale, say the word "relax" to yourself (or use the other word that you selected during Off-Duty Exercise 1, such as "calm," "focus," "control," "easy," "center"). It's important to stick with the same word and use only this word every time.
7. Repeat for 2 to 3 minutes.

It is not uncommon for your mind to get distracted as you first begin these breathing exercises. If that happens, do not get discouraged. Guide your mind gradually back to your breathing and focus on your breath. Some people find it helpful to visualize the breath as a type of energy or flame that goes in and out of the body; this metaphor helps some to stay focused on their breathing. In addition, the consistent use of your chosen word as you exhale will help keep you focused, too.

Officer Mike

 When I was a field training officer, I would notice that when my trainees were dispatched to a potentially dangerous call (domestic, fight in progress, burglar alarm, etc.), they were extremely tense. As a passenger in the squad car, I could look over and recognize this immediately. I would remind them to breathe and then discuss how we would likely handle the situation we were about to face. I wanted them to think about a positive outcome, even if it meant physical control tactics. My goal was always to encourage them to breathe and think about their strategy and tactics for a positive outcome once they were on solo patrol.

After learning the techniques off duty, you will benefit from practicing them on duty. As you gain mastery, you will naturally experience better stress management merely through control of your breathing.

On-Duty Breathing Exercise I

1. Sit in a comfortable position in the cruiser.
2. Breathe in through your nose for 2 to 3 seconds.
3. Hold in your breath for 2 to 3 seconds.
4. Breathe out through your mouth for 2 to 3 seconds, and as you breathe out, say the word you selected during the Off-Duty Breathing Exercises.
5. Repeat for a minute unless your shift is "uneventful," in which case you can practice for a longer time.

On-Duty Breathing Exercise 2

1. Have a clock or a watch available with a second hand.
2. Silently count 4 seconds on the clock as you breathe in through your nose.
3. Silently count 4 seconds on the clock as you breathe out through your mouth.
4. Repeat for at least a couple of minutes until you feel noticeably more relaxed.

If you are interested in the latest technology, there is equipment out there that helps you monitor your breathing and heart rate and provides you with feedback through an app on your mobile device.

Progressive Muscle Relaxation

After learning the breathing exercises, you can begin to incorporate progressive muscle relaxation (PMR) to boost your stress management skills. With PMR, you are adding a muscle relaxation component to your breathing skills. When you can control your breathing and prevent your muscles from tensing (excessively and/or at inopportune times), you remain safely in your optimal stress zone. When you practice PMR off duty, you can achieve a level of relaxation similar to getting a deep tissue massage. Try to practice at least once every day. After a few weeks, you should feel as though you've mastered the skill and can readily make yourself quite relaxed. When you use the technique on duty, the goal is not to obtain deep relaxation. It is to prevent you from getting increasingly tense throughout your shift. Doing this on duty is a way to quickly prevent interfering muscle tension and stay relaxed enough to perform at your peak.

Off-Duty PMR Exercise 1

1. Find a quiet place at home or outdoors and sit or lie in a comfortable position.
2. Close your eyes and take two or three slow, deep breaths.
3. Mentally scan your whole body and pay attention to any areas of tension or tightness.
4. Take another slow, deep breath and tell yourself to relax the tension you identified.
5. Beginning at your toes, tighten the muscles in your feet for 3 to 5 seconds and then release.
6. Move to your calves and tighten your muscles for 3 to 5 seconds and then release.
7. Then, move to your thigh muscles (quads and hamstrings), tighten them for 3 to 5 seconds, and release.

8. Move to your glutes (butt muscle). Tighten them for 3 to 5 seconds and then release.
9. Next, tighten your stomach muscles for 3 to 5 seconds and release.
10. Move to your chest, tighten and hold your muscles for 3 to 5 seconds, and release.
11. Next, pull your shoulder blades together and hold for 3 to 5 seconds and release.
12. Raise your shoulders (as close to your ears as you can) and hold for 5 to 6 seconds and release.
13. Next, tighten your arm muscles (biceps and triceps) for 3 to 5 seconds and release.
14. Then, make fists and hold them tightly for 5 to 6 seconds and release.
15. Next, tighten your neck and face muscles for 3 to 5 seconds and release.
16. Finally, tighten all your muscles (listed previously) at the same time for 5 to 6 seconds. Feel the tension, then release.
17. Breathe slowly, in through your nose and out through your mouth.
18. Relax all your muscles completely; notice your heart rate slowing.

Off-Duty PMR Exercise 2

After performing PMR Exercise 1 for several weeks, some people continue as outlined earlier, whereas others find that they no longer need to tense their muscles to achieve a level of deep relaxation. Instead, you begin with the slow, deep breathing. Following the same progression from the toes to the head, you can simply visualize each muscle in your body becoming relaxed without tensing and releasing it. While doing this, some people feel as though their body gets heavy, like it is sinking into the floor. Other people have an opposite reaction and feel as though their body begins to float as it gets more and more relaxed. The exercise should take 12 to 15 minutes each time you practice it.

On-Duty PMR Exercise

1. As you sit in your cruiser or at your desk, take a couple of slow, deep breaths, breathing in through your nose and out through your mouth.

2. Mentally scan your body and focus on three muscle groups where you feel the most tension (for example, your quads, traps, and jaw muscles).

3. Focus on your thighs, tighten your quads and hamstrings for 2 to 3 seconds, and release.

4. Then, move to your shoulders, tighten your trapezius muscles for 2 to 3 seconds, and release.

5. Next, tighten your jaw muscles by clenching your teeth for 2 to 3 seconds and release.

6. Relax all your body muscles completely while taking several slow, deep breaths.

7. You can choose a different set of muscles each time you practice this or select the three sets of muscles where you seem to carry the most tension.

Bonus: Relaxation With Focused Imagery

Once you learn how to create a comfortable state of relaxation through the PMR exercises, adding a mental image can significantly enhance your ability to remain in your optimal stress zone, even during the most critical times. Again, this takes some practice off duty to benefit from the skill on duty.

Off-Duty Exercise: PMR With Focused Imagery

1. Using PMR, take 10 to 12 minutes to make yourself relaxed.
2. Once relaxed, picture a place that will become your oasis. It can be somewhere you've been or a place you've only dreamed of visiting. Whatever you select, it should contain nothing but relaxing, pleasant imagery because you are going to take in all the sensory experiences you would encounter there.
3. Focus on every visual detail of your private haven. Take in the objects, the colors, the brightness, the shadows.
4. Next, move on to the sounds you hear. Do you hear birds? Waves? The rustle of leaves on the trees?
5. Then, identify what you can smell. Is there a campfire? Freshly mowed grass? Sea air or swimming pool chlorine? Sunscreen?
6. Last, what physical sensations do you feel? Is there sun and/or a warm breeze on your skin? Are you floating on a pool raft? Is there warm sand under the towel on which you are lying?
7. Practice getting relaxed and then bringing the image and all those sensations to mind.

By adding the visual image to your relaxed state off duty, you will become more relaxed whenever you bring that image to mind on duty. Obviously, it can't be the deep state of relaxation you can achieve off duty, but it is a darn good approximation. First, however, you have to successfully train yourself off duty to pair your state of relaxation with the mental image.

On-Duty Use of PMR With Focused Imagery

1. Take a slow, deep breath and think about your oasis.
2. Then, bring the image to mind to feel flooded with the sights, sounds, smells, and physical sensations from that image.
3. At that moment, you will become more relaxed (i.e., you will get your stress level back into your optimal zone).

One of Officer Mike's officers shared his use of focused imagery:

> The most relaxing thing I do is float on a raft in my brother's backyard pool. So, when I started doing the relaxation exercises, I decided to make that my focused imagery. After getting relaxed, I concentrate on the gentle rocking of the raft, the sun on my face, the birds flying around and chirping, the sound of the pool filter churning away. I could go on and on. I mean, I can mentally make myself feel like I am actually back in that pool. Then, during a shift, if I get a call that could be hairy, you know, a DV or man-with-a-gun call, the first thing I do is take a deep breath and bring that image of myself floating in the pool into my mind. I do it with my eyes open as I'm rolling code, but my body does not get all tense like it used to before I learned this stuff. And if some yahoo is mouthing off during a traffic stop, or if I get chewed out over a typo in a report, before I react, I take a deep breath and quickly bring that swimming pool to my mind. It takes just a second, and I am literally more relaxed and less likely to lose my cool.

STEP 6. MINDFULNESS AND GROUNDING

You've probably heard about mindfulness and, perhaps, your agency provided you with some training to become "mindful." *Mindfulness* means staying mentally sharp and focused in the moment. It involves a type of meditation that clears your mind of distracting thoughts. A lack of mindfulness makes you vulnerable to becoming distracted or inappropriately reactive. It is a skill that has been shown to be beneficial for reducing posttraumatic stress disorder symptoms,[7] as well as general stress and anger[8] among police officers. To achieve mindfulness, however, some effort is required. This is because our minds often drift to things from the past or worries about something in the future. Mindfulness exercises help you to focus on the present moment by accurately observing your thoughts, emotions, and physical reactions without any negative judgments. Mindfulness is another tool to recognize and eliminate irrational thoughts because it keeps you focused only on the facts at hand even when there isn't enough evidence to know for sure what's what.

Off-Duty Mindfulness Exercises

According to the Mayo Clinic,[9] there are three simple mindfulness exercises that you can practice every day:

- Body scanning. Lie on your back with your legs extended and arms at your sides, palms facing up. Focus your attention slowly and deliberately on each part of your body, in order, from toe to head or head to toe. Be aware of any sensations, emotions, or thoughts associated with each part of your body.
- Sitting. Sit comfortably with your back straight, feet flat on the floor, and hands in your lap. Breathing through your nose, focus on your breath moving in and out of your body. If physical sensations or thoughts interrupt your meditation, note the experience and then return your focus to your breath.
- Walking. Find a quiet place 10 to 20 feet in length, and begin to walk slowly. Focus on the experience of walking, being aware of the sensations of standing and the subtle movements that keep your balance. When you reach the end of your path, turn and continue walking, maintaining awareness of your sensations.

While initially doing these exercises, it's common for you to lose focus. You are developing the skill to avoid being distracted by random thoughts, sounds, or sensations. As you progress, it will become easier to refocus away from the distraction. You know that you have mastered the exercise when you can do the activity for 5 to 10 minutes without anything causing you to lose focus.

On-Duty Mindfulness

Rather than making time to do mindfulness exercises on duty, the goal is to *be* mindful on duty. The more you practice the exercises to avoid becoming distracted by unnecessary thoughts and remain mentally focused off duty, the better you will be at staying focused on duty. Many people use props, such as a wristband, as a reminder to stay focused; whenever they look at or adjust it, they take a slow, deep breath and clear their minds of anything distracting. Others set an hourly silent alarm on their Fitbit; when it goes off, they take a slow, deep breath and remind themselves to stay focused in the present moment.

Grounding

Staying grounded is the opposite side of the mindfulness coin. Where mindfulness keeps you focused in the present moment, being grounded anchors you to your present surroundings. Both skills keep you highly attuned to the task at hand and prevent your mind from wandering.

Off-Duty Grounding Exercise

A couple of times per day, try this exercise to stay focused. You can do it anywhere, such as while you are walking, exercising, shopping for groceries, or watching TV.

- Select three things that you can SEE right now (e.g., a person, a street, a vehicle, a piece of furniture), and SAY each of those things to yourself.
- Select three things that you can HEAR right now (e.g., a fan, a vehicle, the TV), and SAY each of those things to yourself.
- Identify three things that you can FEEL touching you right now (e.g., the seat, the watch on your wrist, wind), and SAY each of those things to yourself.

On-Duty Grounding Exercise

- Say one thing you can SEE around you right now (e.g., people, vehicles).
- Say one thing you can HEAR around you right now (e.g., vehicles, radio).
- Say one thing you can FEEL touching you right now (e.g., seat, air-conditioning, equipment belt).

It may not feel like these exercises are accomplishing anything, and that's the point. They are a simple way for you to train yourself to remain in the moment without letting any thoughts distract you.

STEP 7. ADDITIONAL STRESS MANAGEMENT ACTIVITIES

Each of the following techniques can be performed on duty and off duty.

Hang Ten

Bruce Lee used to say, "Be water, my friend." Without getting overly philosophical here, let's just say that there are times when you make things more distressing for yourself than they need to be. Resisting or trying to change things over which you have no control will cause you to feel more frustrated and, ultimately, burned out. Like struggling in quicksand, it's just going to cause you to sink faster. Instead, when you face a difficult situation that cannot be changed, imagine yourself as world-renowned professional surfer Kelly Slater. Paddle out past the breakers, see a big wave coming, hop on your board, and hang ten as the water carries you to shore. You've found a fun way to avoid fighting against the powerful force of the ocean.

Positive Self-Talk

Don't underestimate the value of reassuring yourself from time to time. You probably do this a lot with your kids, maybe with your colleagues, and even with victims you encounter on the job. You say things such as, "You did the best you could," "It wasn't your fault," "Things will get better," "This too shall pass," and "You tried your hardest." So, treat yourself as well as you treat others. At randomly stressful times, and especially after a rough situation, give yourself a verbal pat on the back: "I will be okay," "I am a good cop," "I know I can do this," and so forth. Sometimes you need to be your own cheerleader!

Use Physical Senses

Each of your senses can be used to help you de-stress. It's best to have a large repertoire, so spend some time developing a list of sensory-based relaxation activities. The goal is to focus on the calming impact of the specific stimulus that is hitting your senses. For example,

- Sight. Look up at a star-filled sky; watch a baby, dog, or cat video on YouTube; identify a couple of specific photos on your phone that always bring a smile to your face.
- Sound. Find one song that you can play that calms you down every time you hear it; listen to a child laughing hysterically (again, YouTube has a bunch); identify some sounds of nature, such as birds chirping or waves crashing that help you relax.
- Smell. Identify smells that relax you, such as the aroma of a certain food cooking, cinnamon, coffee, or freshly mowed grass.
- Touch. Find a tactile sensation that you can use to calm yourself quickly, such as petting your dog (or cat), snuggling with your kids, or slipping into an old sweatshirt.
- Multiple senses. Some situations can quickly make you relaxed by engaging multiple senses, such as sitting by a fireplace with a roaring fire or lounging in a hammock on a spring day.

Your success with focused imagery means that you don't necessarily need the actual stimulus to help you de-stress. It's great if you can physically experience these sensations, but a decent alternative is mentally to bring the sensation to mind.

One Thing at a Time

Cops are great multitaskers. However, juggling too many things at once increases the chance that our stress level will exceed the optimal zone. Of course, sometimes it's inevitable that you will have to multitask. Nevertheless, whenever possible, a good practice is to prioritize and tackle one thing at a time. This is easier to do if you've been practicing the mindfulness exercises. Focus your attention on what you are doing at the moment without thinking or worrying about what you have to do tomorrow, next week, or next month.

One of Officer Mike's officers shared the following tip:

> Whenever I knew that I had to go to court, it would weigh on my mind for weeks before the date. I wasn't nervous, but I would rehearse over and over in my mind what I would say and what the defense lawyer would likely ask and mentally review my case report. It got distracting. So, I developed a way to deal with it. I scheduled time in my calendar to focus on and rehearse in my mind the upcoming trial and made sure that I only let myself think about it during that scheduled time. During the rest of the day, I concentrated on focusing only on what I was doing right then.

Stress inoculation helps us withstand many stressors and better manage our internal level of stress. As mentioned earlier, an important component is to establish a well-rounded wellness routine as outlined in the first five chapters of the book. However, no matter how well you eat and sleep, how fit you are, and how many friends or recreational activities you enjoy, your performance will suffer if you are not able to keep your internal level of stress in your optimal stress zone throughout every shift. To do that, in addition to your wellness routine, it is important to learn proper breathing and relaxation techniques, practice mindfulness, and incorporate a few additional stress management techniques. This is what will get you in and keep you in the best mental shape possible to cope with the routine demands of police work.

Why is this so important? Because we all know that police work is rarely "routine." In the following chapter, we discuss resilience and what you can do to best deal with the impact of exposure to traumatic incidents. Think of it this way: Olympic athletes train for years to compete on the world's stage. Do they practice only in the best conditions, or are they ready to perform at their best even when conditions, such as terrible weather, are far beyond their control? Likewise, you can learn to be mentally prepared to handle even the worst aspects of police work successfully.

CHAPTER 10

GROWTH THROUGH ADVERSITY

Just as we discussed in the previous chapter that you can train yourself to handle the routine stress of police work, in this chapter, we focus on strategies to successfully cope with the potentially traumatic incidents that officers encounter on the job. We briefly discuss some common reactions following exposure to traumatic incidents. We also want to introduce you to a few more serious outcomes that some officers develop following these events. The bulk of the chapter focuses on resilience and provides some techniques that you can use to boost your resilience. When you are resilient, you are better equipped to prevent problems from developing following adversity and more likely to bounce back from any problems that might crop up. But resilience is more than bouncing back; we show you how you can grow through adversity.

At the same time, despite our attention in this chapter to your encounters with the more harrowing aspects of police work, traumatic incidents are not the only kind of adversity you face in law enforcement. There are many organizational challenges, as well as operational setbacks beyond anything traumatic, that officers are forced to deal with. So, even though the emphasis here is on trauma, the strategies to boost resilience are appropriate for use regardless of the adversities you experience.

An important caveat is necessary as we begin our discussion of trauma. You already may be aware of how potentially traumatic events have impacted you. You might even still be experiencing some reactions to what you have encountered on the job. Or, perhaps, for the first time while reading this chapter, you may become aware of some of the ways that exposure to these incidents has begun to take a toll on you. Our goal is to provide you with an understanding of some effects of exposure to traumatizing incidents, but this is not intended as a substitute for counseling or psychotherapy with a mental health provider. If you are struggling or bothered in any way because of the traumatic aspects of police work, we encourage you to seek professional assistance with a licensed practitioner who has experience working with cops. For that matter, if some of the nontraumatic aspects of the job have got you down, and you don't feel as if you are performing at your best, it would be a good time to talk with someone.

STEP 1. TRAUMA TERMINOLOGY

Like a discussion about stress, when we start talking about traumas, there is a lot of confusion about terminology. The word *trauma* comes from the Greek "τραύμα" (travma), which means "to wound" physically. These days, however, we know that trauma can cause an emotional or spiritual wound, not just a physical wound. When we mention a traumatic incident, we are essentially describing an external event that is potentially traumatizing to the individual who experiences it. Those events are not traumas per se. Trauma is the impact of that event on those who were exposed to it.

Moreover, in police work, we have to differentiate between the traumatic incidents you respond to and any trauma that you experience related to that exposure. As you are probably aware, police officers average hundreds of responses to traumatic incidents over the course of their careers. This refers to all the physical, emotional, and spiritual wreckage that you see on the job. As a first responder, you routinely encounter and have to provide exceptional service to traumatized people. You see people at their worst. You are directly exposed to death, victimization, violence, abuse, terrible accidents, disasters and catastrophes, and a lot of horrible outcomes from others' carelessness and stupidity. This is referred to as *secondary* or *vicarious traumatization*[1] because even though you may have been first on scene and administered aid and assistance, you were not a direct participant in the traumatic incident itself.

There are three general circumstances in which you can experience work-related disruptions due to trauma. First, your exposure, indirectly, to the traumatic incidents you respond to can cause you to experience emotional and spiritual reactions. This is intensified if the incident in question bears some similarity to something (or someone) in your personal life. Second, while on duty, you can be directly involved in an event that can traumatize you, such as a shooting, a fight, a needle stick while searching a suspect, an accident, or any number of other critical incidents in which your health and safety are jeopardized. Third, sometimes something traumatizing happens in your personal life that weighs on your mind while you are on duty. Even if you are coping adequately with that off-duty situation, your emotional reaction to it may inadvertently take you out of your optimal stress zone while you are on duty.

STEP 2. TRAUMA REACTIONS

Regardless of whether you were involved directly or indirectly, reactions to potentially traumatic incidents run the gamut from mildly upsetting to psychologically debilitating. It is quite appropriate to have a reaction, even if it is only a quiet acknowledgment to yourself that you just witnessed someone else's suffering. As you know, several officers involved in the same incident may have completely different reactions. This depends on many factors, including the extent to which you use a strong wellness program, stress inoculation techniques, and the strategies discussed throughout this book. It also depends on how well you have resolved reactions to past traumatic incidents, including those from childhood. Of course, it depends on whether you are currently experiencing any traumatic situations in your personal life, such as having a terminally ill parent.

Also, you will find that your reaction to certain traumatic incidents is quite mild, whereas your reaction to other, even apparently similar, traumatic incidents is far more intense. Perhaps you've already experienced being less bothered by a certain critical incident call than your partner, or vice versa. It also is quite common for trauma reactions to intensify over time due to the impact of repeated exposure to these critical incidents. This is why it is crucial for officers to address their reactions to potentially traumatic events as they occur to prevent any cumulative psychological impact. However, many officers find that with repeated exposure to certain traumatic incidents, they experience some sense of immunity to the more intense reactions. This tends to work only when you confront the reactions to events as they happen and avoid suppressing or denying the emotional impact of each traumatic incident.

One of Officer Mike's officers shared the following story:

> Probably every cop remembers their first dead body. I sure remember mine. It was a traffic fatality. For a while, every time I saw a red Honda Civic, I would see that dead driver who got t-boned. I can't count how many more of these calls I've been to, but I can't say that they bother me at all. I guess you get used to it. I mean, it's sad and all, but what can you do?

Although there are some predictable features associated with how the body reacts during a crisis (e.g., tunnel vision and/or other sensory distortions), which is beyond the scope of this book, we focus on some common reactions following a traumatic incident. Whether or not you've had any of these reactions, knowledge is power. Be prepared so that you are not caught off guard if you ever do experience any of them.

Hyperarousal and Hypervigilance

As we mentioned in the previous chapter, the fight-flight-freeze response during a crisis puts your systems on high alert. Then, when the dust settles after a potentially traumatic incident, it may take a while for your mind and body to reset themselves. In the meantime, you may experience *hyperarousal* (often referred to as *hypervigilance*) as the remnants of being in survival mode during the crisis. Although the threat is gone, hyperarousal keeps you in survival mode, as though your safety is still at risk.

Hyperarousal means that you are unnecessarily attentive to everything around you. You become excessively sensitive to your surroundings and may react, sometimes in an exaggerated manner, to stimuli that wouldn't normally cause much, if any, reaction. Hyperaroused officers have, for example, pulled their weapon when hearing a car backfire. In essence, hyperarousal makes officers perceive a threat when none is there. Needless to say, it is extremely difficult to stay in your optimal stress zone when you experience hyperarousal. Feelings of tension and anxiety are common, which contribute to sleep difficulties, including insomnia. All of this negatively impacts concentration and decision making. Of course, the strategies outlined in the previous chapter, especially breathing and progressive muscle relaxation exercises, can help recalibrate you out of survival mode and back into your optimal stress zone.

Avoidance

Although some people can't seem to stop talking about their "close call" or a particularly gruesome critical incident, many people take steps to avoid thinking about the traumatizing event in which they were involved. Avoidance comes in two forms. Most commonly, people bottle up their thoughts and feelings about the event. This is an ineffective technique because pretending that you don't have any reactions to a traumatic event will just increase the likelihood that other, more problematic reactions may develop. However, addressing the trauma reactions without the proper support or without using the best techniques, such as those outlined here, can trigger hyperarousal, intrusive thoughts, and other undesirable responses.

The other kind of avoidance is behavioral. It can start innocuously enough when an officer avoids, for example, driving by the location where a fellow cop was fatally shot, which can be a conscious decision or something that just happens without thinking about it. It may seem like a way of not putting yourself in the place to be reminded of the pain of the tragedy. It can develop into a bad habit when reactions to a previous traumatic event cause the officer to avoid similar incidents. For example, an officer's efforts to resuscitate a child failed. Later, without intentionally deciding this, the officer was slow to respond to similar calls to avoid another such traumatic outcome. The most important thing to do to prevent avoidance is to talk about your reactions to potentially traumatic incidents with confidantes, peer support colleagues, or a loved one. It's ideal if you have one go-to person with whom you have agreed to discuss your postincident reactions. They're just there to listen. And, perhaps, you return the favor by giving them your ear after their potentially traumatic incidents.

Intrusive Thoughts

Essentially, the opposite of avoidance is when people cannot stop thinking about the traumatizing incident in which they were involved. Like a clip from a movie, some aspect of the event just keeps replaying over and over again in your mind. Sometimes the clip is only about some seemingly insignificant part of the traumatic event. Sometimes the clip plays in slow motion. Sometimes, it speeds up. Sometimes it appears distorted or out of the sequence in which it occurred. The worst part of this is that the clip plays even when you don't want it to or when you are trying to do something else. The thoughts are intrusive because they distract you from your task at hand.

It doesn't take a clinical psychologist to understand that your mind is using these intrusive thoughts to get you to deal with your reactions to the traumatic incident. An intrusive thought is like a puppy who won't stop jumping on you because he just wants some attention. Officers who try to ignore these thoughts are vulnerable to experiencing worsening and prolonged trauma reactions. Conversely, when you recognize the emotional wake-up call of intrusive thoughts and begin to address your reactions to the traumatic event, you may be able to prevent the reactions from intensifying. You can try writing about the incident and the aspects of it to which you are reacting. Talking, as mentioned earlier, also is an excellent place to start.

Posttraumatic Stress Disorder

You've most likely heard the term *posttraumatic stress disorder* (PTSD) a gazillion times. The term gets bandied around quite a bit, particularly when someone appears to be struggling in some way following a traumatic incident. We would be remiss not to mention it here because it is often used when people discuss police stress. It's not uncommon, as we've said, for anyone, even cops, to experience some reactions after being involved in a critical incident. Most people report having only one to a few reactions. Their reactions don't usually last long and are not typically intense (i.e., they don't interfere with one's on-duty or off-duty functioning). In such situations, officers who use the techniques outlined in this chapter and throughout the book are often able to successfully resolve any postincident trauma reactions without the need for professional assistance. In fact, most police officers do not develop PTSD, even if many do develop some of the symptoms of the disorder from time to time following exposure to a traumatic event or from the cumulative exposure to many critical incidents. Incidence rates of PTSD among cops are usually reported to be between 7% and 20%.[2]

There is somewhat of a debate about whether a new term, *posttraumatic stress injury* (PTSI), should be adopted. The argument goes something like this: If we call it an injury rather than a disorder, there will be more first responders who seek help because an "injury" is less stigmatizing than a "disorder"; however, there is no evidence that a name change alone would make much of a difference.[3] At the same time, because most first responders do not develop enough of the symptoms to meet the diagnosis for PTSD, but many do experience some of those symptoms, the term PTSI could be used to indicate a less severe form of PTSD. Moreover, the term PTSI could represent many more posttrauma reactions than only those represented by a diagnosis of PTSD.[4] Nevertheless, because police officers hear a lot about PTSD, we think it is important for you to know exactly what it is.

Specifically, PTSD is a formal mental health disorder identified in the diagnostic manuals used by health care professionals. Individuals who have PTSD experience a variety of symptoms, including those mentioned here (e.g., hyperarousal, hypervigilance, avoidance, intrusive thoughts), as well as others, such as flashbacks of the event, feelings of detachment from others, and loss of interest in what you used to like to do. If you or someone you know seems to be experiencing a number of these reactions following exposure to one or more potentially traumatic incidents, especially ones in which serious physical harm occurred or was threatened, consulting an experienced mental health provider may be helpful.

Although PTSD is a name given to a set of symptoms, even a single symptom can be distressing. Therefore, the important thing is to monitor yourself continually. How are you responding when someone does something that upsets you? How are you sleeping? Do you have any nightmares? Do you still participate in your regular recreational activities? Are you enjoying time with your kids and spouse as much as usual? For that matter, you may not always be the best judge of how you are doing. So, ask your spouse, best friend, parents, and so forth to keep their eyes out for any changes they see in you. The quicker you can catch yourself changing, even subtly, from your exposure to potentially traumatic incidents, the better your chances are to turn things around before anything gets too disruptive. A key is to keep tabs on how long after the incident you are continuing to have some trauma reactions. If reactions linger beyond several weeks, it would be wise to consider professional assistance or, at least, seek out some peer support.

STEP 3. ADDITIONAL REACTIONS TO TRAUMA EXPOSURE

We want you to be aware of two other reactions that police officers develop in response to exposure to potentially traumatic incidents. Although not as well researched as PTSD, these reactions have been found to be far more common than PTSD among police officers. One factor is that these additional reactions are the result of your repeated exposure to potentially traumatic incidents. Unlike most of the general public, whose exposure to traumatic events is limited, police officers are regularly subjected to potentially traumatic incidents. This can take a cumulative toll on your health and wellness.

Compassion Fatigue

You respond to multiple critical incidents during your shift, and in many of those incidents, you talk to and support the victims of crimes. Moreover, you answer noncritical calls and see people in desperate and deplorable conditions. We have heard many police colleagues say that they often feel like social workers because they are the only ones who are at the scene to support those who are suffering. You are the one who sits with those victims, and you provide them with sympathy and support until a human services agency worker shows up. Your presence during these traumatic times makes the victim feel safe. This is a big aspect of the "to serve" part of the job.

Compassion fatigue has been referred to as "the cost of caring."[5] Specifically, you may develop feelings of frustration, sadness, disappointment, and helplessness because you are not able to prevent others' suffering. When this happens because of the repeated exposure to others' intense emotional pain, many officers become cynical and withdrawn, which is not an effective coping strategy. As a result, they may look stone faced, act aloof, and become less kind when dealing with victims. Conversely, some officers who develop compassion fatigue may find it hard to disengage; they become overly attached to a particular victim and practically obsessed with helping them.

An antidote to compassion fatigue is *compassion satisfaction*, which we discussed in Chapter 7. This refers to officers' appreciation for the services they provide to victims and the community. For more information, we encourage you to review Chapter 7, specifically the section that discusses compassion satisfaction in policing. Also, continue to recognize how valuable your service is to members of your community.

Moral Injury

In addition to the moral risks of policing we discussed in Chapter 7 and Chapter 8, we want to introduce you to a reaction to certain adversities that is just beginning to get the attention it deserves in the law enforcement literature. *Moral injury* happens when something you did (or didn't do) on duty shatters your values and leaves you feeling some guilt or shame.[6] It may have been through no fault of your own that you didn't make it to a call on time, and someone was hurt or killed. Or perhaps you detained and were a little rough with someone who matched a description but who turned out not to be the perpetrator. Moral injury also happens when a colleague or supervisor does something that goes against your values and leaves you feeling somewhat betrayed by their actions. How did you feel when you saw a colleague mistreat a suspect or talk rudely to a victim? Whether or not you intervened or later conveyed your displeasure to the colleague, just observing that the incident happened can leave you questioning your confidence in that colleague.

Moral injury can be devastating to your health and wellness. Guilt and shame leave you blaming yourself. Anger leaves you blaming others. These feelings jeopardize your spiritual health, which can lead to high levels of cynicism and tendencies to isolate yourself from those who love you. If you notice yourself feeling guilty about some of your behavior or angry about the behavior of a trusted colleague, or if you start questioning your core values, please do not let it fester. It is important that you address these feelings, ideally with a trained professional. At the same time, learning the techniques to boost your resilience can help you grow through these adversities.

STEP 4. BURNOUT

Another term that is not unfamiliar to police officers is *burnout*. It is often used erroneously to refer to the cumulative toll that exposure to trauma takes on officers. That is incorrect because burnout occurs in people who work in all sorts of occupations who are never exposed to traumatic incidents on the job. Burnout is a condition that stems from chronic workplace stress[7] and leads to a significant decline in job performance. It is characterized by feelings of exhaustion and being mentally checked out from one's job, such as not caring anymore about even doing a minimally competent job.

Many factors that lead police officers to become burned out are unrelated to trauma exposure.[8] These are often organizational stressors and stressors related to the larger criminal justice system. Of course, chronic trauma exposure contributes to officers' overall work-related stress, but then it is more appropriate to recognize that the officer may be experiencing compassion fatigue and burnout.

This is an important distinction because each condition deserves separate attention to remedy. Even when officers learn to cope successfully with repeated exposure to trauma, some remain emotionally depleted due to nontrauma-related stressors. Although workers in other professions who experience burnout can go through the motions and get by, police officers do not have that luxury. Burnout leaves officers at increased risk to themselves and others. Using the wellness strategies presented throughout this book can help prevent burnout, as well as help you turn things around if you have already begun feeling somewhat checked out. Boosting resilience through the strategies presented in this chapter can improve your motivation and help prolong your career.

STEP 5. DEFINING AND PROMOTING RESILIENCE

Resilience is a trendy buzzword in the trauma literature. Many law enforcement agencies, maybe even your own, have implemented resilience training for their employees. In part, this is because resilient officers tend to display less anger when feeling stressed.[9] You may have benefited from a workshop on resilience that was offered by your agency, especially if you keep using the tools you learned there. Commonly, resilience is referred to as the ability to manage all kinds of challenging situations successfully. Beyond that basic definition, however, resilience is not simply bouncing back from trauma or stress. Resilience relates to your ability to grow from the challenges you experienced. More specifically, following traumatic incidents, resilience is referred to as posttraumatic growth and represents positive changes that people can make after exposure to traumatizing events.[10] This requires an active approach to making sense of and understanding what happened rather than avoiding or just passively accepting it.[11] In other words, we don't want simply to bounce back and act like the trauma never happened; we are changed by the repeated exposure to traumatic incidents. The question becomes whether the change following trauma will be negative or whether we can find a way for the change to be positive.

Promoting resilience focuses on ways for officers to develop the skills necessary to ensure that changes following adversities are positive. To achieve this, boosting resilience needs to be broad based, involving your body, mind, and spirit. You can take charge so that the random trials and tribulations of the job don't erode your humanity. The first step is developing and maintaining an active, well-rounded wellness program, as we outlined in earlier chapters of the book. Another step is to recognize that change from the adversities you confront on the job is inevitable, but the direction of that change is entirely within your control. In the following sections, we provide some tools that you can use to make those changes positive.

STEP 6. STRENGTHENING RESILIENCE FOLLOWING ADVERSITY

Officer Mike

 I had only been on patrol for about a year. We had a hit-and-run traffic crash. It was my call, and a fellow officer was able to locate the car involved at a local bar. I located the driver in the bar, who was intoxicated. But since he had been consuming alcohol after the crash, I could not arrest him for DUI. However, I did write him a traffic citation for leaving the scene of an accident, to which he did admit. I told him he was in no condition to drive, so I drove him to his residence. He was in his 40s and lived with his mother. When I arrived at his house, he said something like, "My mom is not going to be happy, but it doesn't really matter anymore anyway." I walked him to the front door, and his mother let us into the house. As I was explaining things to her, he walked over near a desk in the living room. I was probably four or five feet from him.

He reached in the drawer, retrieved a revolver, put it to his head, and pulled the trigger. I radioed for an ambulance and noticed he was still alive. He died at the hospital about an hour later. I was advised by my command to help the mother clean up the mess before going in to write my report. There was blood and other matter on the walls and ceiling and a vast pool of blood on the floor. I did the best I could, and then I went to the station to write my report.

Once my report was written, I went back out on patrol. My lieutenant thought it would be a good idea to spend some time with me after shift . . . by going to a bar and getting drunk while telling me he hopes I don't go out and "get all religious," because this is just part of the job. The thing I remember most is the smell of the residence. The odor was quite strong because she owned numerous cats and didn't clean out the litter boxes very often. This smell, even today, makes me think of that call. However, today, my coping mechanisms are positive, not "old-school." I have learned so much since then.

Boosting your resilience involves developing a specific set of coping mechanisms. These active coping mechanisms come in two categories: task focused and emotion focused. There also is a passive coping mechanism called avoidance focused, which can provide some short-term relief but has been found to be the least effective response to trauma. The ability to grow through the adversity of repeated exposure to potentially traumatic incidents develops when you incorporate strategies from each of the two active categories. Some of these have been mentioned earlier in the book as strategies for your general wellness. By doing these regularly, you are already better prepared to cope with the traumatic effects of critical incidents. Also, however, it is important to have a repertoire of some additional strategies that you have on hand to use following your exposure to potentially traumatic incidents. These will make up your posttrauma "first-aid kit."

Each of the two categories helps you to reduce the distress you experience after a traumatizing incident. *Task-focused strategies* start with postincident debriefings, which are not the critical incident stress debriefings you may have been required to do through your agency. These debriefings are done by you or with your spouse or closest confidante. You go through each step of the potentially traumatic incident from before receiving the service call to after you had resolved it. It's your chance to analyze your actions objectively. Did you do everything you could, were trained to do, and expected of yourself? How do you rate your performance? Would you do anything differently if you had it to do over again? What can you learn from the incident to make you an even better cop when something like this happens again?

Off-Duty Exercise

Think of a recent critical incident. Conduct the postincident debriefing now by writing down your answers to the questions posed earlier. Try to make a practice of reviewing your actions within a few days after each critical incident and then again, as necessary, if anything from the incident continues to bother you. This scheduled "appointment" with yourself to evaluate your performance should be the only time you do any Monday morning quarterbacking. Scheduling the time will help you to avoid any intrusive thoughts; if a thought about an incident pops into your head at some random time, remind yourself that you will deal with it during your scheduled "appointment." Also, this will get you in the habit of thinking objectively about how you performed during critical incidents. In this way, you can get ahead of and/or remove any irrational thoughts that you may have following these calls.

In addition to conducting your personal postincident debriefings following each critical incident in which you are involved, a task-focused approach to boosting your resilience involves making changes based on what you learned from your debriefing. This is not a knee-jerk reaction to make a change just to avoid the distress of a future potentially traumatic incident. This involves figuring out ways you can grow as a cop and as a person from your exposure to the traumas you face.

One of Officer Mike's officers related the following:

> For a lot of reasons, I wasn't very close to my father. That changed after I did some of the work they recommended I do after critical incidents. It was a few years ago. I responded to a call. There was an old guy who died. I guess he had no friends or family. We got the call from some neighbors because of the smell. It's a very nice area, nice houses. When I walked into his house, it was a real mess. We figured he had fallen but couldn't get up. Eventually, he just died there on the floor. Now, this wasn't a terrible trauma or anything. But it hit me. It hit me because I didn't want to end up like that old guy. And it hit me because I realized that I didn't want my dad to end up like that guy. So, I decided to bury the hatchet and call my dad. We still aren't that close, but I make a point to visit him every couple weeks now and call him every few days just to see how he's doing.

Emotion-focused strategies are pretty self-explanatory. First, one strategy is to examine your feelings honestly. How did you feel before, during, and after the critical incident? This isn't often as easy as it sounds. Nevertheless, it is important to prevent the unexamined emotions from lingering, festering, and interfering with your future performance. This self-exploration does not need to be shared with anyone. However, if you are comfortable talking about your feelings with some coworkers who've never been through what you've experienced, you could be helping them avoid some future negative postincident reactions.

The goal is to understand yourself and how you reacted emotionally to the potentially traumatic incidents. Officers who fail to look at their emotional reactions after these incidents are at a greater risk of developing a host of problems (emotional, cognitive, and behavioral). As you gain a greater understanding of the different emotional reactions you have to various types of critical incidents, you will become more aware of your areas of vulnerability. Some critical incidents may elicit intense emotional reactions, while others don't seem to register much emotional intensity at all. Then, you can be better prepared when you have to respond to the types of calls that are the most emotionally intense for you.

Off-Duty Exercise

Think about the recent critical incident that you used earlier for the debriefing. Explore the emotions you felt (a) when you got the call, (b) during the call, (c) immediately following the call (i.e., for the rest of the shift), (d) when you got home, and (e) for a few days afterward. Pay attention to (a) the emotions you experienced and (b) the emotions you displayed to others. For example, you might have felt some uncertainty but showed only confidence. Then, add this emotion-focused component to all your future postincident debriefings.

Note: We include this exercise in the optional Journal Pages supplement, which can be downloaded from the Resource Library tab on this book's website (https://www.apa.org/pubs/books/the-power-manual).

Emotion-focused strategies also involve changing how you feel about the potentially traumatic incident in which you were involved. A common approach is called *reframing*. In some situations, this involves looking for the proverbial silver lining. For example, after his first OIS, an officer who was quite shaken up from the shooting said, "Well, at least I know that I can pull the trigger when necessary. The training kicked in. This takes away a big question mark I always had in the back of my mind." Moreover, and in conjunction with the cognitive behavior therapy (CBT) tools we discussed in the previous chapter, reframing helps you recognize that the critical incident happened, and there was nothing you could have done to prevent it. There are situations, including those that evoke intensely uncomfortable emotions, that are simply out of your control. That realization doesn't eliminate uncomfortable emotional reactions following exposure to potentially traumatic incidents, but it may lessen the intensity of those emotions and prevent them from interfering with your performance.

Officer Mike

 After witnessing the suicide mentioned earlier in this chapter, I began to reflect and wonder what I could have done to prevent it. I went through the scenario over and over in my head. When I thought back to the subject saying something to the effect of, "My mom is not going to be happy, but it doesn't really matter anymore anyway," I began to doubt myself, thinking I should have realized this comment was a clue that he may commit suicide. This bothered me for quite a while, and I kept it to myself. Finally, I decided to talk about it with a fellow officer of equal rank who is of great character and is looked up to by everyone. He made me realize that, in this line of work, we all do the best we can in every situation. Hindsight is 20/20, and if we could go back in time, we all have dozens of situations we would have handled differently. Most importantly, we need to recognize that we can't save the world, and we can't prevent every bad thing from happening. I also began to realize that the subject who committed suicide—it was his doing, not mine. However, from that day forward, I began to listen to inferences from citizens who might be a threat to themselves or someone else. I can't go back in time, but I can learn and move forward.

STEP 7. PRACTICAL ON-DUTY AND OFF-DUTY STRATEGIES TO BOOST RESILIENCE

Many of the strategies already described in this book serve the dual purpose of improving your wellness and strengthening your resilience, assuming that you regularly engage in them. For example, when it comes to growing from the adversity you encounter on the job, the exercises discussed in Chapter 5 regarding your spiritual wellness are particularly important. Similarly, you are unlikely to rely on avoidance and isolation following exposure to a potentially traumatic event when you establish and maintain excellent social wellness strategies (Chapter 4). The stress inoculation activities discussed in Chapter 9, especially progressive muscle relaxation with focused imagery and mindfulness, are skills that help you remain resilient after a traumatic incident.

In addition to the techniques that you can use to mitigate your reactions to potentially traumatic incidents before they have a chance to develop, there are several strategies that will boost your resilience after you start to experience some posttrauma reactions. These are particularly helpful when you feel some moral injury–related reactions, such as guilt, anger, or betrayal. These techniques are taken from CBT theory and are designed to help you think rationally and experience manageably intense emotions after a traumatic incident.

Apportioning Blame

Let's face it, we all make mistakes. After a mistake, especially one in which the outcome was quite troubling, we may blame ourselves and take full responsibility for the outcome. This may seem like the noble thing to do, but it also may be irrational, which can really mess with your mind. Rarely are we completely at fault, because there are usually contributing factors that led to our decision that caused the mistake. Thus, you will cope better after a potentially traumatic incident when you take some time to allocate blame to all those who contributed to the mistake (e.g., other officers on scene, supervisor, perpetrator, civilians). Rather than irrationally thinking, for example, "I am responsible for what happened," after recognizing that others played a part in that incident, you more rationally will think, "We messed up there." Then, the intensity of your anger or guilt or frustration will decrease to more tolerable emotions, such as shared sadness, group remorse, or collective frustration.

Off-Duty Exercise

During each of your personal postincident debriefings, whenever you identify feeling any guilt, remorse, anger, betrayal, or intense frustration, add a component of apportioning blame during the debriefing. Focus on realistically assessing your role and the role that others played in how that incident went down.

Imaginary Dialogue

It's easy to start beating ourselves up after making a mistake. Even if allocating blame leaves you with only 20% of the responsibility for something, you may keep kicking yourself. We tend to have a tough time forgiving ourselves. Regardless of the amount of responsibility you take, it's important to cut yourself some slack.

Off-Duty Exercise

In the spirit of self-forgiveness, this exercise provides some support when you have trouble forgiving yourself for something you did or failed to do. After your personal posttrauma debriefings, if you still feel some remorse about your actions, think of the person in your life who was the most caring, compassionate, and forgiving, whether or not they are still living. Maybe it was a grandparent, a coach, a teacher, a parent, or any mentor you had who helped you feel better after you screwed up. In an imaginary conversation with this person, explain what happened and how you are feeling about it. Then, tell yourself what that person would say to you. For example, a sergeant, whose father was no longer living, told us that whenever he has any feelings of guilt, shame, or anger from something that happened on duty, he has a conversation with his father in his mind. He thinks about what his father would have said to him, which would have been nothing but loving support and encouragement.

Making Amends and Self-Forgiveness

After accepting some responsibility for your actions that left you feeling remorseful, a resilient technique that facilitates posttrauma growth is to apologize. First, it helps to apologize to yourself. Just as your mentor would show support and compassion during your imaginary dialogue, this is the time to recognize that you let yourself down; you performed below your expectations. Following the apology, forgive yourself, embrace your fallibility (we all make mistakes), and let go of the remorse. It will help this process if you figure out how you can make it up to yourself by making some amends. You can dive into a home project that you've been postponing. You can give up some bad habit that you've fallen into. It's up to you to decide how you want to do penance, so to speak.

At the same time, if there was someone who you believe suffered in some way due to the actions that left you remorseful, it will be easier to forgive yourself if you also find ways to make amends to others. This does not mean that you necessarily seek out someone to whom to apologize. In many cases, this would not be feasible due to department policy and impending legal proceedings. It means that you do something tangible to facilitate your selfforgiveness. You can dedicate some anonymous charitable time or money to a cause. For example, after a suspected DUI stop, an officer felt nagging guilt for allowing the sober passenger to drive home rather than arresting the mildly impaired driver. A few weeks later, the original driver was involved in a fatal DUI accident. The officer learned of this and thought that had he arrested the driver when he had the opportunity, the fatality might not have occurred. The officer decided to get actively involved as a volunteer with Mothers Against Drunk Driving (MADD).

If your remorse stems from your actions at an incident involving others to whom you could apologize (e.g., a fellow officer), it couldn't hurt to apologize directly. After you do so, a common reply might be, "Thanks, but don't worry about it." Unfortunately, that may not be enough to help you. So, again, find a way to make some amends. For that matter, it doesn't have to be obvious. The goal is not to be forgiven by that person; it's so that you can feel better about yourself and grow through this adversity.

Forgiving Others

Your posttrauma reactions of anger, frustration, or bitterness may stem from feeling betrayed by someone else. These incidents can leave you dispirited and resentful. Rather than walking on eggshells around that person, it is important for you to find a way to forgive them. Again, you may or may not decide to express your feelings directly to the person. Sometimes such a conversation results in something positive, such as strengthening the relationship and building trust. Other times the discussion is disappointing (e.g., the other person was defensive or failed to give a sincere apology). Of course, if their actions reflected a lack of operational competence, their behavior needs to be addressed and corrected by following your agency's procedures. However, for your health and wellness, you have to find a way to let it go.

Letting It Out and Letting It Go

Officer Mike

 A friend of my family shared a story with me about when her mother passed away in the hospital over 30 years ago. She was in her 80s. I had known her my entire life, and she had not mentioned this to anyone before confiding in me. She was by her mother's side in the hospital when one of her mother's best friends arrived. The nurse asked my friend whether it was okay for her to let the friend in to see her mother. She decided to let her mother's best friend come into the room. The friend came into the room and held her mother's hand. At that moment, her mother passed away. My friend told me she thought it was too much for her mother, and she should not have let her mother's friend come in. She felt guilty about this—all this time. I did not realize that she had this on her mind for over 30 years. I'm glad she shared it with me. I told her that it was apparent that her mother would not have lived much longer and that she was probably holding on until she saw her best friend. My friend said she had never thought about it like that.

Guilt can motivate positive change. However, hanging onto the guilt over something you did or failed to do is, perhaps, one of the unhealthiest coping mechanisms you could use. Catholics have the confessional, which, when used appropriately, is a way to obtain forgiveness for a mistake or a transgression. This usually comes with penance, which means that you have to do something to show your remorse before you can receive absolution. The rest of us have to develop our version of the confession booth. Do whatever works best for you: Write it out, talk to someone, pray. Put the incident in question in perspective, and remember that you will have plenty more chances to atone for any mistakes you made. Also, rather than dwelling on the mistake, improve your skills to ensure that you never make it again. Sometimes the best penance is just to work your ass off to get better.

Throughout your law enforcement career, you will perform far more noble and heroic acts than you will make mistakes. The resilient officer understands this and takes active steps to grow through the adversities, which include not just the horrors you encounter on the job but also the times that you were not at your best. There were reasons why you weren't at your best—for example, not maintaining a comprehensive wellness program. The resilient officer figures this out and takes the necessary steps to correct it. Likewise, the bad feelings don't just go away without some effort on your part. The resilient officer tackles the strategies outlined in this chapter and becomes an even better cop following exposure to potentially traumatic incidents. In the next chapter, we focus on two other important components to boost your resilience: self-compassion and positive psychology.

CHAPTER 11

SELF-COMPASSION AND POSITIVE PSYCHOLOGY

In this chapter, we introduce you to the concept of *positive psychology*, which focuses on identifying and enhancing your personal strengths. But first, we want to discuss *self-compassion*. You've dedicated yourself to protecting and serving others. Probably, in addition to at work, you demonstrate these traits in your personal life too—for example, when a loved one is in pain, you provide support, compassion, and care. In this chapter, we discuss the importance of giving some of this attention to yourself. Along with the tips we've already covered throughout the book to take better care of yourself every day, self-compassion also is a way to take better care of yourself when you aren't feeling your best. We give you some Band-Aids that you can use whenever you think you've blown it, when you're feeling discouraged, or when you're struggling with some burnout or compassion fatigue. Self-compassion is a key skill used by resilient people.[1] Thus, you will strengthen your resilience by practicing self-compassion techniques.

STEP 1. ELIMINATING BARRIERS TO SELF-COMPASSION

Self-compassion is nothing more than an approach to being kind to yourself. There's enough unkindness out there toward cops; why not develop some strategies to be kind to yourself? However, for

Self-Compassion: Myth Versus Reality

Myth: Self-compassion is childish.

Reality: Self-compassion provides some kindness when you could use a boost to your morale.

Myth: Self-compassion makes me look pathetic.

Reality: Self-compassion enhances resilience when you are confronted with challenges.

Myth: Self-compassion is all about making excuses for mistakes.

Reality: Self-compassion accepts your fallibility, acknowledges your "humanness," and provides support without denying responsibility for mistakes.

Myth: Being hard on myself motivates me.

Reality: Self-compassion leaves room for honest scrutiny of areas for self-improvement.

some reason, many police officers struggle with the concept of self-compassion. It's most likely a remnant of the "suck it up, tough guy" philosophy, which is, at best, a successful strategy only in the short term. Nevertheless, it is embedded in police culture. So, for those of you who are reluctant to begin being more compassionate to yourself, we start with a chart that shows some misconceptions about self-compassion.[2]

STEP 2. SELF-COMPASSION EXERCISES

Most of us wouldn't know where to start to show more self-compassion. Maybe you already have some ideas, which we hope you will use on a regular basis. In this section, we offer a few specific suggestions for you to be self-compassionate.

Remember the Wins

This exercise helps you to memorialize the wins that you've had on duty. A trophy case (or dedicated bookshelf) is not meant for letting you rest on your laurels or brag about your achievements. It's to remind you of the hard work you put in to achieve some success. It's easy enough to remember the failures, so the trophy case helps us focus on the wins. When you see those ribbons and medals, you can't help but think that all the pain was worth it. For example, after he delivered a baby on duty for a couple who owned a Chinese restaurant, Officer Mike received a bag of fortune cookies with a note that said they named their child after him. That note went straight to his trophy case.

Off-Duty Exercise

Dedicate a shelf or drawer (or start a scrapbook) for reminders of your on-duty wins. Start collecting letters received from grateful community members, commendations, photos sent to you or clipped from newspaper stories, or anything that represents a success you had at work. For past wins for which you have no tangible reminder, write a brief description of what happened and how good it made you feel. Then add it to your collection of work-win memorabilia. Sometimes no one but you will see the incident as a win, but all that matters is that you notice it, record it, and memorialize it in your work-win drawer.

Off-Duty Exercise

In addition to continually adding to your "trophy case" as your wins accumulate, add a reminder in your calendar to spend 10 to 15 minutes per month looking over your achievements. While doing so, remind yourself that there is much about the job that you love.

Kindness Reminders

Another way to show some self-compassion is to add some kindness to your life. We're not talking about all the good deeds you do for others. This is about being kinder to yourself. You can start simply. When you are doing the breathing, relaxation, or mindfulness exercises described in Chapter 9, you can add a simple kindness affirmation. This is especially important when you feel a little down or think that the job isn't fulfilling. Say something supportive to yourself, such as "I appreciate myself," "I'm a good person," "I can roll with the punches," and "I can grow through the adversity." Beyond kindness reminders during relaxation exercises, remember to say these affirmations on duty throughout your shift, especially after interacting with people who aren't kind to you.

Kindness Activities

It's easy to treat yourself when you think you've done a good deed and deserve something special. By all means, keep doing that. However, self-compassion guides you to be kind to yourself even when you might not think you deserve it. You aren't rewarding mistakes, and you aren't neglecting to correct errors; you are telling yourself that your self-compassion is not conditional on how well you do. Even when you aren't happy with your performance or feel as though parts of the job are bringing you down, make time to do something nice for yourself.

Off-Duty Exercise

Make a list of splurges. Be creative. Try to come up with 25 items on the list ranging from free to a bit pricey. The list should contain only things you see as a real treat, which you might only get on a special occasion. It could be a certain meal or dessert (at home or at a favorite restaurant). It could be a sports massage. Maybe it's sleeping in late one morning or adding chocolate chips to your pancakes. Some of the activities can be solitary, but many can involve your spouse, kids, or close friends so that the kindness you show yourself is matched by the love you feel from them.

Off-Duty Exercise

Whenever your morale needs a boost, or you feel discouraged about work, take a look at your list of treats. Pick one, and do that kindness activity for yourself. It may not change the things that are bothering you, but it will be a way for you to tell yourself that you will still make time to be kind to yourself no matter how low things get.

STEP 3. POSITIVE PSYCHOLOGY

Most people think of psychology as the science that describes people's mental and emotional problems. Clinical psychologists are trained to help their patients through mental health challenges, most typically by focusing on and offering guidance to overcome symptoms of psychological distress. However, psychology has a lot more to offer than just dealing with problems. Positive psychology focuses on people's strengths. The goal is not to help someone survive the bad things that happen in life (which remains an important goal of clinical psychology). Instead, the goal of positive psychology is to help people figure out how to have a great life! It's a proactive approach, which fits nicely into our emphasis on wellness. By emphasizing strengths, you can build on them to achieve a sense of fulfillment.

According to those who promote positive psychology, the absence of symptoms (i.e., you don't have depression, anxiety, or other problems) does not mean that everything is hunky-dory. To achieve a great life, you need to develop and use your strengths, including resilience, to not only help you through tough times but also to ensure that you appreciate the good times and continue to thrive during the so-so, ordinary times.[3] Your personal strengths are not just your talents or skills. They are the core components of your identity that reside in your "mind and heart" and help you to maintain healthy relationships with others. However, these are not fixed characteristics that you're stuck with whether you like it or not. You can build on the personal strengths you already possess, and you can identify and develop strengths that you want to have that you believe will make your life more satisfying and complete. Think of it this way: Positive psychology is strengths based, like training to be tactically prepared in the field. The more you train, the more confident and competent you will be to handle everything that comes along.

STEP 4. PERSONAL STRENGTHS

In this section, we describe one model of personal strengths.[4] Strengths fall into six general categories: wisdom, courage, humanity, justice, temperance, and transcendence. You may see some of them as strengths of your own. Others may seem highly desirable to you, strengths you would like to develop. Later in the chapter, we ask you to identify your personal strengths and any others you may want to cultivate. Then, we offer a few exercises for you to keep practicing and promoting your strengths. Each of the strengths is accompanied by an Officer Mike story. This doesn't mean that Officer Mike is a perfect person or possesses each of the strengths

Human Character Strengths for Promoting Resilience and Maintaining Wellness

WISDOM	COURAGE	HUMANITY	JUSTICE	TEMPERANCE	TRANSCENDENCE
Creativity Originality; Adaptive; Ingenuity	**Bravery** Valor; Not shrinking from fear; Speaking up for what's right	**Love** Both loving & being loved; Valuing close relations with others	**Teamwork** Citizenship; Social responsibility; Loyalty; Contributing to group effort	**Forgiveness** Mercy; Accepting others' shortcomings; Giving people a second chance; Letting go of hurt	**Appreciation of Beauty & Excellence** Awe; Wonder; Admiration for skill and moral greatness
Curiosity Interest; Novelty-seeking; Exploration; Openness	**Perseverance** Persistence; Industry; Finishing what one starts	**Kindness** Generosity; Nurturance; Care & compassion; Altruism; "Niceness"	**Fairness** Adhering to principle of justice; Not allowing feelings to bias decisions about others	**Humility** Modesty; Letting one's accomplishments speak for themselves	**Gratitude** Thankful for the good; Expressing thanks; Feeling blessed
Judgment Critical thinking; Thinking things through; Open-mindedness	**Honesty** Authenticity; Integrity	**Social Intelligence** Aware of the motives/feelings of self/others; Knowing what makes other people tick	**Leadership** Organizing group activities to get things done; Positively influencing others	**Prudence** Prudence; Careful; Cautious; Not taking undue risks	**Hope** Optimism; Future-mindedness; Future orientation
Love of Learning Mastering new skills & topics; Systematically adding to knowledge; Ingenuity	**Zest** Vitality; Enthusiasm; Vigor; Energy; Feeling alive			**Self-Regulation** Self-control; Discipline; Managing impulses & emotions	**Humor** Playfulness; Bringing smiles to others; Lighthearted
Perspective Wisdom; Providing wise counsel; Taking the big picture view					**Spirituality** Connecting with the sacred; Religiousness; Faith; Purpose; Meaning

Note. From *The 24 Character Strengths*, by VIA Institute on Character, 2020 (https://www.viacharacter.org/character-strengths). Copyright 2004–2020 by VIA Institute on Character. Adapted with permission.

in large quantities. The stories simply illustrate the strengths from Officer Mike's activities during his long career in law enforcement. As you read the descriptions of the strengths, think of examples from your life that exemplify the strength.

Wisdom

This group of strengths refers to how we acquire knowledge and how we use it.

Creativity is the strength to think of novel ways of doing things in a productive way and finding multiple solutions to an issue through divergent, out-of-the-box thinking, understanding that there is usually more than one way to solve a problem.

Officer Mike

 I had heard another officer had done this, so I thought I would too. I was dispatched to a domestic dispute, and the couple were arguing loudly and had no intention of slowing down. They were several feet apart with a couch in between them. I sat down on the couch and picked up a magazine from the coffee table. The couple couldn't believe their eyes. While I was just sitting there, looking through a magazine, they both got quiet and looked at me. I said, "Can I chat with the two of you and help get this solved? The sooner we get it solved, the sooner I can get back on patrol and leave you guys alone." It had been a verbal dispute only, and she said she would go and spend the night with her sister. It may not have been the most tactically sound plan, but I was more prepared than I appeared.

Curiosity is the strength to explore and discover through an openness to new experiences, never getting stuck in a rut and always willing to try something different, especially when the initial strategy isn't working.

Officer Mike

 When I was sergeant in charge of the field training program, I was curious about anything new that was being taught at the academy, which may not have filtered down to us in the field yet. Every time our new hires arrived after just graduating from the academy, I would ask them about various tactics they were taught. If they explained something that sounded different from what we were doing, particularly if it was something of value for our department that could improve a strategy or tactic, I would ask the new officer to put on a training session. This not only empowered the new officer but it also was a way to update our policies and procedures.

Judgment is the strength to examine things from different viewpoints and to understand thoroughly before making a determination by reading between the lines, always questioning, and never settling for a quick, knee-jerk conclusion without hearing from all sides.

Officer Mike

 I was patrolling the parking lots on Washington Street one night and saw a young teenager, Sean, breaking into a vehicle.[5] I was able to park my squad car and approach, and by the time he saw me, it was too late. He dropped a plastic cup on the ground, and change spilled onto the parking lot. He was obviously finding unlocked cars and getting change from the consoles. Sean pleaded with me not to tell his mom and her boyfriend. He said he was fine with getting arrested, but he would be beaten if they found out. I had been to his apartment in the past for domestic disputes between his mom and her boyfriend and did not doubt him one bit. I asked him why he needed the money, and he said so he could get a slice of pizza at school lunch on Wednesdays. All of his friends get the pizza, and he never has the money. I was familiar with Sean and considered him a good kid living in a bad family situation. I also believed what he was telling me. So, instead of bringing him to the station and calling his mom, I gave him another option. I told him that I would let everything go if he would report to my dojo every Saturday at 9:00 a.m. for the next 5 weeks. He joined in with my junior high–age students and participated in the workouts and lessons involving character and integrity. He ended up coming to class for almost a year until he began to get involved in school sports—a much better outcome than telling his mom and having him get a beating; probably a better outcome than putting him into the system. We can't lose sight of the big picture when deciding how to use our discretion.

Love of learning is the strength of passion for learning something new, mastering a new skill, and improving one's talent. Those who love learning build on prior knowledge in a critical way and never get complacent about what they already know. Learn something from everything.

Officer Mike

 I was a very average high school student, even though I really loved school. I got my associate's degree in criminal justice from our community college when I was 19 years old. This is the highest degree anyone in my family has gotten. Now I just had to wait until I was 21 years old to get hired as a cop! I was set! I was hired by my department at 21 years old. I was also married and had a child. However, when I found out my department would pay for college, I began working on my bachelor's degree. How could I pass up such a good deal? But to work and have a family life, I could only take one class a semester. When I was almost 30 years old, I obtained my bachelor's degree. Then the next step: I started working on my master's degree, one step at a time and one class at a time. When I was in my late 30s, I received my master's degree. Then, I retired as a lieutenant and began working full time at the police academy. I learned that, again, college was free. I was almost 50 when I earned my doctorate. It was a long journey, but now I am the director of the police academy, with just a few years before retirement. You don't have to be brilliant. You just have to be determined, have perseverance, and always want to keep pushing yourself to keep learning!

Perspective is the strength of wisdom, providing guidance and advice to others and inspiring others, especially to make the world better.

Officer Mike

 I remember being a sergeant at shift briefing when I couldn't wait to share this great idea I had. I don't remember what the plan was (probably some great crime-fighting plan), but I do remember discussing it with my patrol officers. Everyone agreed that it was a great idea—except for Officer Ramirez. He spoke up and said he thought it was a bad idea and gave his reasoning. His reasoning made sense to me, so I canceled the plan. I gained a lot of respect for Officer Ramirez that day. It also showed my officers that I am open to feedback and critique and that we needed to work as a team. Thus, I also gained respect that day. The wisdom came from a junior officer, but this was one of his strengths.

Courage

This group of strengths refers to a willingness to achieve a goal despite internal or external obstacles and challenges.

Bravery is the strength to defy a threat; risk danger, difficulty, pain, or sacrifice; and speak up for what is right. It is the willingness to take an unpopular position, defy the crowd, and challenge one's peers.

Officer Mike

 Brave, stupid, or lucky? How often do we ask that of ourselves? An intoxicated man walked into our police department and told the desk staff that he had a gun. He patted his jacket to imply that is where he was carrying the weapon. He told the desk staff that if any cops had the guts (he used other words), he'd be at the bowling alley. I received the call, along with a description of him. All other officers were on dangerous enough calls that they could not clear for backup. So, I parked about a block away from the "Landfill," which was the name the cops gave this bowling alley. I didn't want to be obvious, so I entered a side door. When I walked in, a man was sitting at a table about three feet in front of me. He fit the description—the same farm company on his hat, his blue jean jacket, green shirt, mullet, and so forth. As soon as he stood up, he reached his hand into his jacket. I just reacted—I grabbed his wrist to control his hand, grabbed his mullet (a popular hair cut back in the day), turned him, and smashed his head on a jukebox as we both went to the ground. As soon as we went to the ground, I felt another body jump on my back. Luckily, it was my sergeant. While getting the man handcuffed, my sergeant cussed at me and said, "Why the hell didn't you wait for backup?" We walked the man out the side door, searched him, and guess what—NO GUN. Yes, it was an attempt at a suicide by cop.

Later, Officer Mike had to ask himself some tough questions to see what he learned from that incident:

- Should I be proud of my bravery?
- Should I be proud of my fighting prowess?
- Were my strategies and tactics sound?

The answer to each question was no. Why?

- I got into a hurry, while at the same time wanting to prove to my fellow officers how much "guts" I had. This was more bravado than bravery.
- I am confident of my martial arts skills. But in this situation, while initially thinking I was as quick as Bruce Lee, I realized later that the man's hand probably wasn't going anywhere anyway.
- Strategy and Tactics 101 tell me how awful my plan was. I could have done many things differently: wait for backup, have dispatch call the bar to find out whether the suspect was there and details of his location, try to find a way to bring him outside (where there are fewer bystanders), and so forth. The important part was to do the debriefing and figure out the lessons to learn from this incident. It's not brave to be tactically stupid.

Perseverance is the strength to persist despite adversity and finish what one has started despite obstacles and challenges along the way. It is the willingness to go through hell to complete the mission.

Officer Mike

 I was a lieutenant and only a year away from retirement. I always shot my handgun well but never qualified as an "expert," despite a strong desire to. I had accomplished a lot in my career, and I was proud. I had been an accomplished patrolman, field training officer, investigator, sergeant, control tactics instructor, K-9 supervisor, and so on. However, as my career was ending, I was determined to qualify on the range as "expert." I began my career as a marksman, which meant I met the minimum requirements. I eventually qualified consistently as a sharpshooter, and in the last few years, I was only a few points from my expert badge. The next qualification shoot was in 6 months, so I took advantage of every opportunity I had to practice under the guidance of our master firearms instructor. During my last qualification before retiring, I was pinned with my expert badge. I'm not sure why, out of all my accomplishments, this seemed like such an important ending to my policing career.

Honesty is the strength to tell the truth no matter the consequences, tactfully expressing a genuine opinion, acting sincerely without pretense, and telling it "like it is" without losing compassion or an understanding for how others may receive the truth.

Officer Mike

 I could always rely on Officer Wilcox to be a straight shooter. During shift briefing, if he disagreed with a policy, procedure, or protocol, he would say so. I appreciated him expressing his opinion with respect, and he always had a good argument. Though there were times when I had to explain why we had to do something a certain way, there were also times when he was right and thought of things the administration had not. When other officers realized that I wanted to hear their honest suggestions, more of them shared their ideas and knowledge. This assisted in both improving our department and building the team. Sometimes it takes a lot of guts to speak up.

Zest is the strength of living life with enthusiasm and adventure; seeing life as an opportunity to have fun, excitement, energy, and adventure; and taking action rather than being complacent.

Officer Mike

 I know that when a police officer signs up for this job, it's more than a job. It's about having compassion and wanting to help people who can't help themselves. It's about wanting to protect those who cannot defend themselves. I know this from the officers I have worked with on the street, the thousands of officers I have met around the nation, and our recruit officers entering the academy. That being said, other characteristics are present too: challenge and excitement. You can hear it in their voices after a dangerous but successful situation. Sitting in the briefing room or break room or chatting off duty, I always notice the excitement in their voices when reliving the situation: "Man, you should have been there!" "I was dispatched to . . ."

Humanity

This group of strengths builds strong and honest relationships with others.

Love is the strength of sharing with and caring for others, being able to receive sharing and caring from others, and putting in the effort to maintain relationships through challenges, adversities, and disagreements.

Officer Mike

 I have always believed that nonenforcement contacts are not only crucial for community policing but that they can also help us gain trust, making compliance more likely during arrests. In reality, these contacts actually can be enjoyable, too. Getting to know others and letting them get to know you is a great feeling. I could talk to people, joke around with them, and even make fun of myself as a cop. I remember talking to citizens on the corner of Jupiter and Eagle Drive (an apartment complex). Everyone in the group was Black, except me. I remember one citizen saying, "Officer Mike, you are the only Black officer on the department." Of course, I'm as White as they come, and we had Black officers, but it was a good feeling to hear that. I took it to mean something simple: Those citizens saw our Black officers who didn't interact with them in positive ways as simply Blue, but they saw me as a regular guy who cared.

Kindness is the strength of caring, helping, doing favors, and showing concern for others and being unconditionally compassionate, altruistic, and generous without expecting anything in return.

Officer Mike

One important thing I learned from my parents was that your character is judged by how you treat people who can't do anything to you or for you. My parents treated everyone (young, old, rich, poor, and so on) as if they were the most important people in the world. I remember my dad introducing me to Bob. Bob was someone in my town who was poor and had a developmental disability. I was a kid, and I remember many of my friends mocked Bob. We were walking on a sidewalk downtown one day, and my dad stopped to talk to Bob. My dad said, "Mike, I want to introduce you to a very good friend of mine. Mike, this is Bob. Bob, this is my son Mike." We then had a lengthy conversation. This became an important part of my everyday life and in the way I policed. Though I received many commendations, my proudest two were a commendation for community involvement from the police department and being named volunteer of the year for my village. It doesn't take as much effort as people think to be nice, and the returns are immeasurable.

Social intelligence is the strength of awareness of others' feelings, motives, and desires. This includes multicultural competence and a willingness to engage people on their own terms and the ability to inspire, motivate, and gain the respect of others, even those who are different from oneself.

Officer Mike

It was a beautiful summer night in the mid-90s. My two sons were at Wabash Park, and my oldest son was playing in a baseball game. I was on foot patrol in the park but mostly watching my son play ball. He was an excellent athlete and a darned good third baseman. Standing there in uniform, watching the baseball game, was my younger son, who was probably about 11 or 12 years old at the time. He walked up to me, and with him was Eddie. I had several calls on Eddie in his neighborhood because other kids made fun of him, and sometimes it would result in a physical confrontation. He was the same age as my son and went to the same school. Eddie had an intellectual disability, and this made life difficult for him because we know how mean kids can be. My younger son and Eddie came up to me, and my son said, "Dad, this is my good friend, Eddie." He continued to say, "We are just hanging out in the park." Wow, this was my son teaching me the same lessons my parents taught me. It was a proud moment for me that he was already showing such social intelligence.

Justice

This group of strengths involves civic action, as well as an active and productive community life.

Teamwork is the strength of being a good team member, supporting and being accepted by other members of your team, and prioritizing the team over one's own ego or personal goals. It demands loyalty to the group.

Officer Mike

 In addition to practicing martial arts since the 1970s, I've been involved with police control and arrest tactics since the 1980s. Having my own martial arts school in my village gave me not only the opportunity but also the location for continued training in control and arrest tactics. When I was on shift as a sergeant and lieutenant, during slow times, I would meet with on-duty officers, and we would practice our skills. I felt this increased not only the officers' skill levels but also their confidence.

And it seems the more confident an officer is in their fighting prowess, the less likely they will be to use it. Also, by training together on shift, we learned about each other and how to work as a team while performing the tactics. For example, if we knew we would have to take a resisting arrestee to the ground, they knew that I was going for the legs, and they would control the arrestee's upper body as they were going to the ground.

Fairness is the strength of giving everyone an impartial chance; treating people without bias or, at least, without any discrimination; and following the golden rule (treat others as you wish to be treated).

Officer Mike

 I have always thought it was important to treat everyone with respect and allow them to save face in front of their friends. I knew that there were times when I could gain compliance when making an arrest if I allowed them to curse me up and down. This way, they could show their friends they were tough by cussing me out yet not have to resist arrest. In fact, I can remember arresting Jimmy Withers in the parking lot of the Corner Bar in front of his buddies. He called me things I had never even heard of. However, he was doing this while placing his hands behind his back. And though he squirmed around and stopped from time to time while I escorted him to the squad car, he went along. I got him in the back of the squad car, seat belted him in, and started to drive off the lot. He then said, "Hey, Officer Mike, you know I was just giving you crap because my people were watching me, and I have a reputation." I said, "No worries, Jimmy." He said, "So, are we still cool?" I said, "Yea, it's cool."

Leadership is the strength of organizing, motivating, and leading others. It requires the ability to create a mission, establish the goals to accomplish the mission, and mobilize and inspire those who can achieve those goals. You earn the respect of others by showing others respect and leading by example without hypocrisy or condescension.

Officer Mike

 I worked second and third shift my entire career (minus a small stint in investigations). I hated investigations. I felt I did a good job, but I needed to be out in the community, interacting and handling exciting calls. For some reason, it seemed like so many day-shift officers were more negative and cynical than the younger crew on the second and third shifts. I had been promoting a wellness program for many years. Finally, I got the okay to go ahead with it. The wellness program needed to be positive and encouraging, not forced. I was able to convince the chief that if officers participated in a fitness test twice a year, regardless of their results, they would earn 2 personal days they could use whenever they wanted. Those who were not as fit were allowed to walk instead of run and pick from alternative strength, flexibility, and muscular endurance tests. For the more fit, it became a competition. I convinced the administration to give out a "most fit officer" award at our annual awards banquet.

Temperance

This group of strengths relates to being even handed, measured, and restrained.

Forgiveness is the strength of accepting others' flaws, giving people a second chance, and not being vengeful. It is the ability to forgive when you or a loved one is the injured party.

Officer Mike

 Sometimes, even if you have developed positive relationships with community members, there will be times when you will still have a conflict. I knew Henry well, and we had numerous friendly conversations. Unfortunately, he had a rough life and was someone I would frequently arrest for offenses such as drug possession, disorderly conduct, and battery. Every time I arrested him, he was cool with me. He always complied. However, on one Saturday night, he was involved in a fight at the Corner Bar. This time, it wasn't so simple. Unfortunately, I presumed compliance, which is something I preach never to do. When I told him he was under arrest and to turn around and place his hands behind his back, he punched me in the face! The fight was on. While trying to get control of him, we landed on tables, chairs, and eventually on the ground. Backup officers arrived, and we managed to place him in handcuffs. A couple of days later, I saw Henry while I was shopping with my family at Wal-Mart. He walked up to me and said, "Man, Officer Mike, I'm sorry about the other night. I was drunk and pissed off." I said, "Henry, don't worry about it. I know you weren't mad at me; you were pissed off way before I got there. I have nothing against you. I was just doing my job." I jokingly said, "My face is feeling better, but you can definitely pack a punch. When I'm patrolling in your neighborhood, I'll stop by and chat." I never had an issue with Henry again, even when arresting him.

Humility is the strength of unpretentiousness, not showing off or bragging about accomplishments, never feeling superior to others, and letting your actions speak for themselves.

Officer Mike

 Officers were dispatched to a residence involving a domestic between Marty Smith and his mother. Marty was extremely violent and had been in and out of prison for all his adult life. Dispatch reported that Marty had been smashing everything in the house and threatening to kill his mother. The sergeant assigned me to come up from the rear of the residence; he and another officer would approach from the front. I pulled down the street dark, parked, and ran to the back of the residence.

The sergeant radioed to me that Marty was right at the front doorway on the small front porch, holding a hammer in his hand and his mother with the other arm. I knew the residence well, and because of the yelling, I could work my way close to the front door behind the bushes, which were higher than the front window.

My sergeant began talking to Marty, trying to de-escalate the situation. I was able to work my way within a foot of Marty without him even knowing I was there. I was able to reach out, grab the wrist holding the hammer, and initiate an armbar takedown, bringing him off the porch and onto the ground. The sergeant and other officer ran up and helped me control Marty and get him cuffed. When we debriefed later, the sergeant, along with the entire shift, gave me praise. I admitted to them that I could not have done this without the teamwork—the sergeant coordinating the approach, the sergeant and other officer keeping Marty distracted, and the quick assistance once I got Marty on the ground. He was a tough dude, and I definitely needed help getting him under control. It takes teamwork to do this job.

Prudence is the strength of being careful about one's actions and decisions, avoiding unnecessary risks that could have harmful or irreversible results for the self or other, and being careful to prevent behavior that you will later regret.

Officer Mike

 When I was the patrol sergeant on the midnight shift, not only did I not forget how tough this shift was to work, I was also living it with my officers. Trying to stay up overnight, going to my kids' events during the days and evenings, and attending training and court appearances was stressful on both the mind and body. I told my officers that if they were lacking sleep to let me know. I knew that lack of sleep would affect not only officers' health but also their decision making while on duty.

I told them if they became too tired, they should go into the station and hang out near dispatch to take a nap, if necessary. This way, the dispatcher could wake them should an emergency arise. Meanwhile, I could handle calls with the other officers on shift.

Self-regulation is the strength of regulating how you feel, think, behave, and act. It represents excellent impulse control and judgment under pressure and the ability to act responsibly even in the face of temptation.

Officer Mike

 I can remember interviewing a child who had been sexually assaulted by her grandfather. Of course, she did not deserve this to happen to her, and I felt so bad that it did. Now it was time to interview the grandfather. For years, I had known him through various interactions, both enforcement and nonenforcement, which gave me some trust from him. As I began interviewing him, he eventually gave me admissions but not a confession. This was all I needed, but I wanted more admissions to fill in the gap. Good interviewers know that showing respect and understanding is a good tactic. When he said, "Well, Officer Mike, she was walking up the steps and only had on her nightgown, and she started to fall. When I caught her, my finger accidentally went into her vagina." What did I want to do to him? Or say to him? You can guess. However, I had to remain respectful and say, "I can understand how that can happen, so what happened next?" Keeping my impulses in check helped me secure what we needed to send him away for a long time.

Transcendence

This group of strengths relates to your spiritual health (see also Chapter 5). The strengths allow you to connect with something bigger (e.g., the universe, cosmos, a higher power) and find meaning through those connections.

Appreciation of beauty and excellence is the strength of noticing and appreciating excellence wherever it is found. It represents gratitude and awe for the beauty in art and nature, as well as in simple everyday experiences and activities. You don't take for granted the achievements of others or your own accomplishments.

Officer Mike

 My dad passed away in May of 2018. He was 79 years old. He had suffered the last several months of his life due to the cancer that had taken over his body. He had been gone for about a month when I pulled into the firearms range parking lot at the academy. I had received a text from my mom. It was a lengthy text explaining how she had seen Dad the previous night—and not in a dream. She explained that he had come through the double doors in a hospital and approached her. He looked healthy and was wearing a bright white t-shirt. He told Mom that he was fine and not to worry about him. A nurse then entered through the same doors and said, "Dave, it's time to go now." I called Mom, and she told me more details. We cried together over the phone, but it was a happy cry for her—if that makes sense. I was standing in the middle of the parking lot, out in the middle of nowhere, with fields on all sides of the firearms range. It was a hot and sunny day, and there was no breeze at all—it was completely calm. Right after I finished talking to my mom, a corn husk fell within inches of my face. It was weird—there was no breeze. I have never been a religious person, and I still have questions to this day. But for that moment, I felt it could have been my dad sending me a message. I could not find any scientific explanation for the corn husk. I kept it and appreciate its simple significance whenever I see it.

Gratitude is the strength of appreciation for good things that happen and the ability to express this. You recognize your blessings and say "thank you" to yourself and others.

Officer Mike

 I can remember working two jobs 70 hours a week and my wife working part time. Both of us were going to college (my wife was studying education at the university and I was working on my associate's degree in criminal justice at our community college), and we had a child before the age of 20. Some of the best memories involve working an extra shift so that we could have enough money to order a Domino's pizza for delivery. What a treat! My mom and dad worked hard their entire lives and had no pensions, no investments. Dad has passed away, and my mom lives on Social Security of $1,300 a month. She will accept gift cards and let me help her fix up her house, but she is too proud for anything more than that. When the COVID-19 pandemic began, my mom worked for hours daily making masks out of material she already had. She made over a hundred masks, by hand, for family and friends. She would leave them on her breezeway so that people could come by and get them while maintaining social distancing. Even though my parents did not make financial investments, they made more important investments in my sister, Julie, and me. I wouldn't change a thing. My message: Never forget where you came from.

Hope is the strength of expecting the best possible outcome based on what you can do for yourself, believing in a bright future, and working hard to accomplish this.

Officer Mike

 All the instructors at our academy and I work hard at illustrating the positives of police work and promoting the benefits of nonenforcement contacts. That is the way to get to know civilians as people and give them a chance to get to know the officer as a person, not just a cop. It is rewarding every time I get an email, text, or photo from former recruit officers about their positive interactions with community members—playing with kids at the park, taking selfies with civilians, hanging out with employees at local businesses, coaching a sports team, and so on. Though many officers become negative and cynical, it gives me hope knowing that so many of our graduates are truly making a difference in their community.

Humor is the strength of bringing happiness to others' lives. Using humor with deep compassion can lighten someone's dark days. Use humor to find a silver lining in your own challenging times. As we mentioned in Chapter 3, this is not related to the sometimes-inappropriate or hurtful gallows humor so prevalent among first responders, which often does have its time and place; it reflects the strength to be able to use humor compassionately.

Officer Mike

 A fellow officer, Joe, was walking out of Lt. Mayfield's office and looking pretty down. And now it was time for the shift to go out on patrol. When I asked him what was up, he said that he had just received a discipline letter from the LT for cursing at last night's arrestee. Joe was afraid that if he got one more complaint, he would get a day off. I told Joe we should get out of the station; I said, "Meet me at the Pamida parking lot." Once we pulled up side by side, I said, "Let me guess, your meeting with Lt. Mayfield went something like this. . . ." I did a perfect Lt. Mayfield impression—voice, word choice, everything. Once I was in the role of the LT, Joe started laughing, especially when he realized that the LT had also cursed at him for cursing. We decided that all of us have paper in our files for one thing or another, and if the worse thing is cursing, we weren't doing too badly.

Spirituality is the strength of a coherent higher purpose in your life (again, refer to Chapter 5, too). It involves having faith—in something.

Officer Mike

 Officer Rick and I weren't cops in the same town; however, we both taught control tactics at the police academy part time. When I retired and began full time at the academy, we continued to work together at the academy. We averaged 2 days a week for over 10 years. Then he called me. He said, "Mikey, I let you down." He was referring to me bugging him all the time about his health. He was in good physical shape and had fighting prowess. But I knew that he was working crazy hours, with lots of overtime, and he was at the academy as much as possible (teaching more blocks than just control tactics). I told him that he needed some downtime, that his body and mind needed the rest. He told me he just had a heart attack and was in the hospital waiting for surgery. He developed an infection, and the surgery would be put off until the infection cleared up. When I visited him at the hospital, he was the same old, full-of-shit jokester he ever was. If people didn't know him, they would think that he was a cocky, arrogant, wise-ass cop. But if you really knew him, as I and other cops did, you would know he never took himself seriously—his personality simply made others laugh, and if you got to know him well enough, you figured out that he was genuinely humble. We all made fun of each other, and he was no exception. Recruit officers loved him, his teaching style, and his walk. He had the "coolest" stride up and down the mats. Sometimes a recruit officer would say to the instructors, "That's not fair." Officer Rick would say, "You want fair? It comes to town every August." He had a saying or quote for everything.

I was asked by his family to do his eulogy. The funeral began with heavy metal music playing as friends, family, and cops from all over walked in—just as he would have wanted it. There were many serious parts of my speech; however, the family asked me to put some real "Officer Rick" in it. One of the high points for the family and everyone who knew him was me mimicking his walk—his cool stride. I finished by saying it didn't seem fair that he was taken from us. Then I said, "Officer Rick is looking down on me saying, 'Mikey, if you want fair, it comes to town every August.'" His wrestling shoes hang in the control tactics room with a plaque. His locker remains his locker, with a picture of him on it. As a ritual, every time I teach control tactics, I walk up to his locker and smack him in the face. Then instructors and I tell an Officer Rick story or simply make fun of him. This might be hard for nonpolice to understand, but it is a great release and a way for us never to forget him. His cocky legacy lives on—and I do believe he is looking down at us and looking out for us.

STEP 5. IDENTIFY AND CULTIVATE YOUR PERSONAL STRENGTHS

One method to maintain your wellness is never to stagnate. Keep striving for personal growth and self-improvement. That may mean that you continue your formal education, as Officer Mike did. It could reflect your desire to promote; you take leadership development classes and strive for positions with greater authority and responsibility. However, your efforts at self-improvement need not relate to anything professionally. If you love patrol (or just don't want the responsibility that comes with being a supervisor), there is nothing wrong with staying in patrol for your whole career. Of course, larger agencies offer many opportunities for your career other than promoting, such as positions in investigations, traffic, school resources, and so on. Nevertheless, the key to your overall health and wellness is not to look only for new challenges at work. Many officers may do just that, but it doesn't have to be the path to your self-improvement.

There are many ways you can avoid complacency. We've mentioned some of these in earlier chapters of the book. Learning a new language or how to play a musical instrument are excellent activities that also help keep your mind sharp. Getting involved in a charitable or community-based organization whose mission you are passionate about can refresh your sense of purpose. But in this section, we are focusing on self-improvement that stems from paying attention to your personal strengths. You can improve your resilience and your overall wellness by making the commitment to sharpen your strengths.

Off-Duty Exercise: Identify Your Personal Strengths

In Step 4, we presented six categories, which contained a total of 24 strengths. To identify your strengths, follow these steps:

1. Look over the 24 strengths.
2. Make a list of the strengths that you think best represent your self. Maybe there's only one or a few. Or maybe you identify many that you view as strengths of yours.
3. Think about your personal strengths that were not included on our list. These should be core characteristics that you think define you as the person you are. Add those to your list here.
4. Rank order the list of your strengths from most to least representative of your self. For example, if your list contained zest and bravery, determine which you feel is a stronger strength.

Off-Duty Exercise: Strengthen Your Strengths

When you commit to lifelong learning for self-improvement, one straightforward technique is to find ways to build on your existing personal strengths. Many officers prefer starting with the lower ranked strengths and boosting those. But there are no rules here. You can work on one at a time, several, or all of them at once.

1. Look over your list of strengths.
2. Select the strengths you want to strengthen.
3. Make a plan. What will you do to improve the strengths you chose to boost? It's easy to find ways to improve some of the strengths by just doing more of that characteristic. For example, if you want to be more kind, you can commit to doing three kind things every day. Other strengths are not as behaviorally oriented; they will require you to think differently and to adopt a different approach to life. For example, to boost hope or humility, you will need to focus on improving how you see yourself and others.
4. Put a reminder on your calendar to monitor your progress at least once per week. Take 10 to 15 minutes to review your list and your strength strengthening plan. How well are you progressing? Are some strengths improving more than others? Make the necessary changes to your plan as needed to maintain steady progress.

In addition to boosting your existing strengths, many officers use positive psychology to cultivate new strengths. This is an excellent way to foster personal growth and to promote lifelong learning.

Off-Duty Exercise: Identify New Strengths

1. Review the list of 24 personal strengths in Step 4.
2. Select some strengths you don't currently have but would like to develop. There's no limit to how many you choose, but try to pick at least a few.
3. Do the strengths on this new list come from a variety of the categories we defined, or are they bunched in one or just a few of the six categories?
4. Before finalizing your list, try to ensure that the list of your existing strengths and the list of strengths that you want to cultivate include at least one strength from each of the six categories.
5. Are there any strengths you would like to develop that are not included on our list of 24? Perhaps these are characteristics that you admire in others. If so, add these strengths to your new list.
6. At this point, you have two lists: (a) a list of your strengths that you are strengthening and (b) a list of strengths that you'd like to cultivate. For convenience, combine the lists by adding the new strengths to the bottom of the list of your existing strengths.

STEP 6. CULTIVATE NEW STRENGTHS

Make a plan to cultivate the new strengths you identified. This may take some effort because these are characteristics that you want to develop but don't already possess. Some officers seek the assistance of a mental health professional who specializes in a positive psychology approach. You would share your list of new strengths you want to cultivate and create a plan with the help of the professional on how best to achieve your goal. Some officers have consulted a life coach because they focus on personal growth. Be cautious, however, because there is no degree or license required to call oneself a life coach, although there are certification programs that many have completed. You also can cultivate many new strengths on your own. Ask yourself a few questions:

- Why did I add this strength to my list?
- In what ways will this strength improve my life?
- What are some examples I've seen of this strength being demonstrated to its fullest by someone else?
- What would be the first small but significant sign that I possess this strength?
- How would others become aware that I now have this characteristic?

Once you've answered these questions about each of the strengths you'd like to cultivate, make a plan to begin doing and thinking about ways to boost those strengths. When you monitor the progress of your efforts to strengthen your current strengths, also assess your progress on improving these new strengths. It may sound like a lot when reading this, but once you put the plan into action, you are likely to feel quite gratified by your efforts at self-improvement. And it can be extra rewarding when others take notice of the positive changes you are making.

On-Duty and Off-Duty Strength Appreciation Exercises

Now that you are working to strengthen your strengths, an important way to boost resilience is to monitor and reflect on how your strengths make you a great cop. You typically conduct postincident

debriefings to review tactics so that you can improve future performance. Many officers tend to focus on the details associated with
the call. However, something is missing from this retrospection.
When you review a call, make it a point also to identify the personal
strengths you used to resolve the incident. If you don't have time on
duty, make the time off duty. For instance, you can focus on your
strengths: "I used careful but quick thinking," "I showed compassion
and kindness to the suffering family," "I had a great collaboration
with my partner to resolve the call successfully," "Afterward, I made

a point to thank my partner and congratulate myself for helping the victim." Do this as often as possible as a technique to reinforce your strengths and appreciate your efforts. Likewise, you can acknowledge when your actions did not measure up to your expectations of your strengths. At those times, make a point to increase your efforts to boost those strengths.

Never underestimate the power of your personal strengths. When you make it a regular practice to review and appreciate your strengths, boost your strengths, cultivate new strengths, and reflect on how you effectively used those strengths on duty, you will enhance your resilience and your ability to grow through the adversities that you face on the job. At the same time, you aren't just a cop. As we've reiterated throughout the book, you may have plenty of other stressors to deal with in your personal life. Your personal strengths don't just make you a great cop; they make you a great person. If you didn't already consider this, go back to the personal strength exercises and decide where you can boost and/or cultivate some additional strengths for self-improvement in your personal life. A commitment to self-improvement ought to focus as much on your personal life as it does on your professional life. Your health and wellness depend on you being the best you can be on duty and off duty.

CHAPTER 12

CLOSING THOUGHTS: MAINTAINING BALANCE

We began this book by challenging you to stay committed to achieving balance in your life. The ensuing chapters gave you wellness strategies to use on duty and off duty. In addition to the suggestions to optimize your physical, cognitive, emotional, social, and spiritual functioning, we encouraged you to promote your personal integrity. This involves recognizing the moral risks of policing and taking active steps to keep your moral compass pointed in the right direction. Resilience is a critical skill that helps you to avoid the most destructive impacts of policing. We offered ideas to boost your resilience as you cope with the adversities you will encounter throughout your career.

The book provided you with the tools to achieve balance in your life. Now comes the tough part. You have to practice, practice, practice! You have to make the time to use these strategies, and you have to stay committed to maintaining balance in your life. We can't emphasize this enough. Once you are feeling healthy, it takes some effort to stay that way. As a wise person once said, "Amateurs practice until they get it right, and professionals practice until they can't get it wrong."

The job makes it easy to backslide and fall into some unhealthy habits. Many distractions can derail your efforts. In fact, most of us are quick to put our health and wellness on the back burner when other responsibilities seem so important. In this area, however, it's okay to be somewhat selfish. Unless you achieve and maintain your well-being, you are not doing your best to be there for others who need you.

At the same time, although you are ultimately responsible for your well-being, you are not alone in these efforts. You can start by making wellness a family goal. Most of the off-duty strategies we presented can be shared with your spouse, children, and friends. Fitness and nutrition, recreation and relaxation, and many of the techniques for emotional and spiritual health will be enhanced when you do them with loved ones. For example, you don't have to replace your CrossFit workouts, but you can add walks or bike rides with your family to your repertoire. When you integrate your family into many of your wellness activities, it will make it easier for you to stick to your program.

Another suggestion is to tell your loved ones, friends, and trusted colleagues about your wellness goals. Allow them to offer encouragement for your efforts. It's important to get some positive reinforcement from time to time so that you see that your efforts are being noticed by those closest to you. Perhaps just as important is to make sure that these folks understand that you want them to tell you if they notice any backsliding. We rarely recognize subtle changes in our attitude or behavior, but loved ones are usually aware even though they aren't generally inclined to say anything—until things get bad. Give them permission to say something if they ever see small signs of a lack of balance. They may not understand what's wrong, but the wake-up call might be enough to get you back on track.

There are times when you and your loved ones may not be enough to help you with the struggles you are experiencing. For that matter, there are times when the most comprehensive wellness program will be insufficient to help you through some adversity. This is when outside help may be needed. The support can come from a department chaplain, member of peer support, or licensed mental health professional. First, it takes great insight to know when you might benefit from some professional help, especially when things aren't that bad; seeking support then may be what you need to prevent things from getting bad! Second, when you start from a relatively balanced, healthy position, you won't likely need to spend much time with that support person. These are more like mental health checkups that give you a booster, some reminders about staying healthy, and doing what you know works.

When officers recognize the value of professional help during noncrisis times, it is easier to consider talking to someone when the shit hits the fan. Even the most psychologically healthy officers sometimes encounter something that knocks them down. Rather than struggling to get up on their own, these folks take advantage of available counseling services. If your agency doesn't provide access, use your medical benefits and find a professional who understands and works with cops. Remember, it takes more guts to speak up when you are having issues than to keep it inside. Contrary to popular belief, you most likely won't be seeing the counselor for more than six to eight sessions. However, if the counseling happens to bring up something that is unresolved from the past, you might want to extend the sessions to address the additional issues.

No matter how challenging things are, you can achieve and maintain balance in your life. However, you can't wait for things to calm down before you start practicing the strategies outlined in this book. You don't wait to start brushing your teeth only after the dentist needs to fill some cavities or do a root canal. Likewise, when we talk about health and wellness, we are advocating for a prevention mindset. Sure, plenty of resources are available to intervene when you are struggling, but your well-being depends on taking action now. Figure out what works for you. Commit to making wellness practices part of your daily routine. Develop the mental flexibility to know when you are not performing at your best, and seek help when you might need it.

By design, one of the things that is missing from this book is an emphasis on organizational stressors. We know that the job involves more than what your operational responsibilities entail. The job confronts you with organizational and systemic stressors, many of which could be improved or completely fixed if the bureaucrats made a few logical, even simple changes. Some of those improvements might happen—someday. We've seen changes over the years and, in many areas, the policing profession has evolved. But in other areas, there are impediments to your wellness at every turn. Some issues are so complex that positive change seems like an impossibility. Please don't let that reality prevent you from taking care of your own wellness.[1] Your challenge is to focus on yourself and your loved ones. Your challenge is to live a long, healthy postretirement life and enjoy the retirement benefits for which you worked so hard.

Perhaps it will provide a little reassurance for you to know that we will continue working tirelessly on your behalf to improve organizational and operational stressors. In the meantime, keep using your POWER to take care of yourself and your loved ones, and be safe out there.

Feel free to email us:
Daniel.Blumberg@policepowerproject.org
Dr.konstantinos@aya.yale.edu
Michaelschlosser16@gmail.com

ADDITIONAL RESOURCES

The authors are not affiliated with the resources listed here. They do not explicitly endorse any of these resources (nor does the publisher) but compiled them for the convenience of the readers.

CHAPTER 1: PHYSICAL HEALTH

Video

How a Police Officer Changed His Health, Fitness and Nutrition Through Mindset

https://www.youtube.com/watch?v=UlNmaWW-bI4

- Sergeant Mark of the Los Angeles Police Department explains the effects that his daily food regimen and the amount of physical exercise he implemented in his daily life had on the quality of his life and his relationships.

The authors would like to thank the following research assistants for their dedicated efforts in compiling this list of resources: Prashant Aukhojee, Rebekah Lazarski, Felipe Rubim, and Lucas Rubim.

Websites and Articles

"On-the-Job Stress Negatively Impacts Police Officer Health, Study Suggests"

https://www.ehstoday.com/health/article/21915261/onthejob-stress-negatively-impacts-police-officer-health-study-suggests

- Stress from police work can have adverse effects on the individual's sleep cycle, along with other negative effects on their mental and physical health.

"Impact of Stress on Police Officers' Physical and Mental Health"

https://www.sciencedaily.com/releases/2008/09/080926105029.htm

- A variety of research studies on the topic of police work and job burnout have demonstrated recurrent results, indicating that the accumulation of stress in police work can lead to numerous physical and mental health issues (e.g., high blood pressure, heart problems, posttraumatic stress disorder [PTSD], suicide).

"How Self-Care Can Reduce Police Officer Stress"

https://www.lexipol.com/resources/blog/how-self-care-can-reduce-police-officer-stress/

- Dan Fish explains how to control police work stress by outlining three self-care tools that all officers should employ in their daily lives to inoculate themselves from the harms of daily job anxiety and strain.

"OSH Answer Fact Sheets: Police"

https://www.ccohs.ca/oshanswers/occup_workplace/police.html

- Outlines the health and safety issues that exist in the lives of police officers and discusses some protective and preventive tools that can help avert any problems that threaten officer well-being.

"Building and Sustaining an Officer Wellness Program: Lessons From the San Diego Police Department"

https://www.policeforum.org/assets/SanDiegoOSW.pdf

- This 120-page report on an officer wellness program offered in the San Diego Police Department outlines the type of training, the help resources used, and the results and conclusions established based on the results obtained by the officers involved in the program.

Book

Biddle, S. J., Fox, K., & Boutcher, S. (Eds.). (2003). *Physical activity and psychological well-being.* Routledge.

- This book, written for both researchers and the general public, discusses the science of the "feel-good" effects of exercising. It explains the physical, emotional, and psychological well-being that comes from exercising. It also discusses how exercise can be used to manage stress, anxiety, depression, self-esteem, and much more.

Journal Articles, Government Reports, and Conference Abstract

Andersen, J., Chan, J., Nota, P. D., Planche, K., Boychuk, E., & Collins, P. (2019). Diurnal cortisol variation according to high risk occupational specialty within police: Comparisons between frontline, tactical officers, and the general population. *Psychoneuroendocrinology, 107,* 16–17. https://doi.org/10.1016/j.psyneuen.2019.07.045

- Analyzes salivary cortisol (stress hormone) among officers of specialized high-risk occupations and compares it with the general population.

Hartley, T. A., Gu, J., Baughman, P. J., Violanti, J. M., Andrew, M. E., Fekedulegn, D., & Burchfiel, C. M. (2013, May 16–19). *Comparisons of cardiovascular health in police officers, U.S. general population, and U.S. employed population* [Conference abstract]. American Psychological Association. https://doi.org/10.1037/e577572014-379

- A study on police officers' cardiovascular profile.

Kuhns, J. B., Maguire, E. R., & Leach, N. R. (2015). *Health, safety, and wellness program case studies in law enforcement.* Office of Community Oriented Policing Services, U.S. Department of Justice.

- A report with case studies on various health, safety, and wellness programs.

Neylan, T. C., Metzler, T. J., Best, S. R., Weiss, D. S., Fagan, J. A., Liberman, A., Akiva., Rogers, C., Vedantham, Kumar., Brunet, A., Lipsey, L. T., & Marmar, C. R. (2002). Critical incident exposure and sleep quality in police officers. *Psychosomatic Medicine, 64*(2), 345–352.

- Analyzes research on sleep quality of police officers compared with that of the general population.

Soroka, A., & Sawicki, B. (2014). Physical activity levels as a quantifier in police officers and cadets. *International Journal of Occupational Medicine and Environmental Health, 27*(3), 498–505.

- Summarizes research on the physical activity levels of active duty officers and cadets.

Violanti, J. M. (2012, March). *Shifts, extended work hours, and fatigue: An assessment of health and personal risks for police officers* [Unpublished report] (Doc. no. 237964). https://www.ojp.gov/pdffiles1/nij/grants/237964.pdf

- The effects of shift work on police officers' health and psychological well-being.

Violanti, J. M., Charles, L. E., McCanlies, E., Hartley, T. A., Baughman, P., Andrew, M. E., Fekedulegn, D., Ma, C. C., Mnatsakanova, A., & Burchfiel, C. M. (2017). Police stressors and health: A state-of-the-art review. *Policing: An International Journal, 40*(4), 642–656. https://www.ncbi.nlm.nih.gov/pmc/articles/PMC6400077/

- Various stressors of police work and how these can affect police officers' health.

CHAPTER 2: COGNITIVE WELLNESS

Videos

3 Instantly Calming CBT Techniques for Anxiety

https://www.youtube.com/watch?v=JiDaTi_iQrY

- Cognitive behavior therapy is reviewed, and its advantages and disadvantages are discussed, along with three unique techniques for instant relaxation.

Reframe Your Thoughts | Diane Sawyer and Marcia Perkins | TEDxUWMilwaukee

https://www.youtube.com/watch?v=J6_P5rpfp74

- How transforming one's thoughts to become more resilient can help individuals confront the barriers existent within themselves.

Websites and Articles

"Dealing With Confirmation Bias"

https://www.policemag.com/341175/dealing-with-confirmation-bias

- Explains what cognitive bias is and how law enforcement personnel can prevent it from effecting their daily work and lives.

"CBT's Cognitive Restructuring (CR) for Tackling Cognitive Distortions"

https://positivepsychology.com/cbt-cognitive-restructuring-cognitive-distortions/

- Talks about the role that cognitive restructuring can play in cognitive behavior therapy (CBT) and the different methods that are employed with cognitive restructuring.

Book Chapter

Ellis, A. (2019). Early theories and practices of rational emotive behavior therapy and how they have been augmented and revised during the last three decades. In M. E. Bernard & W. Dryden (Eds.), *Advances in REBT: Theory, practice, research, measurement, prevention and promotion* (pp. 1–21). Springer Nature Switzerland AG. https://doi.org/10.1007/978-3-319-93118-0_1

Journal Articles

Brown, S. G., & Daus, C. S. (2015). The influence of police officers' decision-making style and anger control on responses to work scenarios. *Journal of Applied Research in Memory and Cognition*, 4(3), 294–302. https://doi.org/10.1016/j.jarmac.2015.04.001

- Examines the interaction between anger control and decision making in police officers.

Gutshall, C. L., Hampton Jr., D. P., Sebetan, I. M., Stein, P. C., & Broxtermann, T. J. (2017). The effects of occupational stress on cognitive performance in police officers. *Police Practice and Research*, 18(5), 463–477.

- Gutshall and colleagues attempt to understand the effect that stress has on police officers' working memory and other psychological and biological features.

Healy, H. A., Barnes-Holmes, Y., Barnes-Holmes, D., Keogh, C., Luciano, C., & Wilson, K. (2008). An experimental test of a cognitive defusion exercise: Coping with negative and positive self-statements. *The Psychological Record*, 58(4), 623–640. https://doi.org/10.1007/BF03395641

- Analyzes how positive (i.e., I am whole), negative (i.e., I am a bad person), or neutral self-statements can have an effect on one's ability to manage current psychological stress.

Robson Jr., J. P., & Troutman-Jordan, M. (2014). A concept analysis of cognitive reframing. *Journal of Theory Construction & Testing*, 18(2), 55–59.

- Explains what cognitive reframing is and uses Walker's and Avant's classic framework for concept analysis to define the four features of cognitive reframing.

van den Heuvel, C., Alison, L., & Power, N. (2014). Coping with uncertainty: Police strategies for resilient decision-making and action implementation. *Cognition, Technology & Work*, 16(1), 25–45. https://doi.org/10.1007/s10111-012-0241-8

- Examines how police officers can use specific coping strategies (e.g., reflection in action) to reduce uncertainty during a hostage negotiation event (i.e., a high-stress event).

CHAPTER 3: EMOTIONAL WELLNESS

Video

Officer Wellness Helps De-Escalate Police Calls [HLN Michaela Pereira interview with Linda Webb of RITE Academy]

https://www.youtube.com/watch?v=dq15xLg6ARM

- Dr. Webb explains why police officer training should focus more on emotional intelligence training and communication training.

Websites and Articles

"How Mindfulness Is Changing Law Enforcement"

https://greatergood.berkeley.edu/article/item/how_mindfulness_is_changing_law_enforcement

- Highlights the importance that meditation can have for police officers, especially for the improvement of their mental well-being.

"Managing Law Enforcement Stress Through Emotional Intelligence"

https://www.policeone.com/health-fitness/articles/managing-law-enforcement-stress-through-emotional-intelligence-imPiq2L4NQu3o9nj/

- Mark Bond explains four foundational ideas behind emotional intelligence, including self-awareness, self-management, self-motivation, and social awareness.

Book

Gilmartin, K. M. (2002). *Emotional survival for law enforcement: A guide for officers*. E-S Press.

- Seeks to help law enforcement personnel and their families who have experienced or are experiencing difficult situations due to the nature of their profession.

Journal Article

Baker, R., Jaaffar, A. H., Sallehuddin, H., Hassan, M. A., & Mohamed, R. (2019). The relationship between emotional intelligence and affective commitment: An examination of police officers. *International Journal of Recent Technology & Engineering, 8,* 658–665.

- Baker and colleagues use the four fundamental features of emotional intelligence—self-emotional appraisal, other's emotional appraisal, use of emotions, and regulation of emotions—to understand the interaction between emotional intelligence and effective commitment.

CHAPTER 4: SOCIAL WELLNESS

Book

Kirschman, E. (2018). *I love a cop: What police families need to know.* Guilford Press.

- Details the issues that families of police officers might encounter, including stress and abuse, and solutions that create a healthy and supportive environment for all family members.

Websites and Articles

"Think It's Hard Being a Cop? Try Being Married to One"

https://www.psychologytoday.com/ca/blog/cop-doc/201805/think-its-hard-being-cop-try-being-married-one

- Provides readers with 10 tips for police families to deal with hardships.

"How to Have a Stable Law Enforcement Marriage"

https://www.policeone.com/family-home/articles/how-to-have-a-stable-law-enforcement-marriage-WIL1anBdFRnlCmxt/

- Ron Lyons talks about the issues that couples in police families might go through and provides an in-depth understanding of solutions that can help them create a safe and healthy environment for their families and their marriage.

Journal Articles

Karaffa, K., Openshaw, L., Koch, J., Clark, H., Harr, C., & Stewart, C. (2015). Perceived impact of police work on marital relationships. *The Family Journal*, 23(2), 120–131. https://doi.org/10.1177/1066480714564381

- Karaffa and colleagues examined, by using a needs assessment, the marital problems that exist within the relationship between police officers and their spouses.

Rathi, N., & Barath, N. (2013). Work–family conflict and job and family satisfaction: Moderating effect of social support among police personnel. *Equality, Diversity and Inclusion*, 32(4), 438. https://doi.org/10.1108/EDI-10-2012-0092

- Rathi and Barath examine the moderating effect that police coworker support has on the relationship between work–family conflict and family and job satisfaction.

CHAPTER 5: SPIRITUAL WELLNESS

Video

10% Happier Road Trip: Guided Meditation Session With Tempe Police https://www.youtube.com/watch?v=EazlsdmCZv8

- Meditation teacher Jeff Warren teaches police officers how to meditate in a step-by-step tutorial with real police officers.

Website and Article

"Embracing the Spiritual Dimension of Law Enforcement"

https://leb.fbi.gov/articles/perspective/perspective-embracing-the-spiritual-dimension-of-law-enforcement

- Proposes that for police officers to prosper and succeed in their daily lives and in their jobs, they require the ability to strengthen their spiritual side.

Journal Articles

Pearce, M., Haynes, K., Rivera, N. R., & Koenig, H. G. (2018). Spiritually integrated cognitive processing therapy: A new treatment for post-traumatic stress disorder that targets moral injury. *Global Advances in Health and Medicine*. https://doi.org/10.1177/2164956118759939

- Pearce and colleagues examine the role that spirituality can have on cognitive processing therapy and the extent that such assimilation can have on the effectiveness of PTSD and moral injury treatment.

Van Hook, M. P. (2016). Spirituality as a potential resource for coping with trauma. *Social Work and Christianity*, *43*(1), 7.

- Details the manners in which trauma is experienced by individuals and the benefits that introducing spirituality into one's life can have on the healing prospects of their trauma.

CHAPTER 6: COMMITMENT TO THE NOBLE CAUSE

Website and Article

"Policing With Honor: The Three Levels of Accountability"

https://www.policeone.com/patrol-issues/articles/policing-with-honor-the-three-levels-of-accountability-nimCOgK939bhaCKk/

- Randy Sutton, a police trainer, explains the three synchronous levels of accountability that ensure that police officers abide by and commit to the goals of protecting and serving.

Journal Articles

Cooper, J. A. (2010). Noble cause corruption as a consequence of role conflict in the police organization. *Policing and Society*, 22(2), 169–184. https://doi.org/10.1080/10439463.2011.605132

- Cooper discusses a new social psychological framework, namely the integration of role theory and role conflict, to address issues with police wrongdoing and negligence.

Crank, J., Flaherty, D., & Giacomazzi, A. (2007). The noble cause: An empirical assessment. *Journal of Criminal Justice*, 35(1), 103–116. https://doi.org/10.1016/j.jcrimjus.2006.11.019

- Crank and coauthors explore the defining characteristics of noble cause and various relationships between noble cause and factors such as crime and attitudes toward administrators.

Johnson, R. R. (2012). Police organizational commitment: The influence of supervisor feedback and support. *Crime & Delinquency*, 61(9), 1155–1180. https://doi.org/10.1177/0011128712466887

- Johnson explores the effect that supervisor feedback and perceived organizational support have on police officers' commitment to the organization, among other factors.

CHAPTER 8: MORAL DISTRESS AND ETHICAL EXHAUSTION

Websites and Articles

"The 7 Layers of Police Grief After a Line-of-Duty Death"

https://www.policeone.com/evergreen/articles/the-7-layers-of-police-grief-after-a-line-of-duty-death-87r7e3EReF23yNQV/

- Talks about the stages of police officers' grief for their fellow officers who died in the line of duty.

"No 'One Way' to Deal With Grief"

https://www.blueline.ca/no_-one_way-_to_deal_with_grief-3035/

- Discusses the effects that not acknowledging grief for a fallen officer can have on police officers and how to get around the malformed coping mechanisms.

Books

Kushner, H. (2005). *Nine essential things I've learned about life.* Penguin Random House.

- Rabbi Harold S. Kushner offers spiritual, pragmatic, and practical advice for life's difficult times.

Gottschalk, P. (2010). *Police management: Professional integrity in policing.* Nova Science.

- Discusses corruption inside police culture and addresses this issue by giving insights into the dynamics of police enforcement.

Tuttle, B. M., Blumberg, D. M., & Papazoglou, K. (2019). Critical challenges to police officer wellness. In Henry Pontell (Ed.), *Oxford research encyclopedia of criminology and criminal justice* (pp. 1–27). Oxford University Press. https://doi.org/ 10.1093/acrefore/9780190264079.013.538

- Talks about the role of compassion satisfaction, emotional intelligence, and emotional regulation in aiding officers to maintain balance both in their job and personal life.

Van Droogenbroeck, F., Spruyt, B., Ivkovic, S. K., & Haberfeld, M. R. (2019). The effects of ethics training on police integrity. In K. Ivkovik & M. R. Haberfeld (Eds.), *Exploring police integrity: Novel approaches to police integrity theory & methodology* (pp.365–382).

- Explores the short- and long-term effects of ethics training on police officers.

Journal Articles

Blumberg, D. M., Papazoglou, K., & Schlosser, M. D. (2021, February). Tackling the moral risks of policing. *Police Chief*, 42–47.

- Discusses how organizations can implement comprehensive prevention and intervention strategies to address the moral risks that lead to officers' emotional and spiritual distress and the moral risks that increase the likelihood of officer misconduct.

Papazoglou, K., & Chopko, B. (2017). The role of moral suffering (moral distress and moral injury) in police compassion fatigue and PTSD: An unexplored topic. *Frontiers in Psychology, 8*. https://doi.org/10.3389/fpsyg.2017.01999

- Talks about moral suffering in first responders and the relationship between PTSD and compassion fatigue.

CHAPTER 9: STRESS INOCULATION

Mindfulness Applications

Free mindfulness app and guided meditations: http://counselingcenter. utah.edu/services/mindfulness.php

Free guided meditations (English and Spanish): http://marc.ucla. edu/body.cfm?id=22

Free online mindfulness-based stress reduction 8-week course: http:// palousemindfulness.com/

Book

Jacobs, G. D. (2009). *Say good night to insomnia: The six-week, drug-free program developed at Harvard Medical School.* Macmillan.

- Dr. Gregg D. Jacobs talks about a cognitive behavior therapy program that helps people with sleep problems and sleep disorders, revealing different techniques that help one to fall asleep and stay asleep longer without medication.

Websites and Articles

"Box Breathing"

https://www.policemag.com/342171/box-breathing

- Police Commander Mark Divine discusses the importance of breathing techniques to deal with stress, with a focus on the "box breathing" technique and an explanation of how to apply it to the field of law enforcement.

"Just Take a Deep Breath"

https://www.policemag.com/342152/just-take-a-deep-breath

- Discusses the importance of slow breathing to increase resilience and job performance when under stress.

"How to Incorporate Combat Breathing in Police Pursuits"

https://www.policeone.com/officer-safety/articles/how-to-incorporate-combat-breathing-in-police-pursuits-ER1ZKNdX79tS3XN8/

- How breathing techniques can help officers when in the field, especially in stressful situations.

Journal Articles

Bergman, A., Christopher, M. S., & Bowen, S. (2016). Changes in facets of mindfulness predict stress and anger outcomes for police officers. *Mindfulness, 7*, 851–858. https://doi.org/10.1007/s12671-016-0522-z

- Examines how changes in facets of mindfulness reduces and affects coping mechanisms.

Eddy, A., Bergman, A. L., Kaplan, J., Goerling, R. J., & Christopher, M. S. (2019). A qualitative investigation of the experience of mindfulness training among police officers. *Journal of Police and Criminal Psychology, 36*, 63–71. https://doi.org/10.1007/s11896-019-09340-7

- A qualitative assessment of a mindfulness-based resilience training for police officers.

Grupe, D. W., McGehee, C., Smith, C., Francis, A. D., Mumford, J. A., & Davidson, R. J. (2019). Mindfulness training reduces PTSD symptoms and improve stress-related health outcomes in police officers. *Journal of Police and Criminal Psychology, 36*, 72–85. https://doi.org/10.1007/s11896-019-09351-4

- Examines how an 8-week mindfulness training program reduces PTSD symptoms in police officers.

Kaplan, J. B., Bergman, A. L., Christopher, M., Bowen, S., & Hunsinger, M. (2017). Role of resilience in mindfulness training for first responders. *Mindfulness*, *8*, 1373–1380. https://doi.org/10.1007/s12671-017-0713-2

- A discussion and investigation of how mindfulness-based resilience training can increase psychological resilience and prevent burnout.

CHAPTER 10: GROWTH THROUGH ADVERSITY

Websites and Articles

"Police Officer PTSD & Mental Health"

https://oc87recoverydiaries.org/police-officer-ptsd-mental-health/?gclid=EAIaIQobChMIx__5zJ225wIVkYFaBR1Qmgw8EAAYASAAEgKv8fD_BwE

- An article (and video) about the experience of officers who experienced PTSD.

"PTSD Among Police Officers: Impact on Critical Decision Making"

https://cops.usdoj.gov/html/dispatch/05-2018/PTSD.html

- An informative article on PTSD among police officers.

"Police Mental Health: A Discussion Paper"

https://www.camh.ca/-/media/files/pdfs---public-policy-submissions/police-mental-health-discussion-paper-oct2018-pdf.pdf

- Explores the toll that stress has on the life of officers' mental well-being.

Journal Articles

Arble, E., Daugherty, A. M., & Arnetz, B. B. (2018). Models of first responder coping: Police officers as a unique population. *Stress & Health*, *34*(5), 612–621. https://doi.org/10.1002/smi.2821

- Explains two coping pathways that first responders use to cope with the psychological pressures of the job.

Arble, E., Lumley, M. A., Pole, N., Blessman, J., & Arnetz, B. B. (2017). Refinement and preliminary testing of an imagery-based program to improve coping and performance and preventing trauma among urban police officers. *Journal of Police and Criminal Psychology, 32*, 1–10.

- Explores a Swedish program designed to build resilience in stressful events for first responders.

Trounson, J. S., Pfeifer, J. E., & Skues, J. L. (2017). Perceived workplace adversity and correctional officer psychological well-being: An international examination of the impact of officer response styles. *Journal of Forensic Psychiatry & Psychology, 30*(1), 17–37. https://doi.org/10.1080/14789949.2018.1441427

- Investigates how workplace adversity perception in correctional officers predicts psychological well-being.

CHAPTER 11: SELF-COMPASSION AND POSITIVE PSYCHOLOGY

Websites and Articles

"How Mindfulness Is Changing Law Enforcement"

https://greatergood.berkeley.edu/article/item/how_mindfulness_is_changing_law_enforcement

- Analyzes the effects of meditation on police officers' job performance and well-being.

"The Moderating Effect of Self-Compassion and Dispositional Mindfulness on Police Occupational Stress: Preliminary Results"

https://www.researchgate.net/publication/332603521_The_
  Moderating_Effect_of_Self-Compassion_and_Dispositional_
  Mindfulness_on_Police_Occupational_Stress_Preliminary_
  Results

- Examines the effects of mindfulness and self-compassion in a sample of police officers.

"Leadership Spotlight: Compassion in Law Enforcement"

https://leb.fbi.gov/spotlights/leadership-spotlight-compassion-in-law-enforcement

- Analyzes compassion and empathy in law enforcement work.

Videos

The Edge of Compassion—Françoise Mathieu Giving a TEDTalk for TEDxQueensU

https://www.tendacademy.ca/tag/law-enforcement/

- Psychologist Françoise Mathieu discusses her research as a specialist on compassion fatigue and the development of new tools to help to maintain compassion and empathy for others.

Breaking Point: Addressing Operational Stress and PTSD Among Police

https://leaderpost.com/news/local-news/weekender-the-overflowing-cup-dealing-with-operational-stress-and-ptsd-among-police

- An officer shares his experience with PTSD.

The New Era of Positive Psychology

https://www.ted.com/talks/martin_seligman_the_new_era_of_positive_psychology?language=en

- In this TED Talk, psychologist Martin Seligman discusses the development of positive psychology that he uses in his treatment of patients.

Building Your Strengths

https://www.utsc.utoronto.ca/projects/flourish/building-your-strengths/

- An online guide to building character strengths.

Books

Kushner, H. (2006). *Overcoming life's disappointments.* Random House.

- This book about spiritual wisdom teaches readers how to overcome life's disappointments with faith and strength.

McGonical, K. (2012). *The willpower instinct.* Avery Publishing.

- Talks about what willpower is and how it works from the perspective of current psychological research.

Neff, K., & Germer, C. (2017). Self-compassion and psychological well-being. In E. Seppälä, E. Simon-Thomas, S. L. Brown, M. C. Worline, C. D. Cameron, & J. R. Doty (Eds), *The Oxford handbook of compassion science* (pp. 371–386). Oxford University Press.

- Discusses tools to help individuals be more compassionate.

Journal Articles

Allen, A. B., & Leary, M. R. (2010). Self-compassion, stress, and coping. *Social and Personality Psychology Compass, 4*(2), 107–118. https://doi.org/10.1111/j.1751-9004.2009.00246.x

- Examines the way people high in self-compassion cope when faced with stressful situations.

Andersen, J. P., & Papazoglou, K. (2015). Compassion fatigue and compassion satisfaction among police officers: An understudied topic. *International Journal of Emergency Mental Health and Human Resilience, 17*(3), 661–663. https://doi.org/10.4172/1522-4821.1000259

- Focuses on the current research on compassion fatigue and compassion satisfaction and the various implications that it has for police officers.

Birch, P., Vickers, M. H., Kennedy, M., & Galovic, S. (2016). Wellbeing, occupational justice and police practice: An 'affirming environment'? *Police Practice & Research, 18*(1), 26–36. https://doi.org/10.1080/15614263.2016.1205985

- Looks at well-being and occupational justice in policing.

Birnie, K., Speca, M., & Carlson, L. E. (2010). Exploring self-compassion and empathy in the context of mindfulness-based stress reduction (MBSR). *Stress and Health, 26*(5), 359–371. https://doi.org/10.1002/smi.1305

- Examines the impact of mindfulness-based stress reduction on empathy and self-compassion.

Goodman, F. R., Disabato, D. J., Kashdan, T. B., & Machell, K. A. (2017). Personality strengths as resilience: A one-year multiwave study. *Journal of Personality, 85*(3), 423–434. https://doi.org/10.1111/jopy.12250

- Examines how personality strengths can predict different reactions to negative events.

Grant, H. N., Lavery, C. F., & Decarlo, J. (2019). An exploratory study of police officers: Low compassion satisfaction and compassion fatigue. *Psychology for Clinical Settings*, *9*. https://doi.org/10.3389/fpsyg.2018.02793

- Discusses the relationship between compassion fatigue and compassion satisfaction.

Hamby, S., Grych, J., & Banyard, V. (2018). Resilience portfolios and poly-strengths: Identifying protective factors associated with thriving after adversity. *Psychology of Violence*, *8*(2), 172–183. https://doi.org/10.1037/vio0000135

- Uses the resilience portfolio model to identify protective factors for those who have been exposed to violence and adversities.

NOTES

INTRODUCTION

1. All names and places mentioned in Officer Mike's stories have been changed to ensure confidentiality.

CHAPTER I

1. Risky Business: These 25 Occupations Are Among the Most Dangerous Jobs in America. (2020, January 24). *USA Today*. https://www.usatoday.com/picture-gallery/money/2020/01/24/25-most-dangerous-jobs-in-america/41041127/
2. World Health Organization. (2018). *Physical activity*. https://www.who.int/news-room/fact-sheets/detail/physical-activity
3. U.S. Department of Agriculture. (n.d.). *What is MyPlate?* https://www.choosemyplate.gov/eathealthy/WhatIsMyPlate
4. Geller, A. I., Shehab, N., Weidle, N. J., Lovegrove, M. C., Wolpert, B. J., Timbo, B. B., Mozersky, R. P., & Budnitz, D. S. (2015). Emergency department visits for adverse events related to dietary supplements. *The New England Journal of Medicine*, *373*(16), 1531–1540. https://doi.org/10.1056/NEJMsa1504267
5. Costanzo, S., de Gaetano, G., Di Castelnuovo, A., Djoussé, L., Poli, A., & van Velden, D. P. (2019). Moderate alcohol consumption and lower total mortality risk: Justified doubts or established facts? *Nutrition, Metabolism and Cardiovascular Diseases*, *29*(10), 1003–1008. https://doi.org/10.1016/j.numecd.2019.05.062

6. U.S. Department of Health and Human Services. (2020). *2015–2020 dietary guidelines*. https://health.gov/our-work/food-nutrition/2015-2020-dietary-guidelines

CHAPTER 2

1. See, for example, https://www.azquotes.com/author/9574-Abraham_Maslow
2. Adapted from Ackerman, C. E. (2020). Cognitive distortions: When your brain lies to you. *PositivePsychology.com.* https://positivepsychology.com/cognitive-distortions/
3. Adapted from Ellis, A. (n.d.). *Techniques for disputing irrational beliefs (DIBS)*. https://albertellis.org/rebt-pamphlets/Techniques-for-Disputing-Irrational-Beliefs.pdf
4. Merriam-Webster. (n.d.). Cynical. In *Merriam-Webster.com dictionary*. Retrieved April 2, 2021, from https://www.merriam-webster.com/dictionary/cynical
5. Klinoff, V. A., Van Hasselt, V. B., Black, R. A., Masias, E. V., & Couwels, J. (2018). The assessment of resilience and burnout in correctional officers. *Criminal Justice and Behavior, 45*(8), 1213–1233. https://doi.org/10.1177/0093854818778719
6. Perez, R. A. (2019). *Dispositional optimism effects on stress and police task performance* (Publication No. 10934815) [Doctoral dissertation, Walden University]. ProQuest Dissertations and Theses Global.
7. Reichart, B. (2016). Tunnel vision: Causes, effects, and mitigation strategies. *Hofstra Law Review, 45*(2), 451.
8. Manzella, C., & Papazoglou, K. (2014). Training police trainees about ways to manage trauma and loss. *International Journal of Mental Health Promotion, 16*(2), 103–116. https://doi.org/10.1080/14623730.2014.903609

CHAPTER 3

1. All names and places mentioned in Officer Mike's stories have been changed to ensure confidentiality.
2. Lennie, S.-J., Crozier Sarah, E., & Sutton, A. (2020). Robocop—The depersonalisation of police officers and their emotions: A diary study of emotional labor and burnout in front line British police officers.

International Journal of Law, Crime and Justice, 61, Article 100365. https://doi.org/10.1016/j.ijlcj.2019.100365

3. Mastracci, S. H., & Adams, I. T. (2020). It's not depersonalization, it's emotional labor: Examining surface acting and use-of-force with evidence from the US. *International Journal of Law, Crime and Justice, 61*, Article 100358. https://doi.org/10.1016/j.ijlcj.2019.100358

4. Much of this section is reprinted with permission from: Papazoglou, K., Koskelainen, M., & Stuewe, N. (2018). Exploring the role of compassion satisfaction and compassion fatigue in predicting burnout among police officers. *Open Journal of Psychiatry & Allied Sciences, 9*(2), 107–112. https://doi.org/10.5958/2394-2061.2018.00020.4

5. Manoj, M., Joseph, K., & Vijayaraghavan, G. (2020). Type D personality and myocardial infarction: A case-control study. *Indian Journal of Psychological Medicine, 42*(6), 555–559. https://doi.org/10.1177/0253717620941157

6. University of South Australia. (2020, August 13). When you're smiling, the whole world really does smile with you. *Science Daily.* https://www.sciencedaily.com/releases/2020/08/200813123608.htm

7. Romosiou, V., Brouzos, A., & Vassilopoulos, S. P. (2019). An integrative group intervention for the enhancement of emotional intelligence, empathy, resilience and stress management among police officers. *Police Practice & Research, 20*(5), 460–478. https://doi.org/10.1080/15614263.2018.1537847

CHAPTER 4

1. Aronson, E. (2004). *The social animal* (9th ed.). Worth.

CHAPTER 5

1. Chopko, B. A., Facemire, V. C., Palmieri, P. A., & Schwartz, R. C. (2016). Spirituality and health outcomes among police officers: Empirical evidence supporting a paradigm shift. *Criminal Justice Studies, 29*(4), 363–377. https://doi.org/10.1080/1478601X.2016.1216412

2. Moran, R. (2017). Workplace spirituality in law enforcement: A content analysis of the literature. *Journal of Management, Spirituality & Religion, 14*(4), 343–364. https://doi.org/10.1080/14766086.2017.1376287

3. Laird-Magee, T., Gayle, B. M., & Preiss, R. (2015). Personal values and mission statement: A reflective activity to aid moral development. *Journal of Education for Business*, *90*(3), 156–163. https://doi.org/10.1080/08832323.2015.1007907

4. van Tilburg, W. A. P., Igou, E. R., Maher, P. J., & Lennon, J. (2019). Various forms of existential distress are associated with aggressive tendencies. *Personality and Individual Differences*, *144*, 111–119. https://doi.org/10.1016/j.paid.2019.02.032

5. https://www.bbcearth.com/sevenworldsoneplanet/

CHAPTER 6

1. Blumberg, D. M., Papazoglou, K., & Creighton, S. (2018). Bruised badges: The moral risks of police work and a call for wellness. *International Journal of Emergency Mental Health and Human Resilience*, *20*(2), 1–14. https://doi.org/10.4172/1522-4821.1000394

2. Adam, S. (2020, October). Worlds most respected profession 2020. *University Magazine*. https://www.universitymagazine.ca/worlds-most-respected-profession-2020/

3. Caldero, M. A., & Crank, J. P. (2011). *Police ethics: The corruption of noble cause*. Elsevier.

4. Blumberg, D. M., Papazoglou, K., & Schlosser, M. D. (2020). Organizational solutions to the moral risks of policing. *International Journal of Environmental Research and Public Health*, *17*, 7461. https://doi.org/10.3390/ijerph17207461

5. Aronie, J., & Lopez, C. E. (2017). Keeping each other safe: An assessment of the use of peer intervention programs to prevent police officer mistakes and misconduct, using New Orleans' EPIC program as a potential national model. *Police Quarterly*, *20*(3), 295–321. https://doi.org/10.1177/1098611117710443

CHAPTER 7

1. Rahr, S., & Rice, S. K. (2015). *From warriors to guardians: Recommitting American police culture to democratic ideals*. U.S. Department of Justice, Office of Justice Programs, National Institute of Justice.

2. Li, D., Nicholson-Crotty, S., & Nicholson-Crotty, J. (2021). Creating guardians or warriors? Examining the effects of non-stress training on policing outcomes. *American Review of Public Administration*, *51*(1), 3–16. https://doi.org/10.1177/0275074020970178

3. Bandura, A. (1999). Moral disengagement in the perpetration of inhumanities. *Personality and Social Psychology Review*, *3*(3), 193–209. https://doi.org/10.1207/s15327957pspr0303_3

4. Loyens, K. (2014). Rule bending by morally disengaged detectives: An ethnographic study. *Police Practice & Research*, *15*(1), 62–74. https://doi.org/10.1080/15614263.2013.770941

5. Blumberg, D. M., Papazoglou, K., & Creighton, S. (2020). The moral risks of policing. In K. Papazoglou & D. M. Blumberg (Eds.), *POWER: Police officer wellness, ethics, and resilience* (pp. 49–75). Elsevier.

6. Much of this section is reprinted with permission from Schlosser, M. D., Blumberg, D. M. & Papazoglou, K. (2021, March 11). Tactical respect and tactical empathy. *FBI Law Enforcement Bulletin*. https://leb.fbi.gov/articles/featured-articles/tactical-respect-and-tactical-empathy

7. Papazoglou, K., Koskelainen, M., & Stuewe, N. (2018). Exploring the role of compassion satisfaction and compassion fatigue in predicting burnout among police officers. *Open Journal of Psychiatry & Allied Sciences*, *9*(2), 107–112. https://doi.org/10.5958/2394-2061.2018.00020.4

8. Andersen, J. P., Papazoglou, K., & Collins, P. (2018). Association of authoritarianism, compassion fatigue, and compassion satisfaction among police officers in North America: An exploration. *International Journal of Criminal Justice Sciences*, *13*(2), 405–419.

9. Burnett, M. E., Sheard, I., & St. Clair-Thompson, H. (2020). The prevalence of compassion fatigue, compassion satisfaction and perceived stress, and their relationships with mental toughness, individual differences and number of self-care actions in a UK police force. *Police Practice & Research*, *21*(4), 383–400. https://doi.org/10.1080/15614263.2019.1617144

10. Milliard, B. (2020). The role of compassion satisfaction. In K. Papazoglou & D. M. Blumberg (Eds.), *POWER: Police officer wellness, ethics, and resilience* (pp. 205–218). Elsevier.

CHAPTER 8

1. Papazoglou, K., Blumberg, D. M., Kamkar, K., Mclntyre-Smith, A., & Koskelainen, M. (2020). Addressing moral suffering in police work: Theoretical conceptualization and counselling implications. *Canadian Journal of Counselling & Psychotherapy/Revue Canadienne de Counseling et de Psychothérapie, 54*(1), 71–87.
2. Blumberg, D. M., Papazoglou, K., & Schlosser, M. D. (2020). Organizational solutions to the moral risks of policing. *International Journal of Environmental Research and Public Health, 17*(20), 7461. https://doi.org/10.3390/ijerph17207461
3. Blumberg, D. M., Schlosser, M. D., Papazoglou, K., Creighton, S., & Kaye, C. (2019). New directions in police academy training: A call to action. *International Journal of Environmental Research and Public Health, 16*(24), 4941. https://doi.org/10.3390/ijerph16244941.

CHAPTER 9

1. Tan, S. Y., & Yip, A. (2018). Hans Selye (1907–1982): Founder of the stress theory. *Singapore Medical Journal, 59*(4), 170–171. https://doi.org/10.11622/smedj.2018043
2. Jetelina, K. K., Beauchamp, A. M., Reingle Gonzalez, J. M., Molsberry, R. J., Bishopp, S. A., & Simon, C. L. (2020). Cumulative, high-stress calls impacting adverse events among law enforcement and the public. *BMC Public Health, 20*, 1–9. https://doi.org/10.1186/s12889-020-09219-x
3. Kupriyanov, R., & Zhdanov, R. (2014). The eustress concept: Problems and outlooks. *World Journal of Medical Sciences, 11*(2), 179–185.
4. Teigen, K. H. (1994). Yerkes-Dodson: A law for all seasons. *Theory & Psychology, 4*(4), 525–547. https://doi.org/10.1177/0959354394044004
5. Kwiatkowski, C. C., Manning, C. E., Eagle, A. L., & Robison, A. J. (2020). The neurobiology of police health, resilience, and wellness. In K. Papazoglou & D. M. Blumberg (Eds.), *POWER: Police officer wellness, ethics, and resilience* (pp. 77–96). Elsevier.

6. Dobson, D., & Dobson, K. S. (2017). *Evidence-based practice of cognitive-behavioral therapy* (2nd ed.). Guilford Press.
7. Grupe, D. W., McGehee, C., Smith, C., Francis, A. D., Mumford, J. A., & Davidson, R. J. (2019). Mindfulness training reduces PTSD symptoms and improves stress-related health outcomes in police officers. *Journal of Police and Criminal Psychology, 36*, 72–85. https://doi.org/10.1007/s11896-019-09351-4
8. Bergman, A. L., Christopher, M. S., & Bowen, S. (2016). Changes in facets of mindfulness predict stress and anger outcomes for police officers. *Mindfulness, 7*(4), 851–858. https://doi.org/10.1007/s12671-016-0522-z
9. https://www.mayoclinic.org/healthy-lifestyle/consumer-health/in-depth/mindfulness-exercises/art-20046356

CHAPTER 10

1. Versola-Russo, J. M. (2005). Vicarious victims of trauma: A literature review. *Journal of Police Crisis Negotiations, 5*(2), 59–80. https://doi.org/10.1300/J173v05n02_05
2. Fitzpatrick, A. (2020, July). First responders and PTSD: A literature review. *Journal of Emergency Medical Services.* https://www.jems.com/administration-and-leadership/first-responders-and-ptsd-a-literature-review/
3. Wallace, D., Jallat, E., & Jetly, R. (2020). Post-traumatic stress disorder or post-traumatic stress injury: What's in a name? *Journal of Military & Veterans' Health, 28*(1), 39–44.
4. Anderson, G. S., Di Nota, P. M., Groll, D., & Carleton, R. N. (2020). Peer support and crisis-focused psychological interventions designed to mitigate post-traumatic stress injuries among public safety and frontline healthcare personnel: A systematic review. *International Journal of Environmental Research and Public Health, 17*(20), 7645. https://doi.org/10.3390/ijerph17207645
5. Figley, C. R. (1995). *Compassion fatigue: Coping with secondary traumatic stress disorder in those who treat the traumatized.* Brunner/Mazel.

6. Papazoglou, K., Bonanno, G., Blumberg, D. M., & Keesee, T. (2019, September 10). Moral injury in police work. *FBI Law Enforcement Bulletin.* https://leb.fbi.gov/articles/featured-articles/moral-injury-in-police-work

7. World Health Organization. (2019, May). *Burn-out an "occupational phenomenon": International Classification of Diseases.* https://www.who.int/mental_health/evidence/burn-out/en/

8. Talavera-Velasco, B., Luceño-Moreno, L., Martín-García, J., & García-Albuerne, Y. (2018, September). Psychosocial risk factors, burnout and hardy personality as variables associated with mental health in police officers. *Frontiers in Psychology, 9.* https://doi.org/10.3389/fpsyg.2018.01478

9. Doyle, J. N., Campbell, M. A., & Gryshchuk, L. (2021). Occupational stress and anger: Mediating effects of resiliency in first responders. *Journal of Police and Criminal Psychology.* https://doi.org/10.1007/s11896-021-09429-y

10. Tedeschi, R. G., & Calhoun, L. G. (2004). Posttraumatic growth: Conceptual foundations and empirical evidence. *Psychological Inquiry, 15*(1), 1–18. https://doi.org/10.1207/s15327965pli1501_01

11. Chopko, B. A., & Schwartz, R. C. (2009). The relation between mindfulness and posttraumatic growth: A study of first responders to trauma-inducing incidents. *Journal of Mental Health Counseling, 31*(4), 363–376. https://doi.org/10.17744/mehc.31.4.9w6lhk4v66423385

CHAPTER 11

1. Neff, K., & Germer, C. (2017). Self-compassion and psychological well-being. In E. Seppälä, E. Simon-Thomas, S. L. Brown, M. C. Worline, C. D. Cameron, & J. R. Doty (Eds.), *The Oxford handbook of compassion science* (pp. 371–386). Oxford University Press.

2. This has been adapted from the work of Dr. Kristin Neff (see https://centerformsc.org/5-myths-of-self-compassion/).

3. Watkins, P. C. (2016). *Positive psychology 101.* Springer.

4. VIA Institute on Character. (2020). *The 24 character strengths.* https://www.viacharacter.org/character-strengths

5. All names and places mentioned in Officer Mike's stories have been changed to ensure confidentiality.

CHAPTER 12

1. Blumberg, D. M., Papazoglou, K., & Schlosser, M. D. (2020). The importance of WE in POWER: Integrating police wellness and ethics. *Frontiers in Psychology*, *11*, 614995. https://doi.org/10.3389/fpsyg.2020.614995

INDEX

ABOUT THE AUTHORS

Daniel M. Blumberg, PhD, is a licensed clinical psychologist who has spent more than 3 decades providing all facets of clinical and consulting psychological services to numerous local, state, and federal law enforcement agencies. He is the director of The POWER Project (https://policepowerproject.org), a nonprofit 501(c)(3) Public Benefit Corporation that provides evidence-based and practice-based educational and consulting services on police wellness, ethics, and resilience. In addition to his expertise in workplace stress prevention and trauma recovery, Dr. Blumberg is an authority on the selection, training, and clinical supervision of undercover operatives. His research interests include police integrity, the moral risks of policing, and programs to improve relations between the police and the community. Dr. Blumberg received his doctorate from Clark University in Worcester, Massachusetts. After a postdoctoral internship with the Los Angeles County Sheriff's Department, he was hired as a staff psychologist with the San Diego Police Department. Dr. Blumberg has given over 100 presentations at national and international conferences and has published more than 40 peer-reviewed articles and book chapters. He is the coeditor of *POWER: Police Officer Wellness, Ethics, & Resilience*, published by Elsevier.

Konstantinos Papazoglou, PhD, CPsych, is the founder and director of ProWellness Inc., a psychology professional corporation, as well as the principal founder of the POWER Project, a nonprofit public benefit corporation. He recently completed his appointment as a postdoctoral scholar at Yale University School of Medicine. He earned his doctoral degree in psychology (clinical–forensic area) as Vanier Scholar at the University of Toronto. Dr. Papazoglou is a former police captain of the Hellenic Police Force and European Police College, and he holds a master's degree in applied psychology from New York University as Onassis Scholar. In addition, he is an affiliated researcher with the Loss, Trauma, and Emotion Lab at Teachers College, Columbia University of New York. He has presented his work at numerous scientific conferences and professional events and has published extensively in major scholarly journals and large-scale law enforcement magazines. Dr. Papazoglou's research focuses on performance, wellness, and resilience promotion among law enforcement officers. He is the coeditor of *POWER: Police Officer Wellness, Ethics, & Resilience*, published by Elsevier, which established the theoretical framework for *The POWER Manual*.

Michael D. Schlosser, PhD, is the director of the University of Illinois Police Training Institute and a principal founder of The POWER Project. He holds a master's degree in public administration from Governors State University and a PhD in education from the University of Illinois. He retired as a lieutenant from the Rantoul Police Department in 2004. Dr. Schlosser has conducted and collaborated in numerous research projects at the University of Illinois and is credited for his innovative ideas toward police reform. He has authored dozens of articles, made numerous radio and television appearances, and given over 100 presentations across the country on topics such as police tactics, police training, use of force, de-escalation techniques, control and arrest tactics, the intersection of police and race, diversity, police officer wellness, and police family wellness.